IN HIS GRIP

A Daily Devotional based on incidents and experiences from current and former members of law enforcement and first responders

by

Robert F. Gerken

IN HIS GRIP

ISBN-13: 978-0-578-21263-0

Author contact: inhisgrip2571@gmail.com

Website and blog: http://www.inhisgrip2571.net

DEDICATION

This devotional is dedicated to my Lord and Savior Jesus Christ

whose sacrifice and death on the cross have given me the gift of eternal life

through His grace.

To God be the glory.

To my faithful wife, Joanne, for her encouragement, support,

and countless hours editing this devotional.

Without her commitment to this book, it would have remained

nothing more than a dream.

To the memory of Colonel John K. Schafer, Commissioner, Pennsylvania State Police,

and the late Lieutenant Thomas O. Marakovits,

for the bond of friendship and many great memories both on and off the job,

some of which are recounted in this devotional.

To all the men and women in Law enforcement, First Responders and Military Service

and to

Those Who Paid The Ultimate Price.

To family members waiting for their loved ones to return home each day.

"They also serve, who only stand and wait." John Milton, poet, 1608-1674

ENDORSEMENTS

In His Grip is a must read for all law enforcement officers and their families. Jesus used things familiar to His hearers to drive home important spiritual truths that are critical for everyday living and Bob Gerken does the same with this devotional. Bob takes us from a moment on the job to a biblical principle that challenges and encourages in a day when law enforcement has become harder and more dangerous than ever. Family members and friends of officers will learn what it means to put on the uniform and the desperate need for all of us to be prayer warriors for and encouragers of these "Ministers of God" who keep the rest of us safe. I plan to give this devotional to my sons, their wives, and each officer in our church and community.

Reverend Carl J. Fisher Jr., Pastor and father of three police officers.

As either someone in law enforcement or someone who just wants a closer walk with the Lord, you cannot read these devotionals without experiencing how God has truly worked in Bob Gerken's life. This book will inspire you and give you hope that you, too, can have a stronger relationship with God and peace in your daily challenges.

Melanie Himmelberger, M.A., L.P.C.

Pennsylvania State Police retired Corporal Bob Gerken has hit a home run with this inspirational daily devotional for the benefit of not only police officers, but also people in all professions. I wish it had been available when I was "on the job."

Lieutenant Colonel Rick Periandi, Pennsylvania State Police, retired

It seems that the law enforcement profession gets more difficult and dangerous by the day. In response to these unsettled times, retired PA State Police Corporal Bob Gerken reflects on his personal experiences to describe the daily challenges of the profession. The daily reflections are then woven into larger topics which provide readers personal strength and bring them close to God. Gerken's goals are to help the officer while on-duty, but even more important, to provide balance and perspective for the challenges faced off-duty with family and friends.

Thomas A. Marakovits, Federal Law Enforcement Agent.

ACKNOWLEDGMENTS

Joanne Gerken, Editor-in-Chief, Book Cover Concept

Harry Miller, Co-Editor, Technology Expert/Advisor, Formatting Guru. His endless hours of work, his expertise, wisdom, encouragement, and deepening friendship- all priceless: hmatmc@gmail.com

Lyn and Melanie Himmelberger, Co-Editors. Faithful, wise friends, our cheerleaders, who devoted many, many months to editing, offering insight, and encouraging this endeavor.

Leslie and Howard Vernick, Our first advisors and mentors who graciously offered their time and invaluable knowledge to prepare us for this journey.

Advisors: Joe & Marcia Hackman, Yvonne Bleam, Ned Schillow, Each offered a unique perspective and gave of their time to help us undertake this project.

Contributors: Dirk Ottens: Book Title and story

Stories: Jim Anderson, Frank Bason, Ethan Brownback, Jim Cavallo, Mike Chaplin, Mike Faulkner, Everett Goff, Jan and Dave Hamrick, Carl Harnish, Ed Long, Bob Miklich, Tom Taylor, Laird Thomas, Mike Wall, Matt Zimpfer

Emily New, Graphic Designer, Book Cover: emnew22@yahoo.com

Grace Blenis, web design and blog setup: Shecantoo.net

PREFACE

This devotional is based on the personal experiences of the author, a Pennsylvania State Trooper for twenty-five years, as well as the experiences of others in law enforcement and 1st responders, both current and past. This book is not specific to one Christian denomination; rather it encourages all to develop and strengthen a personal relationship with Jesus Christ. Although those on the job have chosen this field for various reasons, these men and women devote their lives to serving others, protecting their communities, and helping to better the lives of others. At times, their jobs are thankless, especially in today's society where many are critical of the efforts being made by those who run into danger without hesitation. Police departments now have a difficult time recruiting, and some currently on the job are frustrated and even scared. In these times, we often hear of officers being killed in the line of duty for no apparent reason other than they are in uniform and carry a badge. Added to these concerns are the increasing numbers of divorces and suicides and the higher rate of alcoholism among officers.

To find peace in this environment, one must have a strong faith and reach out to our Creator for protection, wisdom, discernment, and compassion. Without this Source, our lives can unravel and become overwhelming. For all of us, time is valuable, and most feel that we do not have enough of it. In addition, because of the demanding schedules, too often our time with God is not our first priority. However, to be ready each day to stay on top of our game, we must spend time calling out to our Lord, and "He will make our path straight." Pastor Chuck Swindoll said, "Make a plan now to keep a daily appointment with God. The enemy is going to tell you to set it aside, but you must carve out the time. If you are too busy to meet the Lord, then you are simply too busy."

"The Lord is my strength and my shield; my heart trusts in Him, and He Helps me." Psalm 28:7

"Be strong and courageous. Do not be terrified; do not be discouraged, for the Lord your God will be with you wherever you go." Joshua 1:9

"Watch, stand fast in the faith, be brave, be strong." 1 Corinthians 16:13

CONTINGENCY PLANS

As we begin the New Year, we often reflect on the past year and contemplate what we have accomplished as well as our plans that never came to fruition. We have taken on a career that is full of danger and uncertainty. I never knew the magnitude of that reality, nor could I, until I came on the job. Some calls that I responded to, I realized afterwards, could have gone very badly, not only for me, but also for those who were in danger. Consequently, I became a planner and was most comfortable when I had a contingency plan. Eventually, that mindset becomes second nature to most of us out of a sense for the need to survive. In our work, we must strive to do our very best because that is what we are called to do.

Ephesians 6:7 tells us to "Serve wholeheartedly, as if you were serving the Lord, not men, because you know that the Lord will reward everyone for whatever good he does." However, our plans should not be restricted only to those hours that we spend on the job. We need to be constantly asking the Lord to show us His will, not only in our work, but also in our everyday lives. So, what is the Lord's plan for us this coming year? We may have some sense, but we need to ask Him and then wait for direction. "For I know the plans I have for you," declares the Lord, "plans to prosper you and not to harm you, plans to give you hope and a future." Jeremiah 29:11.

"And our wise Father in Heaven knows when we're going to need things, too. Don't run out ahead of Him." Corrie ten Boom, author

Proverbs 3:5-6, Ecclesiastes 3:1-22, Romans 8:28

NOW WHERE?

It was 11:15 PM, and my shift was almost over. It had been relatively quiet, but I was tired and ready to go home. Soon, the silence was broken as dispatch directed me to a one-car crash on a rural road several miles away. I began heading to the scene, and upon rounding a bend in the road, I came upon a small vehicle against a tree; flames were pouring out of the interior. I jumped out of my cruiser and approached the vehicle, but the searing flames continued to grow and didn't allow me to get any closer. As I looked toward the driver I noticed that both of his arms were positioned as if he still had his hands on the steering wheel. At a closer look, I discovered that the intensity of the flames and heat had burned off both hands. Despair quickly engulfed me as I realized that there was absolutely nothing I could do to save this person who just minutes ago was traveling this quiet country road. I then began to wonder whose son, husband, brother, or father this person could be. More importantly, where was he now? Where would he spend eternity?

In John 5:24, Jesus assures Christians of their future: "I tell you the truth, whoever hears My word and believes Him who sent Me has eternal life and will not be condemned; he has crossed over from death to life." Romans 10:9 reminds us, "That if you confess with your mouth 'Jesus is Lord,' and believe in your heart that God raised Him from the dead, you will be saved." Plain and simple!

"At the most, you will live a hundred years on Earth, but you will spend forever in eternity."
Rick Warren, pastor/author

Job 14:14-16, John 3:16, 1 John 5:13

THE BROTHER/SISTERHOOD

Recently, three blood-brothers graduated from the NYPD Academy. They joined their father, a Deputy Inspector and a thirty-year veteran of the department. Since those who are on the job often refer to one another as "brothers and sisters," this accomplishment makes these three brothers, "brothers twice." Those in law enforcement who are Believers can be called "brothers/sisters twice," as well, for they are brothers/sisters on the job and brothers/sisters in the Lord. Although their relationship on the job is certainly unique, their bond in Christ is even more special. Those in Christ will remain a part of the family of God for eternity and will be called the sons and daughters of God.

Although the job creates many extra stresses on relationships, Colossians 3:12-14 clearly defines the unique characteristics that we need to display to other Christians: "Therefore, as God's chosen people, holy and dearly loved, clothe yourselves with compassion, kindness, humility, gentleness, and patience. Bear with each other and forgive whatever grievances you have against one another. Forgive as the Lord forgave you. And over all these virtues, put on love, which binds them all together in perfect unity."

A popular song says, "He's (God) got my brothers and my sisters in in His hands; He's got the whole world in His hands."

John 1:12, Ephesians 2:19-22, Romans 12:5

FIGHTING THE GOOD FIGHT

I obtained a search warrant for an apartment occupied by several major drug dealers of methamphetamine. As I approached the door with our team, I recalled that an informant said that these dealers were also using meth. Not knowing the mental or physical condition of the occupants was always an added concern. As we crashed the door, the residents began to scatter. Trying to round up the suspects, I grabbed hold of one and attempted to force him onto a nearby chair. When he did not budge, I recognized that he was on meth, and a physical confrontation was inevitable. However, regardless of what I attempted to do, this suspect would not move and actually became more aggressive. After the other officers began to assist, this person was eventually subdued.

On the job, we often become involved in confrontations both verbal and physical. We must not lose sight that the evil one also wants to go to battle against us. As Believers, it is apparent that Satan's desire is to cause strife, temptations, and turmoil in our lives. He has a greater victory when he is able to cause a follower of Christ to succumb to sin. While Jesus walked in this world, He was also tempted because He came as a human; yet, He continued to be sinless. He wrestled with the knowledge that He would have to bear the weight of all of mankind's sin and be separated for a time from His Father in Heaven. However, He won the greatest battle of all when He willingly went to the cross and paid the full penalty that we so rightly deserve for our sin. As we come to understand the heart and mind of Jesus, we will be able to discern His perfect will for our lives. In 1 Timothy 6:12, Paul tells us to, "Fight the good fight of the faith. Take hold of the eternal life to which you were called."

"God didn't just give a little for us; He gave His best. He gave Himself."
Francis Chen, pastor/ author

John 19:28-30, Ephesians 6:12, Hebrews 12:2-3

THE TRUE LIGHT

Tom had only three months on the job, and his supervisors recently determined that he no longer needed to ride with his Field Training Officer. One morning, the Patrol Sergeant gave Tom a new marked patrol vehicle and emphasized the need to take special care of the car since it had only 600 miles on the odometer. Feeling pleased that the sergeant had entrusted him with this new vehicle, Tom drove to the local magistrate's office to file citations and parked at the top of the hill. When he completed his business, he returned to his vehicle which now was nowhere in sight. At first, he thought that his brothers were messing with him and had taken the new car. However, as he glanced down the hill, he noticed that the red "bubble" light of his vehicle was the only visible part of the new car that was now submerged in a pond below. We can only imagine the ensuing conversation with his sergeant.

"Light" is mentioned over 150 times in the Bible, but it refers to a different kind of light. James 1:17 says, "Every good and perfect gift is from above, coming down from the Father of the heavenly lights, Who does not change like shifting shadows." In John 8:12, Jesus said, "I am the Light of the world. Whoever follows Me will never walk in darkness, but will have the light of life." Matthew 5:16: "In the same way, let your light so shine before men, that they may see your good deeds and praise your Father in heaven."

"If I forget that it was He who granted that ray of light to His most unworthy servant, then I know nothing of Calvary love."
Amy Carmichael, missionary/author

Psalm 119:105, Matthew 4:16, Matthew 5:14

BACK TO LIFE

A call from dispatch directed me to a rural area of the county where skeletal remains had been located by a farmer. As I approached the location with the farmer, it became obvious that the bones were of a human. After the scene was processed, as the lead investigator, I took the bones to a forensic pathologist. Few bones were missing, and the remains were determined to be those of a 25-35-year-old white female. When several frustrating weeks passed without any leads, a colleague suggested that I take the skull to a forensic sculptor. Having never heard of such a person, I was reluctant to leave this vital piece of evidence with him. However, three weeks later when I returned to his studio, there perched on a pedestal was the skull covered with a long wig. The sculptor had placed clay over the skull and obtained frames to fit the glass lenses found at the scene. The glasses were now balanced on her nose. Although somewhat skeptical of the validity of this work, I decided to place a photograph of this reconstruction in the newspaper. Several days later, a man called to say that the photo looked like his daughter who had been missing for several years. Dental comparisons confirmed his suspicion.

Someday, our earthly bodies will be transformed and taken to Heaven. In Mark 13:26, Jesus said: "At that time, men will see the Son of Man coming in clouds with great power and glory. And He will send His angels and gather His elect from the four winds, from the ends of the earth to the ends of the heavens." Then, we will receive new bodies that will last for eternity. No one will have to determine our identity. Our Creator knew us as individuals before Creation and during our life on Earth, and He will continue to know us forever.

"God is the ultimate worker. We are His handiwork."
David Jeremiah, pastor/author

Genesis 2:7, Job 10:8-9, Psalm 139:13-16, Isaiah 64:8

WHOM DO WE TRUST?

Over time in my law enforcement career, I learned that developing confidential informants can be critical in solving crimes. Lynn was a heroin addict and dealer. When I arrested her for prostitution, she revealed that she had recently been released from state prison. Since this new arrest would send her back on a parole violation, she agreed to provide information on illegal activity that she was aware of. However, as sincere as she could sometimes appear, I never knew how much to trust her. The first time I was going to meet with her, she told me she would be at a certain location at 9:00 PM to discuss those dealing heroin in the area. By 9:30, she still had not arrived. Although I knew where she lived, it was not safe to meet her at her residence. Having worked with many informants in the past, I knew that they usually were not very reliable and most could not be trusted. At 9:45, she finally arrived with a flimsy excuse. My trust level for her at this point was very low.

I was regularly exposed to those who tried to circumvent the law and were involved in questionable activities. When we work with a partner or even when calling for backup, we must feel secure in knowing that help is on the way. We also realize that we must trust the firearm that we carry and the patrol car we drive. As important as these all are, we cannot lose sight that any or all of these could fail us. However, we never need to be concerned when we continue to put our trust in our Creator, our Solid Rock, who will never leave us. Psalm 20: 7, "Some trust in chariots and some in horses, but we trust in the name of the Lord our God." Proverbs 3:5, "Trust in the Lord with all your heart and lean not on your own understanding; in all your ways acknowledge Him, and He will make your paths straight." Isaiah 12:2, "Surely, God is my salvation; I will trust and not be afraid. The Lord, the Lord, is my strength and my song; He has become my salvation."

"Trust whatever He has for you. It will be better than anything you can plan yourself."
Francis Chan, pastor/author

Psalm 84:12, Isaiah 43:1-3, John 14:1, Romans 15:13

PRIDE ABOUNDING

I had done well. I had managed to endure the grind, both mentally and physically, through many months at the PA State Police Academy. Now, I was entering into a profession which was usually highly respected. People were turning to me for advice and direction and even, at times, for comfort. We all have been there. As we move on with our career, we often have great successes. We land a new position or assignment and may even get the long-sought-after promotion. At these times, we may not identify the source for our success, and we start to think that we have done it all on our own. This may be the time when the evil one will cause us to think that we really are exceptional. After all, we fix problems, often those which others cannot.

The Bible mentions "pride" 49 times, "proud" 48 times, and "haughty" 10 times. Apparently, God knew that this was going to be a problem for His creation. We are reminded in Proverbs 16:18, "Pride goes before destruction, a haughty spirit before a fall." Although we may not sense our attitude of pride, it becomes evident to those around us. It never goes unnoticed; in fact, it diminishes our witness. Proverbs 29:23: "A man's pride brings him low, but a man of lowly spirit gains honor." When Peter addressed the elders and young men, he included a quote from 1 Peter 5:5-6: "Young men, in the same way be submissive to those who are older. All of you, clothe yourselves with humility toward one another because, 'God opposes the proud but gives grace to the humble.' Humble yourselves, therefore, under God's mighty hand that He may lift you up in due time."

"Whoever God is blessing, we can expect the devil to be opposing."
Greg Laurie, pastor/author

Isaiah 23:9, Jeremiah 9:23, James 4:6

CONVERSATIONS

While on the job, it is very unlikely to go out on a tour of duty without having multiple conversations during the shift. Most often, the conversations occur because there is a problem or a difficult incident that we have entered into. The shiny, red sports car flew by my unmarked patrol car. As I began to follow the vehicle, the driver's speed continued to increase. At 90 miles per hour, I knew it was time to make the stop. The driver pulled over and immediately began walking back to my car. When told to get back into his vehicle, he began to argue with me at the side of the road. I knew this encounter and any further conversations were not going to go well. "Why don't you guys go out and catch real criminals?" he asked. "You know, I pay your salary." "It's not nearly enough," I barked back. In some encounters, we have to use strong words to admonish others for their inappropriate actions. In other conversations, we can offer words of encouragement that convey an attitude of caring, but this could not happen with the driver of the sports car because of his aggressiveness.

We need to remember that the Lord wants us to enter into His presence, talk to Him, and then just listen. Psalm 46:10 says, "Be still, and know that I am God; I will be exalted among the nations, I will be exalted in the earth." He wants us to come to Him often, and doing so will help to keep us on track. In Jeremiah 29:11-14, the Lord says, "For I know the plans I have for you... plans to prosper you and not to harm you, plans to give you hope and a future. Then you will call upon Me and come and pray to Me, and I will listen to you. You will seek Me and find Me when you seek Me with all your heart. I will be found by you."

"God waits for you to communicate with Him. You have instant, direct access to God."
Wesley Duewel, missionary

Luke 11:2, James 1:19, 1 John 5:14

IN GOD WE TRUST

We received a call that an elderly woman had wandered away from her home and had not been seen for several hours. It was now time for her to be taking her much-needed medications. When the State Police Bell Jet Ranger landed in the field adjacent to the barracks, I agreed to go with the pilot in search for this woman. As I climbed into what appeared to be a huge bubble that surrounded the cabin, the only thing that seemed to be somewhat secure was the floor. As the pilot lifted off the ground and made a turn which seemed far too sharp, I realized that there was no room for error should this helicopter go down. Although I did not know the pilot, I had no choice but to trust him. Even more important was that I had to trust God to bring me back to Earth safely. When we located the elderly woman, we directed those on the ground to her location. Approximately one year later, the same helicopter and pilot crashed on a similar mission, and the pilot died.

I often wonder how many people truly trust God, and if so, what do they fully turn over to Him? Do they trust that He will grant wisdom and direction with solutions which ultimately will be better for them? Often, my trust is tested. Sometimes, I am consciously willing to turn over trying situations and rely on the Lord to handle them. At other times, I seem to think that God still needs my help. As Believers in Christ, our trust in God should not be haphazard, nor should we trust only when there seems to be no other option-- like having to get in a helicopter. Our very survival is often dependent upon our trust in Him. However, we cannot know what His plans are for us tomorrow. Although I fully trusted in God, my helicopter ride could have ended just like the one a year later. If so, that would not have meant that He did not hear my prayer, but rather that He had something much better for me– being in Heaven for Eternity.

"I do not come to God so that Jesus can give me what I want. But I must come to God so that Jesus will grant me what I need." Alistair Begg, pastor

Proverbs 3:5-6, Proverbs 16:3, Philippians 4:19

SATISFACTION

Late one Saturday morning, I received a radio call that a theft had just occurred at a residence in a suburban neighborhood. Pulling up to the home where I had been directed, I saw a six-year-old boy sitting on the front step. When I approached him, tears filled his eyes. His mother came out of the home and explained that her son's new bicycle had just been stolen. This certainly was not the crime that I had expected nor an encounter as serious as it could have been. After getting a description of the bike, I told the boy that I would attempt to locate it. As I began to scour the neighborhood, I believed that I had only enough time for a cursory search. However, I kept thinking about the boy's loss and that to him, this was a major crime. Driving by a school, I observed a group of young boys playing on a field, and several bicycles were parked nearby. One matched the description of the stolen bike. As I approached the group, a boy jumped on the bike and attempted to drive away. After he was "apprehended," I put the bike into the patrol car and headed back to my victim. The look on his face when he realized that his bike had been returned was worth every minute that I had spent attempting to recover it. The next day, the boy and his mom came to the station with a plate piled with homemade cookies, a reward for solving this case. However, what I felt inside was even more satisfying.

When we accept Christ as our Savior, He, too, will provide a reward for us that will far surpass anything that we will ever experience in our time on this earth. He has left this earth to prepare a place for us in His home that has "many mansions" awaiting our arrival. Hebrews 11:6 encourages us: "And without faith, it is impossible to please God, because anyone who comes to Him must believe that He exists and that He rewards those who earnestly seek Him."

"We should never take for granted the reality that when the God of the Universe became a man, He chose to come as a Servant." Joseph Stoll, pastor/author

Matthew 5:12, Luke 6:23, 2 Timothy 4:8

WHAT CRIME?

We are all very familiar with trials since they are a significant part of the judicial process. Anytime we bring an action charging someone with a violation of the law, whether criminal, or motor vehicle, the possibility exists that the outcome and any consequences will be determined through a trial, a judge, or jury. Whenever I had a trial, a preliminary hearing, or any other proceeding that would require me to justify charges or actions that I had taken, I prepared my case carefully and extensively. I never wanted to lose; none of us does. Yet, in spite of the public oath that I had given to tell the truth, during the cross-examination of my testimony, defense attorneys often insinuated that I was not truthful. In a sense, I was being put on trial.

We also face trials of many kinds in our off-duty hours. Perhaps when we first became Believers, we thought that our trials would be minimized. The Bible gives no indication of that; instead, we are told that God will provide peace, power, and wisdom during difficult times. Sometimes in our trials here on Earth, false accusations are made against us as was the case with Jesus. In the most significant trial in history, the trial that Jesus faced, He stood blameless and sinless before Pilate. As the Jews demanded that He be crucified, Pilate said that he found in Him no crime and no grounds to put Him to death. However, Pilate succumbed to their demands to crucify Jesus. Thankfully for us, Christ is our ultimate and righteous judge. When we face Him, we will have the assurance that His death and sacrifice set us free from any penalty that we deserve for our sins. "Let us fix our eyes on Jesus, the author and perfecter of our faith, who for the joy set before Him endured the cross, scorning its shame, and sat down at the right hand of the throne of God." Hebrews 12:2.

"Trials are to see if you believe what you say you believe."
Tony Evans, pastor/author

John 19:4-6, Matthew 27:32-56

DISAPPOINTMENTS

Many jobs that I had came with some disappointments. In law enforcement, there are always plenty of them. So often, they were not even caused by what I did or did not do. Fairness is never guaranteed in any profession, and even on the job, "politics" may become more important than what is right or wrong. Evangelist Billy Graham said, "Comfort and prosperity have never enriched the world as much as adversity." Could our need to grow be the reason why we face adversity? When we take our requests to the Lord, and the answer that He provides is disappointing, it can be difficult to accept. However, Pastor Timothy Keller reminds us that, "The basic purpose of prayer is not to bend God's will to mine, but to mold my will into His."

When difficult times come our way, often our first response is to give up, give less, or maybe even to quit. If we have sought God's will, sensed that we were following His lead, and still do not agree with the outcome, we need to realize that these thoughts are probably from Satan. Dr. David Jeremiah describes Satan at work: "He can imitate God, but he cannot duplicate Him. God is the only one who can deliver us from our pain and suffering." Our Creator has always been in control since He first created this world. He knows our every need. Even though we face trials, tribulations, and disappointments, He still has the very best in mind for us. Accepting that is the only way to receive real peace. After Paul endured countless trials and suffering, his faith allowed him to say in Philippians 4:6-7, "Do not be anxious about anything, but in everything, by prayer and petition, with thanksgiving, present your requests to God. And the peace of God, which transcends all understanding, will guard your hearts and your minds in Christ Jesus."

"Refuse to let your situation determine your attitude."
Charles Swindoll, pastor/author

Psalm 29:11, Colossians 3:15, 1 Peter 5:7

SKILL SET

I always find it interesting to see how those on the job are so much alike, yet, they also have many differences and abilities. Some seem to have a sense that something is about to go wrong. Others are able to "read" people and know whether they are being truthful. A nationally-recognized criminal profiler that I worked with is able to study a crime scene and from it describe characteristics of the person who perpetrated the crime. God gives certain skills and abilities to every person that He creates. He may have given us keen insight, great strength, a compassionate demeanor, and even the ability to be a leader. We also have some abilities that may not be spiritual in nature. As Believers, we learn that He expects us to use all of our abilities in a way that will cause Him to be honored and glorified.

At the time when we become Believers, God imparts upon us a very special skill set that we know to be the indwelling of the Holy Spirit. 2 Corinthians 1:21-22 says, "Now it is God who makes both us and you stand firm in Christ. He anointed us, set his seal of ownership on us, and put His spirit in our hearts as a deposit, guaranteeing what is to come." Colossians 3:23-24 says, "Whatever you do, work at it with all your heart, as working for the Lord, not men, since you know that you will receive an inheritance from the Lord as a reward." When we are faced with a decision or a challenge that we feel we do not have the skills to handle, all we need do is to reach out and pray in the Holy Spirit to help us… and He will!

"I may not be better than other people, but at least I'm different."
Rousseau, author/philosopher

1 Corinthians 10:31, 1 Corinthians 12:4-6, Jude 1:20, Romans 8:14

FEAR

In law enforcement, danger is ever-present, and we can be exposed to life-threatening situations every day. When I first entered this career, I felt somewhat fearless until the first time I joined my partner to search a building for a person who had just committed an armed robbery. As I moved quickly toward the building, trying to keep out of range and away from windows, I was scared, perhaps even more so after others arrived, and the suspect was apprehended. Then I had time to realize what had just occurred or could have happened. Only foolish people say that they have no fear, especially during those times when we cannot predict the outcome. Unfortunately, some people like this are on the job, and we do not want them alongside us in times of peril. They can be reckless and cause harm, not only to themselves but also to others around them.

Some have said that fear at times is healthy, for it causes us to be on top of our game. However, when fear becomes overwhelming for us as Believers, we know the true source of peace and comfort. Hebrews 13:6 says, "The Lord is my helper; I will not be afraid. What can man do to me?" Isaiah 41:10 says, "So, do not fear, for I am with you; do not be dismayed, for I am your God. I will strengthen you and help you; I will uphold you with my righteous right hand." In John 14:27, Christ says, "Peace I leave with you; my peace I give you. I do not give to you as the world gives. Do not let your hearts be troubled, and do not be afraid."

"Any time we open ourselves up to fear, we fall prey to his (Satan's) deception and intimidations. Yet, if we submit our hearts to God and stand in faith, we can resist those first fearful thoughts. As we yield to God, we can master our reactions to fear, and the enemy will soon flee."
Francis Frangipane, pastor/author

Psalm 16:8, Psalm 46:1-3, Psalm 118:14-16, John 16:33

THE TRUTH

While sitting in my office reviewing an investigative report, I received a call from dispatch alerting me to a possible homicide and also to an assault, each at a different location. I advised that I was going to the scene of the murder first. When I arrived, I saw the body of a young woman lying on her back in a field a short distance from the highway. It was obvious that she was dead. Stab wounds were scattered about her face and chest. On that cold day, the woman wore a short wool coat. One of her hands had a wool mitten on it, but the other was bare. As the body was removed and the scene was being processed, I proceeded to a residence located several miles away to meet with the victim of the assault. When I entered his residence, I noticed that his hands were bleeding and appeared to have been cut. He told me that he and his girlfriend had been walking in a field when they were attacked by an unknown assailant. As he described the location, it was evident that it was the same scene that I had just left. He indicated that when the attacker began to stab his girlfriend, he tried to intervene, and the attacker ripped a gold chain from his neck. Soon the ambulance that he had called earlier arrived, and he was transported to the hospital.

As I walked out of this home down a long walkway to an alley, I saw a garbage can at the curb. From past experience in drug investigations, I instinctively grabbed the garbage inside. As I examined it back at the barracks, I found a glove matching the one of the homicide victim. Inside the glove was a knife and a gold chain. Sometimes, it is not easy to discern the truth when we engage in conversations with those we encounter. However, we do know without a doubt that what we read in God's word is the truth, the whole truth, and nothing but the truth. "O Sovereign God! Your words are trustworthy." 2 Samuel 7:28.

"If you tell the truth, you don't have to remember anything," Mark Twain, author

Psalm 119:160, John 1:14, 1 John 3:18

EVIL AROUND US

It is not uncommon, even for Believers, to question at times why evil is so prevalent in our society. News headlines nauseate us with details about a mother and her boyfriend who plotted for a year to carry out their rape/murder fantasy on her fourteen-year-old adopted daughter. Afterwards, they dismembered her, stored her in moth balls, and months later buried her remains. Almost daily, stories from around the world describe man's inhumanity to man. Recently, the first-known family to include their children as suicide bombers all strapped on explosives and blew themselves up as they inflicted death and damage on innocent bystanders. MS-13 gang members, some who are barely in their teens, systematically rape, torture, and murder people they randomly choose to be victims. Because those in law enforcement often see the very worst in people, awareness of the presence of evil may become even more intense and cause us to lose heart.

Until the Lord establishes His kingdom on Earth, we will be faced with evildoers. Romans 8:7 tells us: "The sinful mind is hostile to God. It does not submit to God's law, nor can it do so." However, Psalm 37:7-11 encourages us as it reminds us that the Lord will both punish and reward justly. "Be still before the Lord and wait patiently for Him; do not fret when men succeed in their ways, when they carry out their wicked schemes. Refrain from anger and turn from wrath; do not fret--it leads only to evil. For evil men will be cut off, but those who hope in the Lord will inherit the land. A little while, and the wicked will be no more; though you look for them, they will not be found. But the meek will inherit the land and enjoy great peace."

"The only thing necessary for the triumph of evil is for good men to do nothing."
Edmund Burke, author/orator/statesman

Psalm 97:10-12, Proverbs 8:13, Ephesians 5:8-12

GIVE AN ANSWER

As law officers, we are often called upon to resolve an issue, solve a problem, and answer difficult questions. Prior to giving testimony in a hearing or court case, we must prepare extensively to answer any challenges that may be presented. Our friends and family may turn to us from time to time, believing that because of our background and ability to think on our feet, we will have the answers or at least a possible solution. A big challenge for Christians is to act differently as we seek to be Christ-like in all that we do and say although we sometimes will fail. Hopefully, others will see the differences in us, even in subtle ways. When they do, we need to be prepared to answer if asked, "Why are you different?" When our behavior and speech set us apart, we have greater credibility to testify as to why we trust God's word. Our testimony about the Lord's work in us is far more important and has greater consequences than anything else.

The Bible tells us that we must be ready, but careful, to give answers to those who ask about the way we live. In 1 Peter 3:14-15, we read, "But even if you should suffer for what is right, you are blessed. Do not fear what they fear; do not be frightened. But in your hearts, set apart Christ as Lord. Always be prepared to give an answer to everyone who asks you to give reason for the hope that you have. But, do this with gentleness and respect." When we honor the Lord by sharing our faith and living a God-centered life, we will be rewarded: "God will give to each person according to what they have done. To those who by persistence in doing good seek glory, honor, and immortality, He will give eternal life. But for those who are self-seeking and who reject the truth and follow evil, there will be wrath and anger." Romans 2:6-8.

"The Bible is not a book of principles to live by but rather a Person to live for."
Peter Driscoll, pastor/author

Hebrews 4:12, James 1:22-25, 2 Timothy 3:16-17

EVERY CRUCIFIXION

In his book, *Lessons from a Father to his Son,* John Ashcroft, the United States Attorney General under President George W. Bush, wrote, "My theory about elections is mirrored in what I hold about all in life; for every crucifixion, a resurrection is waiting to follow." For law officers, the crucifixions that Ashcroft refers to could be our disheartenment in not getting a promotion in rank, having to adjust to an unexpected change in our duty assignment, losing an important case in court, or even the tragic loss of a fellow officer. Sometimes, the reason why things happened as they did became evident to me only after time. In other cases, I now realize that it may not have been for me to know on this side of Heaven. When I get to Heaven, it probably will not be important anymore.

The Scriptures are replete with verses of encouragement as we wait for our "resurrection" experience. Proverbs 3:5-6 says, "Trust in the Lord with all your heart, and lean not on your own understanding; in all your ways acknowledge Him, and He will make your path straight." Psalm 62:6, "He alone is my rock and my salvation; He is my fortress, I will not be shaken." In 2 Corinthians 12:7-9, Paul tells of having to deal with an undefined problem, "To keep me from becoming conceited...there was given me a thorn in my flesh, a messenger of Satan, to torment me. Three times I pleaded with the Lord to take it away from me. But He said to me, 'My grace is sufficient for you, for My power is made perfect in weakness.' Therefore, I will boast all the more gladly about my weaknesses, so that Christ's power may rest on me." In Philippians 4:6-7, Paul tells us how to get past such hard times: "Do not be anxious about anything, but in everything by prayer and petition, with thanksgiving, present your requests to God. And the Peace of God, which transcends all understanding, will guard your hearts and your minds in Christ Jesus."

"Put your expectations on God, not on people." John MacArthur, pastor/author

Psalm 9:10, Isaiah 41:10, Jeremiah 17:7-8

DON'T GIVE UP

Upon acceptance to the PA State Police Academy, future cadets are told that there is a component to the training that will be physically demanding. For many of us, that is an understatement. One of my vivid memories of PSP Academy life occurred on a typical morning at daybreak when we went for our regular five-mile run. As I began to jog down the long, steep roadway leading away from the PSP Academy, I knew that the worst was yet to come, for we would eventually have to return up this same hill. By the time we were about midway up the hill and anxious to complete the run, a shiny Corvette slowly began to pass us. Then I remembered that this was the day for testing potential cadets. As the driver came alongside me at a very slow speed, he rolled down his window, and with a pained look on his face, he asked, "Do you have to do this every day?" With almost my last breath of air, I responded, "Yup." He then drove a short distance to the top of the hill, turned around, drove back down the hill, and was never seen again.

Often when we choose to accept the Lord as our Savior, we have the misconception that our life is suddenly going to be easier. Instead, we may encounter especially difficult situations, and we begin to realize that our expectations were unfounded. However, as we trust Him and persevere, we start to understand that the Lord allows our trials to develop more Christ-like qualities in us. James 1:2-4 shows us a way to face such times: "Consider it pure joy, my brothers, whenever you face trials of many kinds, because you know that the testing of your faith develops perseverance. Perseverance must finish its work so that you may be mature and complete, not lacking anything."

"An inconvenience is only an adventure wrongly considered."
G. K. Chesterton, philosopher/poet

Isaiah 40:29, Philippians 4:19, 2 Peter 1:3-4

WHAT'S IMPORTANT?

At some point in our career, we, like most others, will question whether the things that we do are of real value. During any given shift, a young mother may call for help in getting her stranded cat out of a tree, or a babysitter may desperately ask for help in finding the toddler who wandered off in the park. I could be called upon to go to the scene of a suicide or perhaps to investigate a creased bumper in a parking lot. In the latter incident, I would question whether this was something that should demand my attention, but then the crestfallen face of the young owner who had worked so hard to buy his first car would touch my heart. If we subscribe to the values of society, the news media, Hollywood, and so many of the songs that fill the air waves, our values and priorities will be far off target.

In Gordon MacDonald's book, *The Effective Father,* he writes, "Our bosses might underestimate us; our families might under-appreciate us; but the judgment we really ought to shoot for, the one that counts the most, is being written in the Heavens. God keeps the eternal record." Ephesians 1:4-5, "For He chose us in Him before the creation of the world to be holy and blameless in His sight. In love He predestined us to be adopted as His sons through Jesus Christ, in accordance with His pleasure and will." Everything that we do should be done to bring honor to our loving Lord--even those things that may not seem, in our humanness, to be important. Colossians 3:17: "And whatever you do, whether in word or deed, do it all in the name of the Lord Jesus, giving thanks to God the Father through Him."

"Be faithful in small things because it is in them that your strength lies."
Mother Teresa, nun/missionary

Luke 12:6-7, Colossians 3:17, Colossians 3:23

SURPRISED

Drug investigations often begin at a very low-level: street dealers selling to support their own habit. When I arrested Jimmy, I was surprised to learn that he did not use the heroin he was selling but was dealing only for a profit. With a lengthy record, he knew that this arrest would put him back in jail for a long time. Eager to make a deal, he told me that his supplier was flying into a private, remote airstrip with 10 kilos of heroin. Our team got into place, and soon we heard the aircraft circling the strip. As it approached the landing site, the lights on the plane went out in an effort to avoid being detected, but we could hear the aircraft touching down. Within minutes, a vehicle on the ground drove toward the plane. After a few more minutes passed, our team converged on the plane from all directions. The pilot and crew of three were shocked that their plan had been foiled as we placed all of them under arrest.

Those who believe in God our Creator know that when we get to heaven, we will be greeted by our Lord. There will be no surprises for us regarding this welcome. Although the Bible gives us some descriptions about our new home for eternity, no doubt, we will be in awe at the magnificence of this place that God has lovingly prepared for us. In his book, *Revealing the Mysteries of Heaven,* Dr. David Jeremiah tells us, "When we stand before the Judgment seat of Christ, it's not about whether or not we are going to get into Heaven. We will be there already. When you get to Heaven, you're not going to have to stand before the Judge and give an account for your sins." Hebrews 10:10 says Christ came to do God's will, "And by that will, we have been made holy through the sacrifice of the body of Jesus Christ once for all."

When you accepted Jesus Christ as your Savior, all your sins--past, present, and future-- were forgiven. His blood covered them all and paid the debt forever."
David Jeremiah, pastor/author

Ephesians 2:8-10, 2 Peter 3:7-13, Revelation 21:2-3

WELL DONE

After working a ten-day rotation, I had fallen into a sound sleep when the ringing phone woke me. It was rare for the lieutenant to call me directly, so I knew that the call was about something significant. Officers responding to a 911 call had learned from the parents of a 20-year-old college student that their son, Tony, had been kidnapped, and a ransom of $200,000 was required for his release. My partner and I quickly began the two-hour trip to the campus where we interviewed many persons over a sixteen-hour period. Finally, a lead took us to a fraternity brother of the missing son, and he soon confessed. Having accumulated significant debts from his gambling addiction, he was receiving physical threats if he did not come up with the money. Tony, who had been locked in a room at a cabin owned by the fraternity brother's parents, was located and released unharmed. Returning to the barracks, we found the grateful lieutenant who thanked us for a job well done.

As Believers in Christ, though, we have already received the highest and the greatest reward from our Lord. Furthermore, it is not based on our level of performance; rather, we receive it without having to do anything other than to acknowledge Jesus Christ as the Son of God and our Lord and Savior. Because we live in a work-oriented society always looking for gratification, it is not uncommon to lose sight of what our Savior has done for us which will last for eternity. Ephesians 2:8-9 says, "For it is by grace you have been saved, through faith--and this not from yourselves, it is the gift of God--not by works, so that no one can boast." Although it is pleasant to receive accolades for what we have done in this world all that really matters is that when we enter into His Kingdom, God will greet us with, "Well done, good and faithful servant." Matthew 25:21.

"Aim at Heaven, and you get Earth thrown in. Aim at Earth, and you get neither."
C.S. Lewis, author/theologian

John 14:6, Romans 6:8-9, Galatians 6:8-9

ANY SIGNS?

When we begin our career in law enforcement, it is impossible to fully understand what may be expected of us as we experience new trials and challenges on the job. Because we are interacting with people each day and not working on an assembly line or at a desk in a single office, our work can become very trying at times. Perhaps a superior officer, unaware that you had been working on your own time to gather information, challenged your lack of results over the past weeks. Maybe a member of the public berated you when stopped for an indisputable driving offence. Discouragement and doubt may cause us to think, "Is God still here? Does He know what is going on?" On some difficult days, it is harder to see Him, but those are the days when we most need to find Him.

When we take the time to look around at God's creation and ask the Holy Spirit to make us aware of all that is here for us during our earthly "visit," we will see endless evidence of His presence. Consider the beauty and varieties of the sunrises and sunsets, with no two alike. Count the different birds at the feeder and understand that He could have made only blackbirds. Realize that our creative God surrounds us with his loving touches of beauty, and this omnipotent and omniscient God is eager to hear from us. Indeed, the best it yet to come!

> The earth You created/ how pleased You must be:
> sun, moon, and stars /the mountains and the sea,
> the deserts, the fields/ oceans, prairies, and sky,
> the sea filled with creatures/ many birds on the fly,
> wild animals and livestock/each to its kind.
> Not difficult at all/ God's gifts to find.
>
> rfg

Psalm 19:1, Jeremiah 32:17, Romans 1:20

WHERE IS THE POWER?

It is no wonder that over time, some in the law enforcement profession will crumble under the pressures of the job. These casualties cause the divorce and alcoholism rates to be higher than in most other professions. This stress can also manifest itself in physical ailments, alienation from family and friends, and broken relationships. In his book, *Too Busy Not to Pray,* Bill Hybels says, "Prayerless people cut themselves off from God's prevailing power, and the frequent result is the familiar feeling of being overwhelmed, overrun, beaten down, pushed around, defeated. Surprising numbers of people are willing to settle for lives like that. Don't be one of them. Nobody has to live like that. Prayer is the key to unlocking God's prevailing power in your life." Satan knows that, too, so he will do everything he can to take away any desire you have to pray. Remember: those times when you least want to pray are the times when you most need to pray!

A simple but powerful command in I Thessalonians 5:17 says, "Pray continually." 1 Timothy 2:1-4 says, "I urge, first of all, that requests, prayers, intercessions and thanksgiving be made for everyone--for kings, and all those in authority, that we may live peaceful and quiet lives in all godliness and holiness. This is good and pleases God our Savior, who wants all men to be saved and to come to the knowledge of the truth." God is ready and waiting to hear from us. "For the eyes of the Lord are on the righteous, and His ears are attentive to their prayer..." 1 Peter 3:12.

"Prayer is God's ordained way to bring His miracle power to bear in human need."
Wesley Duewel, missionary/author

Psalm 6:9, Philippians 4:13, Hebrews 4:16

ACCEPTED

Early one morning, I responded to a call from a woman pleading for help. Her husband was out of control, very angry, and becoming more and more violent. Upon my arrival, she told me that he had not taken his prescribed medication. On another occasion, I arrested a young teenage girl who was highly addicted and working the streets for funds to obtain her next high. Many of the people with whom we come in contact each day have serious mental and/or emotional problems. While we do not always know the root cause of their behavior, most are probably experiencing an overwhelming feeling of dejection and a lack of self-worth. Many have scars that are not visible. Although our first response to any incident is to protect those involved as well as any bystanders, we still may be given an opportunity to make a positive impact that could ultimately change a person's life.

Believers in Christ know that there is a better way to live. We may do nothing more than treat people with dignity and respect, something which some may rarely experience. We may even be able to tell them about the hope that is in us. They may not be able to experience love and acceptance from others around them, but we can point them to the One who accepts us unconditionally and will do the same for them. Romans 8:38-39 says, "For I am convinced that neither death nor life, neither angels nor demons, neither the present nor the future, nor any powers, neither height nor depth, nor anything else in all creation, will be able to separate us from the love of God that is in Christ Jesus our Lord."

"Accept one another, then, just as Christ accepted you, in order to bring praise to God." Romans 15:7

John 3:16, Romans 5:5, Galatians 2:20

HOW DO YOU PLEAD?

Enforcing the laws that we swore to uphold and living on the right side of the law, we likely find it difficult to relate to the feelings one must have when found guilty of a crime, and a sentence of incarceration is imposed. The long-awaited day in court arrives; the prosecutor presents the case, and the jury now deliberates. After a time, the jury comes back into the courtroom, and the judge asks the foreman for the verdict. The jury foreman says on behalf of the jury, "Your honor, in our hearts, and based on the evidence presented, we find the defendant guilty beyond any reasonable doubt. But, your honor, because of our unconditional love for the defendant, we ultimately find him not guilty of any of the charges brought here today."

Although this scenario sounds bizarre, it is a verdict not unfamiliar to Believers. When we enter into Heaven and stand before the judgment seat, God will look at us, knowing all too well all of our sins of a lifetime. Then Jesus, our advocate, our defense attorney, will say to His Father that He (Jesus) has already paid the price in full for all of our sins through His shed blood on Calvary's cross. John 5:22-23 tells us that, "Moreover, the Father judges no one, but has entrusted all judgment to the Son, that all may honor the Son just as they honor the Father…"
Our record has been expunged, and we have been set free for eternity from the penalty that we deserve. Hallelujah! What a Savior!

"God does not regret saving you. There is no sin which you commit which is beyond the cross of Christ." Matt Chandler, pastor/author

Romans 6:18, Galatians 5:1, 1Timothy 2:5-6

ARE WE BELIEVABLE?

For five years, Lynn had been one of my most reliable informants. However, her addiction to heroin continued in spite of her claims that she would kick it. One day, I insisted that she allow me to take her to a treatment center, and she agreed to go. Eventually, she progressed to the point of becoming a counselor there before she reentered society. Those we come in contact with, especially people living on the wrong side of the law, may find any of our acts of kindness or common respect for them to be insincere or hypocritical. However, during those times when we are considered the adversary, we can still project the image and love of Christ. Our brief time with someone whom we have been charged to bring to justice probably will not result in an immediate life-changing conversion, but if the love of Christ is evident in us, the seed may be planted, and, ultimately, we will be blessed when we enter eternity. If we are living appropriately, it will not take much for others to see that we are different.

In his book, *Daily with My Lord,* W. Gwynn Evans says, "Lord, as a disciple of yours, I must not only believe, but be believable. My influencing others to follow Christ must begin with my believing in them. That is, I must convince them that they are the proper objects of God's love and Christ's redemptive sacrifice, that they are, in themselves, of infinite worth and value to God; that will guarantee every effort to save them, if only they will turn to Him." Matthew 10:42 says, "And if anyone gives even a cup of cold water to one of these little ones because he is My disciple, I tell you the truth, he will certainly not lose his reward."

"Kind words can be short and easy to speak, but their echoes are truly endless." Mother Theresa

Luke 6:35, Ephesians 4:22, Hebrews 6:10

NOT MY HOME

Desperate women work the streets until the early morning hours to support their drug addiction. Drug dealers, in order to increase the quantity of heroin they have for sale, add anything to it that resembles the drug, including rat poison. A single mom ignores her infant child as she crashes for days after having injected "speed" for extended periods of time. A young "gang banger" shoots someone on the street for taking a parking space that he felt belonged to him. A father, out of work and trying to meet the financial needs of his family, takes the life of his wife and children and then his own to end the pain. It is easy for those on the job to fall into despair as we regularly see the depravity of man in this fallen world. When we look around us, we can find many reasons to question the future of our society. As we experience difficulties even in our own lives, we may wonder at times if there is much for which to be thankful.

Despite the times filled with negativity, Believers must remember that this world is not our home. 1 Peter 2:11 tells us that we are traveling as "aliens and strangers" in the world while the Lord is preparing a home for us in a life and a place that are yet to come. Isaiah 25:8-12 reminds us, "He will swallow up death forever. The Sovereign Lord will wipe away the tears from all faces; He will remove the disgrace of His people from all the earth." We also have the promise of a life that will last forever. When we get to Heaven, we will know that we are finally home. In John 14:1-3, Jesus says, "Do not let your hearts be troubled. Trust in God; trust also in Me. In My Father's house are many rooms; if it were not so, I would have told you. I am going there to prepare a place for you. I will come back and take you to be with Me that you may also be where I am." Heaven is the best gift we could ever receive, and since it is a gift, it is free!

"For victory in life, we've got to keep focused on the goal, and the goal is Heaven."
Lou Holtz, college football coach/author

Matthew 13:44, I Corinthians 2:9, James 1:12

DIVINE PROTECTION

An officer on routine patrol heard another officer advising dispatch that he was stopping a vehicle and wanted backup. After determining the location of the stop, he proceeded to assist. When he arrived, the other officer and the driver were standing at the side of the highway. As the assisting officer approached the two, the operator appeared to become nervous. Suddenly, he bolted from the two officers who then began a foot chase. The assisting officer was able to get close to the subject who appeared to be reaching for something in his waistband. He tackled the suspect from behind, and when he turned him over, he saw that he was trying to pull out a firearm. The suspect was then taken into custody.

At home that evening, the assisting officer described to his wife the close call that he had that day. His wife asked him what time the incident had occurred. When he told her, his wife said that at the same time, she and their five-year-old son were home and ready to eat lunch. Their son told his mom that he wanted to say grace. In his prayer, he said, "Father, please protect my daddy from the bad man standing by his patrol car." Isn't it great that as Believers, we do not believe in coincidences? The Holy Spirit can lay on the heart of even a small child those things that we need to offer for divine intervention...something that we should never take for granted. In Mark 10:14, Jesus said, "Let the little children come to me, and do not hinder them, for the kingdom of God belongs to such as these."

"You're a soul made by God, for God, and made to need God, which means you were not made to be self-sufficient." Dallas Willard, author

2 Samuel 22:3-4, Isaiah 41:10, 2 Thessalonians 3:3

NOT FOR WIMPS

When I was in the PA State Police Academy, "Big Joe" was easily recognized by his huge biceps which required custom-made uniform shirts. Sitting next to him during a graphic video-training session on assisting in emergency childbirth, I noticed him squirming in his seat as beads of sweat ran down his face. Shortly, I heard a thud and looked down to see that he had passed out and fallen to the floor. Anyone entering the law enforcement profession soon realizes that it is not for the meek at heart. It is often necessary to be strong, sometimes even forceful, especially toward those who seek to disregard the law and become aggressive. However, I do hope that Joe was never called upon to perform emergency obstetrics.

It is also important for Believers to be bold in our stand for Christ and the Christian values that we attest to. However, we can become conflicted and wonder if others around us, especially others on the job who see a sensitive side and a caring, compassionate, Christ-like attitude in us will interpret that as a sign of weakness. What they need to see is our firm stand for Christ. They need to know that our true strength, our abilities, and our power all come from God. Although living up to our convictions is not always easy, it is not optional. In Acts 4:29, Peter and John knew to call out to the Lord and ask for strength and power: "Now, Lord, consider their threats and enable your servants to speak Your word with great boldness." We need to follow their example and first talk **to** the Lord before we speak **about** Him.

"Nothing of spiritual significance comes without sacrifice. Your spirituality will always be measured by the size of your sacrifice." Jerry Falwell, pastor

Psalm 138:3, Proverbs 28:1, Ephesians 6:19-20

SECURITY ISSUE

In our profession, we are expected to maintain order, admonish those who do wrong, and seek to provide a secure environment for those we are sworn to protect. This has become a greater challenge every day as respect for law enforcement has plummeted to an all-time low. Even when officers have the best possible training and are willing to go in and quell an out-of-control situation, they are often told to "stand down" by politically-motivated leaders. Active shooters have become so commonplace that the mayhem they cause no longer has the same impact that it once did. Since many soft targets have now been identified, society has begun to wonder if true security is even possible.

After we have been saved through Christ, we may wonder if we will lose eternal security if we continue to sin. Certainly, out of our love for Christ and in recognition of His sacrifice, we will not blatantly continue to pursue sinful acts, but we are likely to slip at times. God's word repeatedly asserts that no one is sinless. For example, Romans 3:10 says, "There is no one righteous, not even one." Yet, in John 10:27-28, Christ says, "My sheep listen to My voice; I know them, and they follow Me. I give them eternal life, and they shall **never** perish; no one can snatch them out of My hand." There is no security issue when it comes to our salvation. Hebrews 7:25 assures us: "Therefore, He is able to save completely those who come to God through Him, because He always lives to intercede for them." Pastor Charles Stanley reminds us, "The timing of your sins is irrelevant since they were all in the future from the perspective of the Cross. To disregard eternal security is to take away what happened at Calvary." His word reiterates that once we sincerely accept Christ as our Lord and Savior, we are secure in Him for eternity.

"God takes our sins--the past, present, and the future--and dumps them in the sea and puts up a sign that says, 'No fishing allowed.'" Corrie ten Boom, Holocaust survivor/author

John 10:29, John 14:2, 1 John 2:1-2

OUR CALLING

Every day, men and women in law enforcement are called upon to confront situations that most would run from. Hostage situations often require officers to enter a residence in an attempt to prevent lives of innocent people from being snuffed out. Twenty-five years ago in a standoff at the Branch Davidian Cult Compound near Waco Texas, four federal agents sacrificed their lives in the line of duty. Firefighters often enter burning buildings to determine if anyone is still inside in spite of the smoke that is so dense that visibility is drastically diminished. A perfect example occurred during the World Trade Center tragedy when almost 500 first responders died trying to save those who were trapped. Cameras recorded that one of their biggest obstructions was getting past those who were rushing to get out of the building. Each day, brothers and sisters on the job are called to do their work well and without regard for their personal safety. We consider our profession a calling, not a job, and it is definitely not for everyone.

Some in law enforcement have what might seem to be a strange way to deal with the stark realities to which we are often exposed. It may be through exchanging sarcastic comments back and forth which we justify by saying that they are only in jest. Our language can be coarse or our joking inappropriate as we attempt to put on what is sometimes a false bravado. However, as Believers, we are called upon to be a testament to our Lord in all aspects of our lives. We are to honor and serve Him with all our heart. Ephesians 4:29 cautions us, "Do not let any unwholesome talk come out of your mouths, but only what is helpful for building others up according to their needs, that it may benefit those who listen." The more effective and appropriate behavior is that which allows others to see the peace and confidence that we have in Christ.

"Every believer is a witness whether they want to be or not."
Donald Barnhouse, pastor/author

Ephesians 6:14, Philippians 4:7, Colossians 3:15, Hebrews 12:14

UNSELFISH SERVING

After a busy shift, the young officer was looking forward to taking his fiancé out to dinner. Traveling home in his personal vehicle, he saw a car on the side of the road, and the trailer in tow was partially on the highway. An elderly man was in a dangerous position as he tried to secure the load in the trailer. The officer, still in uniform, pulled behind the car and approached the driver to offer help. Suddenly, he heard screeching tires as an oncoming vehicle headed toward him. The officer tried to jump over the guardrail, but to no avail. The oncoming vehicle plowed into him, knocking him over the barrier and down a fifty-foot embankment. He was air-lifted to a local hospital and barely survived. Upon awakening several days later, his first question was, "Is the old man okay?" He seemed relieved when the nurse said that he was uninjured.

Most people know that one recurring responsibility of our job is to tell others what they can and cannot do. However, many do not realize that we are also frequently involved in acts of service. Often, service to others is not even recognized by the person receiving the help nor by witnesses at the scene. Recognition is not, however, what members on the job are looking for and is not why they chose this profession. Although we may never know all of the details of the circumstances when we are assisting someone in need, we are all called to serve others in all situations. In law enforcement, serving is not only a significant part of the job but also one of the most rewarding aspects, even when recognition does not come. In addition, as Believers, we have a clear calling to, "Serve one another in love. The entire law is summed up in a single command: 'Love your neighbor as yourself.'" Galatians 5:13-14.

"A test of your love for God is to examine your love for others."
Henry Blackabee, pastor/author

Matthew 5:14-16, 2 Corinthians 9:6-9, Hebrews 6:10

KEEP THE FAITH

It seems that more often than not, it is difficult for those in law enforcement to maintain a high level of faith. Perhaps this is the result of witnessing and dealing with negative, sinful behavior every day. Maybe it results from seeing the courts fail to administer proper justice consistent with the severity of the crime. Watching hoodlums destroy public property without facing arrests or consequences can make us question the very foundation of our legal system. Consequently, we can become so disheartened that we begin to wonder if God really is still watching over us.

God's word is replete with examples of those who did not hesitate to show great faith for extended periods of time. Genesis 21:1-3 tells how Abraham and Sarah had to wait into old age before having a son, Isaac. In Matthew 15:21-28, the Canaanite woman whose daughter was demon-possessed had faith that Jesus could heal her, and He did. When the Israelites were pursued by the Egyptians, God parted the Red Sea, and the people confidently crossed over. Hebrews 11:29, "By faith the people passed through the Red Sea as on dry land; but when the Egyptians tried to do so, they were drowned." Reading God's word on a regular basis is a sure path to a deeper relationship with our Creator. Psalm 119:105 says, "Your word is a lamp to my feet and a light for my path." Remembering to call on the Lord in all situations will provide the strength we need to achieve a stronger and more consistent faith. Hebrews 10:22-23 advises, "Let us draw near to God with a sincere heart in full assurance of faith, having our hearts sprinkled to cleanse us from a guilty conscience and having our bodies washed with pure water. Let us hold unswervingly to the hope we profess, for He who promised is faithful."

"Don't measure the size of the mountain; talk to the One who can move it." Max Lucado, author

Romans 3:21-22, Galatians 2:16, Ephesians 2:8-9, Hebrews 11:1

MINIMIZE THE RISK

In our profession, we never know when we might be called upon to take what many would consider to be heroic actions. While conducting drug investigations, I quickly learning that serving a search warrant on a residence during the daytime could result in serious consequences. Whenever possible, I then began serving warrants at times when it was most likely that the suspects would be sleeping and less likely to cause us physical harm or destroy valuable evidence. Those in uniform minimize their risk by equipping their duty belts with mace, batons, handcuffs, Tasers, and firearms and wearing Kevlar vests. When we are dispatched to an incident that we know could be of a greater risk, such as a domestic dispute, we request backup or even a two-officer vehicle to assist.

Of greater importance, however, is the need to protect ourselves from attacks by the evil forces. Spending time in God's word is certainly the first and most important step to strengthen our faith. There, we learn how to equip ourselves with heaven-sent armor to protect us in our walk with God as well. "Therefore put on the full whole armor of God, so that when the day of evil comes, you may be able to stand your ground, and after you have done everything, to stand. Stand firm then, with the belt of **truth** buckled around your waist, with the breastplate of **righteousness** in place, and with your feet fitted with the readiness that comes from the **gospel of peace.** In addition to all this, take up the shield of **faith,** with which you can extinguish all the flaming arrows of the evil one. Take the helmet of **salvation** and the sword of the Spirit, which is the **word of God**. And **pray** in the Spirit on all occasions with all kinds of prayer and requests." Ephesians 6:13-18.

"A God wise enough to create me and the world I live in is wise enough to watch out for me." Philip Yancey, author

Psalm 5:11, Romans 13:12, 2 Thessalonians 3:3

ON MY WATCH

On June 7, 2009, Pennsylvania State Trooper Joshua D. Miller was shot and killed in an exchange with an estranged father who had kidnapped his young son. Prior to his shift, Trooper Miller had sent a text via his in-vehicle computer to other officers on the shift which said, "I will never let anything happen to my brothers on my watch." Trooper Miller paid the ultimate price and laid down his life so that others could live, especially this young boy. On December 30, 2016, Trooper Landon Weaver, twenty-three years old, on the job for one year, and married for six months, was murdered by a lone gunman while responding to a domestic complaint. These senseless tragedies stand to remind us of how evil dwells in the hearts of many who think nothing of taking a human life.

No matter what we face, the Lord keeps watch on His sheep. Psalm 32:8: "I will counsel you and watch over you." Psalm 33:13-14: "From heaven the Lord looks down and sees all mankind…He watches all who live on earth." Psalm 34:15: "The eyes of the Lord are on the righteous, and His ears are attentive to their cry." In His loving concern for us, God the Father sent His only Son, Jesus, to Earth to give His life for the sins of all humanity. John 3:16 assures us, "For God so loved the world, that He gave His one and only Son, that whoever believes in Him shall not perish but have eternal life." All that He asks from us is to believe in Him and accept Jesus as our Lord and Savior.

"If you accept Jesus as your Savior, you, too, will become a child of God and be among those who will meet Him in the air."
Corrie ten Boom, Holocaust survivor/author

1 Corinthians 15:3-7, Philippians 3:10, 1 John 5:20

OUT OF CONTROL

The snow had continued throughout the night, and a heavy accumulation now covered the roadways. When the Sergeant met with the first shift on that snowy morning, he emphatically told the officers not to leave the barracks until they had put chains on the tires of their patrol vehicles. About an hour after roll call, dispatch received a phone call from a man reporting that traffic was at a standstill, not because of the snow, but because a police cruiser was now on its roof in the middle of the highway. The befuddled caller then added, "The strangest thing is going on. The trooper is putting chains on the overturned patrol car."

At any point in life, things can spin out of control so quickly, and especially in our profession, we may begin to believe that society is becoming unmanageable. We may even question whether God is in control. However, we need to be mindful that God does not always reveal the details of His plans. In 2 Corinthians 5:7, Paul encourages and reminds us that, "We live by faith and not by sight." In 1 Peter 5:8-9, we find the challenge that we should live by: "Be self-controlled and alert. Your enemy the devil prowls around like a roaring lion looking for someone to devour. Resist him, standing firm in the faith because you know that your brothers throughout the world are undergoing the same kind of sufferings." Hebrews 11:40 reminds us that God's plans are always better than any we might have, and that is a promise which He has given to us: "God had planned something better for us so that only together with us would they be made perfect." We need to ask God continually to reveal what His plan is for us. He may not respond immediately, but He certainly will respond--in His perfect timing.

"In the day of prosperity, be happy, but in the day of adversity, consider: God has made the one as well as the other." Charles Swindoll, pastor/author

Jeremiah 29:11, Romans 8:28, Philippians 4:6-7

COVER MY BACK

With two undercover officers for backup, I entered a bar that was frequented by drug-dealing, motorcycle-gang members. As we walked through the front door, all eyes were riveted on the three of us, who were unknown patrons. About twenty minutes later, I recognized someone whom I had previously arrested. He began to circulate among the others in the bar, and soon they all were staring at me. Obviously, we had to make a quick retreat, so we headed toward the door, hoping that we would not be confronted. One of my quick-thinking partners started yelling at me and pushed me toward the door. He was shouting and making threats against me and calling me names. Everyone in the bar watched in surprise, and none of them interfered in this amusing outburst. On the job, it is critical to have dependable partners with us during those dangerous situations which we may not be able to handle on our own. As strong and self-sufficient as we want to be, we must recognize that there will be times when we will need help. To think otherwise is foolish.

We Believers received spiritual backup at the very moment when we accepted Christ as Savior. In Ephesians 1:13-14, Paul explains, "...Having believed, you were marked in Him with a seal, the promised Holy Spirit, who is a deposit guaranteeing our inheritance..." In John 14:26, Jesus said, "But the Counselor, the Holy Spirit, whom the Father will send in My name, will teach you all things and will remind you of everything I have said to you." In 1 Thessalonians 1:4-5, we read about the presence of the Holy Spirit: "For we know, brothers loved by God, that He has chosen you, because our gospel came to you not simply with words, but also with power, with the Holy Spirit and with deep conviction." The Spirit is always with us, but we must remember to call upon Him.

"The Holy Spirit is God's seal that you will arrive."
David Jeremiah, pastor/author

John 15:26, John 16:7-8, 2 Corinthians 1:21-22

HUMBLED

If someone were to take a poll of society and ask members to describe attributes that are necessary to be a good law enforcement professional, they may include: self-control during stressful situations; willingness to do whatever it takes to protect society; the ability to quell a difficult situation. Some may say, however, that many on the job are proud and arrogant, and unfortunately, at times, this may be an accurate assessment. Without trying to make excuses for those who do fit that description, we may find some logical reasons for such behavior. One could result from the fact that people in need are dependent upon us, and in most situations, we are able to help them. Consequently, when someone questions our authority or purpose in responding as we do, we may go into the "we are in control" mode. Because we become accustomed to trying to "fix" everything and everyone's problems, we can begin to think more of ourselves than we should. It was always frustrating to me when someone had been promoted through the ranks without having a varied experience. They were then telling me how to do my job, one that they had never done themselves.

God's word often reminds us that Believers must be humble. Galatians 5:26 says, "Let us not become conceited, provoking and envying each other." 1 Peter 5:6 commands us: "Humble yourselves, therefore, under God's mighty hand, that He may lift you up in due time." Pastor Charles Stanley said, "None of us does everything right. None of us is so wise that we always speak the right word or so strong that we always do the right thing. Remembering this keeps us humble."

"Knowledge is proud that he has learned so much; wisdom is humble that he knows no more."
William Cowper, English poet

Matthew 23:12, Philippians 2:3-11, James 4:6

February 10

WEARY

Any profession that requires physical, mental, and emotional stamina is very challenging. Law enforcement certainly demands all three, often during a single shift. I had just parked my car after completing an especially busy 3:00-11:00 PM shift. As troopers were exiting the barracks, I learned that a young college student's lifeless body had just been found in an abandoned quarry at 10:30 PM. Although I was drained after my shift, my adrenaline kicked in, and I headed to the scene to assist. When I arrived, it was apparent that the young woman had been strangled, and the perpetrator then drove over her body. For the remainder of the night and into the morning hours, I assisted in processing the crime scene. Since the weather forecast indicated that rain was going to begin in several hours, the pressure to obtain possible evidence also added to the stress. On those days when we feel that we do not have the strength or the wisdom to go on and that we cannot right one more wrong or resolve one more issue, we need to look up.

During such times, we should step back and know that God's word is always available to encourage us. That is why it is so important to study at the start of each day and remember what we read in Scripture. Then, His word can be our source of strength during difficult times. In the midst of a trying time, we can always call out to the Lord. He is always there, and He hears us. We may not have time for a lengthy conversation or request for Him, but all we need say is, "Jesus, help me." He wants us to call on Him often. In Matthew 28:20, Christ promised, "And surely I am with you always, to the very end of the age." Isaiah 41:10: "So do not fear, for I am with you; do not be dismayed, for I am your God. I will strengthen you and help you; I will uphold you with My righteous right hand."

"God never said that the journey would be easy, but He did say that the arrival would be worthwhile." Max Lucado, author

Romans 8:31, 2 Corinthians 4:16-18, Philippians 4:13

ALL ARE WEAK

A family reported what they believed was abuse to their elderly mother who was in a nursing home. As I began the investigation, it was evident that personnel at the home were very uneasy about my presence and my questions. One attendant was quick to explain that the elderly woman often got out of her bed unassisted and then fell. I suggested to the family that their mother should be taken from the home to receive a full physical examination, and they agreed. The following day, I met with the family and the doctor who had conducted the examination. He indicated that not all of the injuries were consistent with a fall. In further interviews of the staff, I learned that one of their colleagues had little patience with the elderly woman and frequently was verbally abusive to her. When I interviewed her, she admitted to being abusive and attributed her actions to the stress of a recent, nasty divorce, her kids who were out of control, and her mother's recent passing,

All people will experience times of weakness. Even strong Believers who are intent on doing what is right need to recognize that Satan will always attempt to get us off track through our weaknesses. At times, he will launch a spiritual battle as well. These battles will continue until we are with Jesus for eternity. In the meantime, we need to ask the Holy Spirit to guard our minds and hearts continually and help us to walk in the center of His will. Although nothing is new under the SON, things seem to be pointing toward a time when the Lord will finally say, "Enough is enough." Until that time, we who know Him as Lord and Savior need to be strong in our stand for what we know is His will. "Finally, brothers, whatever is true, whatever is noble, whatever is right, whatever is pure, whatever is lovely, whatever is admirable--if anything is excellent or praiseworthy, think about such things." Philippians 4:8.

"You can't understand where someone is going unless you understand where they've been."
Jerry Jenkins, author

Luke 6:45, Ephesians 6:12, Philippians 4:8

DO I DESERVE IT?

Most of us were taught very early in life that if we work hard, we will be rewarded. Children come to expect that good behavior, good grades, and athletic achievements will be recognized in a special way. On the job, exemplary work may lead to public recognition as Officer of the Year, an award for valor, or a medal of honor. At times, however, if we do not receive a reward for our labor, we may become frustrated. Many of us have known people who became bitter when they did not receive an expected promotion or assignment. Their hearts were no longer in their work, and they just went through the motions during their shift. However, we cannot allow ourselves to become discouraged; we must push on.

Hard work is a part of the human experience. In Genesis 3:17&19, as the consequence of Adam's sin, God told him that thereafter, "Cursed is the ground because of you; through painful toil you will eat of it...By the sweat of your brow..." In Colossians 3:23 we are told that, "Whatever you do, work at it with all your heart, as working for the Lord, not for men." James 2:17 explains that the natural result of our accepting the gift of salvation will be our desire to do good works: "In the same way, faith by itself, if it is not accompanied by action is dead." However, it is important that we do not begin to think that the good works that we accomplish here on Earth make us deserving or are required to receive salvation. If that were true, the gift of eternal life would not be a gift from Jesus because we would have had to work for it. Ephesians 2:8-9, "For it is by grace you have been saved, through faith-- and this not from yourselves, it is the gift of God--not by works, so that no one will boast."

"If our identity is in our work, rather than Christ, success will go to our heads, and failure will go to our hearts." Timothy Keller, pastor/author

Galatians 2:16, Colossians 3:23, Titus 2:11-14

FILLING THE VACUUM

Every day we encounter people who have a significant void in their lives. After retiring from the job, I was asked to create an executive protection detail around the clock for a high-profile individual, a multi-billionaire, and his extended family. Although the contingency of agents and I were initially awed by the lifestyle and the seemingly endless wealth of this family, within a brief period of time, it became evident to all of us that their wealth did not fill their emptiness. Others in society who are searching to fill that same emptiness think that material things, prosperity, popularity, or meaningful relationships will bring them happiness, but they are unable to satisfy their inner longings. Consequently, they may turn to ways that are not only sinful, but also unlawful or harmful. They often resort to criminal acts, drug or alcohol abuse, or even ending their lives over a broken relationship.

Although most of us may never interact with a billionaire, as Christians, we have a responsibility to be a living testimony to the power of Christ to change lives in a positive way. Like Paul, we should say, "I am not ashamed of the gospel, because it is the power of God for the salvation of everyone who believes." Romans 1:16. The manner in which we respond to any human being--regardless of their social status--should cause them to realize that we are different. A kind word or an action may be the first step in planting a seed. We may even have the opportunity to share why we have the peace that they are looking for. Romans 15:13, "May the God of hope fill you with all joy and peace as you trust in Him, so that you may overflow with hope by the power of the Holy Spirit."

"Oh, Divine Master, grant that I may not so much seek to be consoled but to console, to be understood as to understand, to be loved as to love."
Francis of Assisi, Catholic priest

Matthew 10:32, Philippians 1:3-6, 1 John 5:10-12

WHERE IS THE LOVE?

Love in this world
is often hard to find,
but the love of Christ
should remain on our mind.

It is He who first
gave true meaning to "love."
He chose death on the cross
then returned to the Father above.

God gave His Son,
a true love act for sure,
a Son so innocent,
so loving, so pure.

His love didn't stop there
and continues today.
If we have doubts
see what His word does say.

Once we know this love,
we must share it with others-
those whom Christ created
called our sisters and brothers.

rfg

"God proved His love on the cross. When Christ hung, and bled, and died, it was God saying to the world, 'I love you.'" Billy Graham, evangelist/author

John 3:16, John 15:12, Romans 8:37-39, 1 John 4:9-12&16

FORSAKEN

As we work with our brothers and sisters, we often become very close to them. Sometimes, this may be out of necessity, for we realize that we have to cover each other's back. When serving a search warrant, I was always comforted by having the biggest, strongest member of our team alongside me. Since he was also a close personal friend, I knew without a doubt that he was committed to protecting me. Admittedly, at times, I got in over my head physically, but he ensured that I was going to go home safely at the end of my shift. For one reason or another, perhaps as the result of a changed assignment or a promotion, these relationships undergo change, and someone we felt close to is no longer there.

God, on the other hand, continues to love and care for us regardless of our circumstances or whether we choose to turn away from Him. David knew that his relationship with Bathsheba was adulterous, but in Psalm 51:1, he has the confidence to approach God, knowing that he will not be rejected as he confesses his sin: "Have mercy upon me, O God, according to Your unfailing love, according to Your great compassion blot out my transgressions. Wash away all my iniquity and cleanse me from my sin." Even when we mess up, the Lord never holds that against us or walks away from us. In Joshua 1:5, the Lord spoke of His eternal love, "No one will be able to stand up against you all the days of your life. As I was with Moses, so I will be with you; I will never leave you or forsake you."

"Jesus was born to clean up your mess. But He must be invited to do His work."
Joe Henseler, pastor

Joshua 1:9, Psalm 41:9-11, Hebrews 10:24-25, Hebrews 13:5-6

THE FISHBOWL

The first time that I put on the uniform and went on patrol in a marked police vehicle, I was somewhat surprised at how closely people on the street seemed to be watching every move that I made. I also soon realized that in my own neighborhood where some people may not have known my name, even those living blocks away eventually seemed to know where "the trooper" lived. Because our lives can become very public, people tend to expect more from us and hold us to a higher standard. It is not uncommon for society to watch us to see if we are hypocritical in our behavior and whether we follow the letter of the law, the laws that we have sworn to enforce. When someone in our profession does something inappropriate, the case typically becomes very high profile, and often it is suggested that the greatest penalty available be applied.

In our humanness, we **will** fail in our spiritual walk. Proverbs 24:16 says that those seeking to live a godly life will stumble many times, "For though a righteous man falls seven times, he rises again..." Note that the verse says the righteous who stumble **will** rise again. In spite of our failings, our objective should be to continue to live in an upright manner. In addition, if others know about our missteps, their perception of us can create another source of pressure if we allow it. We Christians must remember that we always have a resource who can make dealing with our trials easier. The Holy Spirit is present both to convict us and to help us with all of life's challenges. In John 14:16-17, Jesus said, "And I will ask the Father, and He will give you another Counselor to be with you forever--the Spirit of Truth."

"We don't really get through life by solving problems in a final way but by responding more adequately as we move along." Tim Hansel, author

John 16:13, Romans 8:26, 1 Timothy 6:11-12

UPTIGHT

While working in law enforcement, it was nearly impossible for me not to become anxious at times because of the significant situations that I often faced. High-profile cases which I had developed and was now responsible to present accurately in court, the quest to solve a gruesome homicide, knowing that the longer it went unsolved, the less likely it would be resolved, even a "routine" car stop when indicators suggested that the operator has been involved in high level crime in the past--all contributed to that anxiety. The job can affect us both emotionally and physically, and if pressures are left unchecked, it will likely have an adverse effect not only on us but also on our relationships with family and friends.

Fortunately, we do have a resource that keeps us from crashing, and we can call out to Him, knowing that He is always there. We will also find peace in studying His word. Jesus is there to supply all our needs, and He should not be a last resort, but, rather, our first. Philippians 4:6-7 advises us, "Do not be anxious about anything, but in everything, by prayer and petition, with thanksgiving, present your requests to God. And the peace of God, which transcends all understanding, will guard your hearts and minds in Christ Jesus." He is not waiting for only the big concerns. He wants to hear them all. At times, an extended prayer is impossible because of the gravity of the situation and the speed with which it is unfolding. Yet, He still hears us when we simply say, "Help me Jesus."

"The Christian needs to walk in peace so that no matter what happens, they will be able to bear witness to a watching world." Henry Blackabee, author

Judges 6:23-24, Psalm 4:8, Colossians 3:15-17

FEARLESS

Pennsylvania folklore tells of a sheriff who, when confronted with a riot by miners in a coal town, called the Pennsylvania State Police for assistance. Soon afterward, a trooper on horseback rode into town. When he approached the sheriff, he heard him frantically bellow out, "Where are the rest of your men?" The trooper responded, "There's only one riot, isn't there?" When people in our communities come to us in law enforcement for help, they usually believe that we can not only right a wrong, but that we can also resolve many bad situations. Most of us in law enforcement are very reluctant to admit that there is any person or situation we might face that would cause us to be fearful. Being strong and being in control are what we believe is expected of us. In reality, there were times when fear did grip me. That is not only normal, but it is also healthy. When we begin to think that we are invincible, that is when things are more likely to go wrong.

We need to remember Psalm 28:7, "The Lord is my strength and my shield; my heart trusts in Him, and I am helped." However, throughout the Bible, we are also told to fear the Lord. Fear, in this sense, means to be in awe of His power with a deep respect and a desire to serve Him with reverence. Proverbs 9:10 tells us of the direct benefits that we will receive by doing so: "The fear of the Lord is the beginning of wisdom, and knowledge of the Holy One is understanding."

"Believers, look up--take courage. The angels are nearer than you think."
Billy Graham, evangelist/author

Deuteronomy 6:24, Psalm 33:8, Psalm 112:1, Revelation 14:7

HARDENED

The many situations that we experience on the job can cause us to become calloused. The abuse of a young child, a tragic loss in an accidental death, brutal attacks, obvious lack of concern over human life, carnage on the highway, or a scene where a person who believed that he could not continue with the hardships of this world took his own life--all can harden us. As a result, we may say "strange" things to others or appear to act indifferently at the scene of a tragedy. The officers were called to the home of an elderly man who lived alone in a trailer. Upon entry, they found the man who had been dead for many days. The officers contacted the coroner and gathered outside to wait. Their conversation was light, and at times they even joked and laughed. A next-door neighbor approached them and said, "Don't you have any respect for my neighbor who is dead?" Certainly, this person had no idea how many times these officers had witnessed similar tragedies during their careers, which they had to personally process and then move on. Although such behavior may result from our attempt to cope, we should be careful not to project an impression to others that we are unsympathetic or unloving, which certainly is not accurate.

Our God calls us to be different, so failure to show concern for others is not acceptable. In John 13:34-35, Jesus said, "A new command I give you: Love one another. As I have loved you, so you must love one another. By this all men will know that you are My disciples, if you love one another." In Galatians 5:13-14, Paul instructs us: "...serve one another in love. The entire law is summed up in a single command: 'Love your neighbor as yourself.'"

"It is the understanding of others and the awareness of their needs that the ambassador of Christ should strive to cultivate." Larry Crabb, counselor/author

Matthew 14:14, Romans 5:8, 1 Peter 2:21

ON TOP OF OUR GAME

We live in a fast-paced world with many demands, so it is easy to become distracted from our true purpose in life, especially for those in law enforcement. Because many of us view the job as a higher calling and feel a personal responsibility to make things right and to help those who cannot help themselves, we push ourselves to stay on top of our game. When we solve a complicated case, arrest and prosecute someone responsible for abusing a child or elderly person, or prevent someone from taking his or her own life, we find great satisfaction. One morning about 10:00, I was called to the location of a homicide. After many hours assisting with the processing of the crime scene, others joined me, and we began to canvas the neighborhood. After I had been working fourteen hours straight, I was exhausted. Although there was much more to do and many people to interview, I knew that I was not going to be "on top of my game" during this critical time. When two other officers who had joined the team later in the day offered to continue with leads through the night, they provided me a welcomed relief.

God's word tells us that as Believers, we have a higher calling--not as law soldiers--but as ambassadors for Him. In Mark 10:45, Jesus said, "For even the Son of Man did not come to be served, but to serve, and to give His life as a ransom for many." In Matthew 16:24-26, Jesus told His disciples, "If anyone would come after Me, he must deny himself and take up his cross and follow Me. For whoever wants to save his life will lose it, but whoever loses his life for Me will find it. What good will it be for a man if he gains the whole world, yet forfeits his soul? Or what can a man give in exchange for his soul?" Only the Lord can help us to focus on our real "game" and help us to stay on top of it. In fact, He encourages us to do just that.

"God's work done in God's way will never lack God's supplies."
Hudson Taylor, missionary

John 12:26, Colossians 3:23-24, Hebrews 6:10

ALWAYS COMPLAINING

It was not uncommon for me to get caught up in negative conversations while on the job. These often started with one person complaining about the job, a duty assignment, the behavior of supervisors, or poor conditions. Soon, others began chiming in with their dissatisfactions, and the negativity seemed to become contagious. In the communities where we serve, some people that we come in contact with also seem to be complaining much of the time. Daily news clips suggest that those who ignore the laws of our society as well as God-given laws often appear to be the most disgruntled and often the most violent. Although we will always face challenges in life, we cannot lose sight of the fact that we are extremely blessed in spite of difficult times.

In 1968, the well-known jazz trumpeter, composer, and singer, Louie "Satch" Armstrong, made famous a song called "What a Wonderful World:"

"I see trees of green, red roses too,
I see them bloom for me and for you.
I see skies of blue and clouds of white,
the bright blessed day, and the dark sacred night.
The colors of the rainbow so pretty in the sky
are also on the faces of people going by,
and I think to myself,
what a wonderful world."

The Satch obviously knew what to look for in order to keep focused on the blessings we have been given. God's creation is certainly one of them. Armstrong's faith was evident, so perhaps we will even hear his trumpet when we get to Heaven.

"The remarkable thing is, we have a choice everyday regarding the attitude we will embrace for that day." Chuck Swindoll, pastor/author

Genesis 1:1, Genesis 1:26, Psalm 148:1-13

ON THE READY

We must be alert at all times during each day on the job. We never know when we may be confronted with situations that could be harmful not only to ourselves, but also to those whom we have sworn to protect. Incidents such as an active shooter, a hostage situation, a domestic altercation, stopping a suspicious vehicle, or conducting a raid could be more dangerous than we had anticipated. On September 12, 2014 at 10:50 P.M., a lone gunman, secreted in a dense forest across from the Blooming Grove barracks, fired shots at two Pennsylvania Troopers. Corporal Bryon Dickson was killed, and Trooper Alex Douglass was critically injured. Corporal Dickson was not scheduled to work that shift but had agreed to fill in for a trooper who wanted to attend his son's football game. Corporal Dickson is a hero who paid the ultimate price. Trooper Douglass, a hero for trying to assist Dickson, sustained injuries that will affect him for the remainder of his life. Such cowardly assaults on officers occur all too often in our country today. More than ever, officers need to be on the ready, poised and prepared to jump in to deal with a dangerous issue at hand.

Believers must also be ready and prepared at all times to tell others of the good news of the saving grace of the Lord. 2 Corinthians 4:6 tells us, "For God who said, 'Let light shine out of darkness,' made His light shine in our hearts to give us the light of knowledge of the glory of God in the face of Christ." He knows we are weak, and we may say that it is not convenient or comfortable or easy to share the gospel, but He will empower us to shine His light to those in darkness. If we do not tell others of our hope in the power of God for salvation through Christ, we may miss the only opportunity someone may ever have to hear about Jesus.

"We know exactly what needs to be done to advance the Gospel and fulfill The Great Commission. The question is, will we do it?" David Jeremiah, pastor/author

Isaiah 55:11, Romans 1:16-20, 2 Timothy 3:16

ONE MORE SIN

As much as we try to abide by the laws ordained by God, it is impossible to be sinless while in this world. Romans 3:22-24 says, "There is no difference, for all have sinned and fall short of the glory of God, and are justified freely by His grace through the redemption that came by Christ Jesus." As we in law enforcement look around us, we regularly see the depravity and sin of man. We may even start to believe that some with whom we come in contact have sinned so often and so offensively that it seems impossible for their total forgiveness. Noted psychologist, Dr. James Dobson, had the last interview with serial killer Ted Bundy shortly before he was executed. He had confessed to 30 murders of women and girls, and some authorities suspect that his victims may have numbered 100. In that interview, Bundy expressed his remorse and accepted the salvation offered to him by Christ. Many people, even some Christians, were outraged by the thought that one who had committed such heinous crimes could still be cleansed by the blood of Christ.

The evil one will want us to wonder, "Isn't there a time when sins are just so many and beyond forgiveness?" If we accept that possibility for a minute, we are questioning whether Christ's sacrifice was full and complete. That is a hurtful insult to Him when we understand the fullness of the pain that our Lord was ready to take upon Himself for the punishment which we deserve. Hebrews 10:17 says, "Their sins and lawless acts I will **remember no more**." Psalm 32:1-2 tells us, "Blessed is he whose transgressions are forgiven, whose sins are covered. Blessed is the man whose sin the Lord does not count against him and in whose spirit is no deceit."

"Believe in God's instant forgiveness. The estrangement of a lifetime may be forgiven in the twinkling of an eye." F.B. Meyer, pastor/author

Matthew 6:14-15, Romans 4:7-8, 1 John 1:8-10

COMPASSION

On an early morning shift, one of my friends on the job responded to a call about a motor vehicle accident. At the scene, he quickly determined that the young operator in the single car crash was already dead. After clearing the scene and identifying the deceased, he knew that the toughest part was still before him: notifying the next of kin. Although he had delivered death notices so many times while on the job, it never got any easier. Recognizing the weight of the situation, he said a quick prayer, asking the Lord to give him the words to say and the right way to say them. After he arrived at the family home and shared the news with the victim's mother, she broke down and began to cry inconsolably. The officer, a Believer in Christ, noticed a Bible nearby and asked the distraught mother if he could pray with her. She quickly responded, "Yes, please do." Certainly, it was not by chance that this officer, who knew Jesus as his Lord, was able to bring some comfort to the grieving mother. Although the news she received that day was tragic, she will probably remember the officer's response and his willingness to attempt to give her some peace.

When we become Christians, we become part of a worldwide community, and we have a responsibility to support our new brothers and sisters in prayer and sometimes in tangible ways. Galatians 6:2 tells us that we are to, "Carry each other's burdens, and in this way you will fulfill the law of Christ." 2 Corinthians 1:3-4 describes the example that God the Father wants us to follow: "Praise be to the God and Father of our Lord Jesus Christ, the Father of compassion and the God of all comfort, Who comforts us in all our troubles, **so that we can comfort those in any trouble** with the comfort we ourselves have received from God."

"Our attitude toward others reveals our genuine attitude toward God."
David Jeremiah, pastor/author

2 Thessalonians 2:16-17, 1 Peter 3:8, 1 John 4:7

SACRIFICE

Often, people are asked to put something or someone before themselves. Some sacrifices certainly require more effort, time, or work from us than from others whose jobs do not have the same unpredictable demands. While on the job, we are often asked to make sacrifices, some of which mean that our families have to give something up as well. It is not uncommon for us to work weekends and holidays and be subject to unplanned call-outs. Over the years, I, like most other officers, missed children's birthday celebrations, their sports games, anniversaries, and other special events. Sometimes, I felt as if I did not have a life of my own.

We do not have to look far to recognize a previous sacrifice, the ultimate sacrifice, that makes anything that we are asked to do pale in comparison. Jesus came to Earth knowing that His purpose was to make the supreme sacrifice for all those who were created by God in His image, even for those people who rejected and/or hated Him. His sacrifice is made even more significant because the charges brought against Him were against a sinless Savior who was willing to pay the price that we deserve to pay. Hebrews 10:5-7 says, "Therefore, when Christ came into the world, He said, 'Sacrifice and offerings you did not desire, but a body you prepared for me; with burnt offerings and sin offerings you were not pleased.' Then I said, 'Here I am-- it is written about me in the scroll--I have come to do your will, O God.'"

"Jesus didn't come to tell us the answers to life; He came to be the answer."
Timothy Keller, pastor/author

John 15:13, Ephesians 5:2, Hebrews 9:28

MOTIVATION

At times on the job, I investigated crimes that were difficult to resolve. Even after implementing the best resources and techniques available, including extensive examination of forensic evidence, I found it impossible to reach a successful conclusion. This frustration was especially difficult to handle when a life had been taken, and I knew that the evil perpetrator was somewhere out there living his daily life and perhaps waiting to strike again. At other times, when an investigation resulted in a successful conclusion, I felt buoyant, as if I had just received the ultimate reward. When justice is served or a wrong has been righted, that provides both great satisfaction and further motivation to continue on.

When we initially accept Christ, we often feel a similar sense of elation and look forward to living thereafter with less stress and fewer complications. However, God's promised "peace that transcends all understanding" (Philippians 4:7) refers to an internal peace which is unlike anything we have enjoyed before our inviting Christ to take over our lives. This peace is not a promise that we will have no more difficult times while we remain on Earth. However, in Matthew 5:12, Christ did make a promise when He reminds us, "Rejoice and be glad because great is your **reward in heaven**, for in the same way they persecuted the prophets who were before you." Therefore, we can take heart that we have the assurance of a perfect reward from Christ: we will someday spend eternity with Him, experiencing no more pain, sickness, despair, loneliness, or discouragement.

"No circumstances, person, or difficulty can stop the plans and the promises of God."
David Jeremiah, pastor/author

Luke 6:23, John 14:3, Hebrews 10:35-36

RUTS

In any profession as well as in all aspects of our lives, we often develop patterns of behavior; some are good, while others are not. For example, the way that we have been trained to approach a stopped vehicle has been determined to be the best approach to ensure the safety of an officer. However, even routine situations can spiral into confusion. The first search warrant that I obtained and served led to the seizure of large quantities of drugs found throughout the home. Upon entry, everyone on the team began to search a separate room. After the raid and while documenting the evidence, it became evident that our procedure led to confusion as I attempted to accurately determine where items were found and by whom. Consequently, I learned that in any future searches, it would be critical to have a pattern while searching and to follow it without change.

If we begin thinking that the job is the most important part of each day, we can be distracted from what should matter most in life. Although we may know the power of prayer, we can easily forget to make praying a priority. Because we have a choice of whether or not to take time to pray, Satan will often throw obstructions and distractions in our path. Before we realize it, we have gone through another day without spending quality time with the Lord. In Philippians 4:6, we are encouraged to participate in prayer as a way of life: "Do not be anxious about anything, but in everything, by prayer and petition, with thanksgiving, present your requests to God." He is not a remote being, but a caring, personal God. "This is the confidence we have in approaching God: that if we ask anything according to His will, He hears us." 1 John 5:14.

"The prayer offered to God in the morning during your quiet time is the key that unlocks the door of the day. Any athlete knows that it is the start that ensures a good finish."
Adrian Rogers, pastor/author

-

Jeremiah 33:3, Matthew 7:7-8, 1 Thessalonians 5:16-1

GETTING THE WORD OUT

When I was doing drug investigations, one informant, a user who was attempting to get clean, provided information about ongoing heroin activity within the city and surrounding areas. Because of his involvement, he knew when major heroin dealers were bringing drugs back from two nearby cities. As I received information almost daily, I obtained search warrants and arrested the dealers, most of whom did not use drugs, but made much money poisoning others. After working with this informant for many months, he provided information about one of the largest heroin dealers in the area. I obtained a search warrant and went with my team to the residence. After entering and rounding up the suspects, I handed the dealer a copy of the search warrant. He carefully examined the bottom of the warrant. Seeing my name, he said, "I heard about you. I knew you would eventually be here." It was obvious that the word got out about the many recent arrests and seizures.

People need to know how they can have a peace that does not require getting high on drugs. Romans 10:14 reminds Christians that each of us must take on this challenge of getting the word out to this hurting world. "How then can they call on the one they have not believed in? And how can they believe in the one of whom they have not heard? And how can they hear without someone preaching to them?" We should never assume that someone does not want to hear this message. Psalm 96: 2-3 says, "Proclaim His salvation day after day. Declare His glory among the nations, His marvelous deeds among all peoples." Nothing offers a greater reward in this life than to present The Good News to someone who eagerly accepts it and begins a changed life. Isaiah 52:7, "How beautiful on the mountains are the feet of those who bring good news, who proclaim peace, who bring good tidings, who proclaim salvation."

"The same Jesus who turned water into wine can transform your home, your life, your family, and your future. He is still in the miracle-working business. His business is the business of transformation.   Adrian Rogers, pastor/author

Matthew 24:14, Mark 16:15-16, Romans 1:16, 1 Corinthians 15:1-4

"PROFESSION"

This profession I have chosen
was ordained by God above.
He gave me something special,
a job I really love,

A profession that is meaningful
when I show a caring way
when citizens do listen
and adhere to what I say.

I don't have all the answers,
but if my compassion shows,
my witness may be evident--
sometimes no one knows.

What is most important
throughout each working day
is that those I interact with
see me in a different way.

They need to know my attitude
even in times of despair
makes me unlike many others.
I truly seem to care.

So much woe fills our world today:
conflict, pain, and strife.
Lord, help me to help others
as I sojourn through this life.

rfg

LOST

At times, when I was sent to an incident at a location where I had not been before, I easily got lost. In the past, before GPS Systems were in police vehicles, critical time could lapse before an officer found the location of someone in need. A call from dispatch advised that a male had been found in a rural area. The location was unfamiliar to me, and as I headed toward the scene, I heard over the radio that the supervisor of the detective bureau was also on his way. This added to the anxiety that I was already feeling, as I thought that it was important for me to be at the scene when he arrived. As I pulled in, I was relieved to see that I was first to arrive. I quickly determined that the man was dead and that foul play was involved. Today, technology provides a GPS even on our cell phones to get us on track. As critical as it is in law enforcement to know where we are going during our shift, even more critical is the need to know where we are going at the end of our time in this world.

Those who do not know Christ are spiritually lost, and although someday they may hope to find heaven, unless they have accepted the saving knowledge of Jesus, heaven will not be found. In our daily contacts with people, we have a responsibility to those who are lost and hurting, and it goes beyond the here and now. We can be their GPS, realizing that just planting the seed or asking them if they have a faith may open a conversation that could lead someone to accepting Jesus as Lord and Savior. "For the Son of Man came to seek and to save what was lost." Luke 19:10. The Son of Man wants us to be a part of that process.

"Every Christian is either a missionary or an imposter."
Charles Spurgeon, pastor/author

Isaiah 25:8-12, Matthew 28:19, John 3:16

A POLICEMAN'S PRAYER

When I start my tour of duty, God, wherever crime may be,

as I walk the darkened streets alone, let me be close to thee.

Please give me understanding, with both the young and old.

Let me listen with attention, until their stories are told.

Let me never make a judgment in a rash or callous way,

but let me hold my patience; let each man have his say.

Lord, if some dark and dreary night, I must give up my life,

protect with understanding my children and my wife.

author unknown

CHRIST'S BLESSING

"Blessed are the merciful, for they will be shown mercy.

Blessed are the pure in heart, for they will see God.

Blessed are the peacemakers, for they shall be called sons of God.

Blessed are those who are persecuted because of righteousness,

for theirs is the kingdom of heaven.

Blessed are you when people insult you, persecute you,

and falsely say all kinds of evil against you because of Me."

Matthew 5:7-11

"We are a force for good in society and must take our encouragement from knowing that we are vigorous opponents to all types of evil."

Frank Gale, National 2nd Vice President, Fraternal Order of Police. July 2016

Matthew 5:12, John 10:11, 1 Peter 1:3-7

PEACE

Back in the mid 60's, many in our society were publicly searching for peace. A large number of them believed that they could find peace through the use of illegal drugs. At this time, my lieutenant recruited me for undercover work, and my image changed dramatically from clean-cut uniformed trooper to an unkempt hippie. I adopted their peace sign hand gesture and worked my way into their culture which quickly revealed its empty promises of peace. Instead, theirs was a turbulent world of demonstrations and openly rebellious acts attacking the traditional values of society. A good number of these disenchanted young people, however, were too stoned to know what they did and did not believe in and why. Those in law enforcement had to carry many extra burdens as they were sent out to quell riots and civil unrest in an attempt to restore order and some semblance of civility.

The misguided efforts of those who are trying to find peace in things or places where it cannot be found will ultimately lead to despair and even death. Unless those searching for peace finally discover that it can be found only in a personal relationship with Jesus Christ, they will continue to be lost, discouraged, and lacking in the joy that could be available to them. Jesus Christ said, "Peace I leave with you; my peace I give you. I do not give to you as the world gives. Do not let your hearts be troubled and do not be afraid." John 14:27.

"God has promised to every single one of us that even in our hardest times, if we would just hang on long enough, the blessings will come."
Beth Moore, author/evangelist

Isaiah 26:3, John 16:33, Philippians 4:7

CHOSEN FEW

Most likely there will be many times when we will be called upon to do things that others cannot imagine doing nor would want to do. Trying to talk someone off the ledge of a bridge, telling next-of-kin that their loved one is not coming home, advancing on an active shooter who is holding hostages, or investigating the death of a child in a horrific crash are but a few examples. This is the profession we chose, realizing that at times there would be danger and difficult situations. However, not until we joined the ranks and became immersed in the job could we fully understand the magnitude of this calling. It is often more than we had imagined. The job requires exceptional strength, compassion, dedication, sacrifice, and clarity of mind. That is a tall bill that can be overwhelming. Yet, we are able to stay the course because we realize that we can and do make a difference.

As Believers, we have an incredible resource that we should never overlook. That is the power of God. In Luke 24:49, after the Resurrection, Jesus appeared to His disciples and told them, "I am going to send you what my Father has promised; but stay in the city until you have been clothed with the power from on high." As I look back at some exciting but also potentially dangerous situations that I faced, I now see very clearly that I came through them only because God was with me. Paul asked God to fill the Colossians with "knowledge of His will through all spiritual wisdom and understanding" with words that should still lift our hearts: "And we pray this in order that you may live a life worthy of the Lord and may please Him in every way, bearing fruit in every good work, growing in the knowledge of God, being strengthened with all power according to His glorious might so that you may have great endurance and patience, and joyfully giving thanks to the Father." Colossians 1: 9-12.

"Today, see each problem as an invitation to prayer."
John Ortberg, author/pastor

Psalm 62:11, Acts 1:8, 2 Corinthians 13:4

THE PENALTY

Both the criminal and vehicle codes require that those who violate established laws are to be cited and arrested. Typically, they will have to pay a fine for their noncompliance, which can be only a monetary one or one that includes incarceration. Many lose sight of the fact that not only the perpetrator of the crime is punished, but also the victim, the victim's family, and even the family of the perpetrator because they, too, may be losing a family member for a significant period of time. When we consider our sins toward a perfect and holy God, we, too, deserve a penalty. We know that not one of us is sinless, regardless of how well we may try to live. So then, what about our penalty?

Jesus Christ offers to be our advocate when we stand before God the Father in the Heavenly Courtroom. Is there something that we must do in return? Yes, and it is so simple: believe in God; believe that Jesus is His Son, and believe that Jesus paid the full price for our sins through His brutal death on the cross. The "get out of hell" pass will be freely given to us when Jesus says in essence, "Yes, this child is mine, and I want his/her sins to be pardoned because I paid the penalty due through my sacrifice." To entertain thoughts that God will surely forgive some of our sins but not others that are far too egregious is an insult to our Lord. When we trust with a "child-like" faith (Matthew 18:3) that our penalty has been fully paid by Jesus, our salvation is complete, once and for all. Although Eternity is far beyond our understanding, what better promise than to know that we can spend it in Heaven?

"You don't need to beat yourself up in order to make God love you. Jesus already took your beating." Mark Driscoll, pastor/author

Romans 6:23, Matthew 25:46, 2 Corinthians 5:21

BOLO

When I entered the law enforcement profession, I quickly became aware of the need to be observant and alert as I sensed that it was a critical means of survival. When we get a call to be on the lookout, bolo, we increase the intensity of our awareness. We know it may be for a lost child, a deranged gunman, a suspect in an armed robbery that just-occurred, a confused elderly person, or someone intent on taking their own life. Whenever I received a "bolo" radio call, I immediately became apprehensive, knowing that the situation was probably going to be tense and perhaps even life-threatening for someone. The call over the radio was directed to me and dispatch said, "Be on the lookout for four Hereford cattle that got loose and are walking down the interstate highway." I was somewhat relieved knowing that this was not as serious as it could be, but I still found it challenging as I was a guy from the suburbs who really did not know a Hereford cow from any other. Having been involved in a "chase" like this in the past, I knew that this could be a long shift.

Sometimes, when we encounter someone in need, we realize that the situation does not appear to be as significant as had initially been indicated. Particularly at such sensitive times, we need to "be on the lookout" for the opportunity to show ourselves to be different as we interact with this person. Hopefully, it will become evident that the difference is because of our faith in Christ. In Acts 1:8, Jesus said, "But you will receive power when the Holy Spirit comes to you; and you will be my witness in Jerusalem, and in all Judea and Samaria, and to the ends of the Earth." We need to BOLO for anyone who may be in need of the best news we can provide; that God loves us and wants the very best for us.

"Men give advice; God gives guidance." Leonard Ravenhill, author

2 Corinthians 5:20, 2 Timothy 1:8, 1 Peter 3:15

LIES

I went to Nick's house as I believed him to be a suspect in a homicide. Nick was a known drug dealer and a bicycle gang member whom I had arrested in the past. Tony, his friend and gang associate, had been killed the previous night while standing outside a problem bar. I asked Nick if he knew anything about it, but he adamantly denied any knowledge. When I told him that the external cameras revealed the entire incident, Nick seemed unsettled. After I told him that Tony had been shot and a gun was observed in his right hand, Nike immediately blurted out, "He shot at me first. It was self-defense." Without the camera evidence, the lies that surrounded the incident could have made it difficult to discern the truth. The fact that Tony was left-handed was resolved when footage revealed a young woman running over to Tony's body while he lay on the ground and pulling a gun from his waist band and putting it in his open, right hand. It was further determined that the woman was Nick's "Old Lady."

Someday, each one of us will face our Maker. Regardless of what we have done in our lifetime, God cannot be deceived. He already sees all the lies. Our Creator, who knows the very number of hairs on our head, (Luke 12:7) the exact day and time of our birth and death, and everything else in between, certainly knows all that we have done, as well as every word we have said in our lifetime. That thought can be overwhelming. However, the good news is found in many books in God's word. 1 John 1:9 reminds us, "If we confess our sins, He is faithful and just and will forgive us our sins and purify us from all unrighteousness." God's promise to us goes as far back as the Old Testament, "as far as the east is from the west, so far has He removed our transgressions from us." Psalm 103:13.

"The best evidence of the Bible's being the word of God is to be found between its covers. It proves itself." Charles Hodge, theologian

Isaiah 43:25, Matthew 6:14-15, Ephesians 4:31-32

DEPENDENCE

Not everything we deal with on the job has an easy resolution. Sometimes, the answers just do not seem to be there. Nevertheless, we will not be able to resolve what is before us if we continue to try to do it in our own power, our own strength, or our own way. We may even fall into the trap of believing that we are dependent on no one and can eventually work out a solution. Many times, when working in the detective unit, I had exhausted all possible leads and felt that there was nothing more that could be done to determine who was responsible for committing a crime. To my advantage, eight of us in two separate offices regularly interacted at the start and end of our shift. During these times, we discussed ongoing investigations, especially the difficult cases with no obvious resolution. Often, my colleagues came up with a possible avenue for me to pursue, which frequently lead to a successful conclusion.

God sees everything beforehand and allows difficult situations to be a part of our job, as well as our lives. In His providence, He will carry us through anything that is in accordance with His will and a part of His plan. "And we know that in all things God works for the good of those who love Him, who have been called according to His purpose." Romans 8:28. Therefore, the first step is to love Him. "And He made known to us the mystery of His will according to His good pleasure, which He purposed in Christ." Ephesians 1:9. The next step, then, is to be prepared to see how God is going to work in accordance with His purpose. Sometimes we forget that His purpose is always better than ours.

"We may not receive the things we want because they don't contribute to God's higher purpose." Charles Stanley, pastor/author

Psalm 121:1-2, Proverbs 3:5-6, Isaiah 41:13

UNCONDITIONAL

Some crimes are so heinous that the perpetrators are sentenced to life in prison or even death as the final consequence for their behavior. For many other crimes, the penalty is less severe, and the offender is given a second chance. The most difficult crimes for me to tolerate were those when children were victims. I could not comprehend the mindset of an adult, often a family member, taking advantage of an innocent child. In my first investigation of such a crime, I was able to determine the perpetrator, who ultimately confessed. A five-year-old girl had trusted this nearby neighbor during her brief lifetime. As I thought about what this little girl had experienced, my first impulse was to leap over the table and grab this coward by the throat. When we respond to situations where people are behaving beyond the limits of what society expects or tolerates, it is easy to forget that each of those people must be treated in the same way--unconditionally. That is the oath we have sworn to uphold: "I will serve honestly, faithfully--without any consideration of class, color, creed, or condition." (PA State Police Code of Honor).

Sometimes it is hard to believe that the sins which we continue to commit are truly forgiven by our righteous God. Fortunately, we do not get just a second chance, but God continually and unconditionally forgives us because Christ has paid the ultimate price for our sins. Psalm 32:1-2 says, "Blessed is he whose transgressions are forgiven, whose sins are covered. Blessed is the man whose sin the Lord does not count against him and in whose spirit is no deceit." Satan loves nothing more than when we start to second-guess God's word and promises about unconditional forgiveness. Regardless of what we may think about the level of our sins, God does not pick and choose which ones He will forgive and which He will not. He forgives all sins for all who have accepted Jesus as Lord and Savior.

"My main ambition in life is to be on the devil's most wanted list."
Leonard Ravenhill, pastor/author

Isaiah 43:25, Acts 10:43, Colossians 1:13-14

IN CONTROL

Thankfully, we usually do not face many times when we feel that we are quickly losing control. On one occasion, it was easy to identify the leader of the angry, unruly workers who had been laid off for four weeks. As this large, red-faced man began to approach me with a club in his hand, I knew that this situation was about to erupt into a physical confrontation that could result in injuries, including my own. I quickly called for backup and was relieved to hear the sirens of the responding officers. Once again, a potential tragedy had been averted. When we have success in quelling such outbreaks, we can become accustomed to our power, and we may begin to feel that we must, therefore, always be in control.

However, when we face a situation that we cannot control, we may become very frustrated, especially if it is a situation involving our family members. We think, "I can fix things for other people; why can't I fix everything for those in my own family?" Our frustration can be minimized if we remember that God is truly the only One who is always in control. This world and everything in it belongs to Him. In Isaiah 45:7, God says, "I form the light and create darkness, I bring prosperity and create disaster; I, the Lord, do all these things." In Isaiah 14:24, "The Lord Almighty has sworn, 'Surely, as I have planned, so it will be, and as I have purposed, so it will stand." In Romans 8:28, Paul reminds us, "And we know that in all things God works for the good of those who love Him, who have been called according to His purpose."

"God does not give us everything we want, but He does fulfill His Promises, leading us along the best and straightest path to Himself,"
Dietrich Bonhoeffer, WW II German pastor/martyr

Proverbs 19:21, Matthew 6:34, Matthew 19:26

WAIT

The work we do on the job often requires a quick response. After several arsons had been committed in a small town, it became evident that the same method of operation was being used. As the fires continued, our concern was that someone was going to perish if the perpetrator were not captured. A gas station owner in an adjacent town notified us that a person was regularly filling a number of gas cans. A surveillance of the gas station revealed a person matching the station owner's description of the suspect. When a plain-clothed officer decided to approach the station as the suspect was putting the cans in his vehicle, the spooked suspect raced off. I was frustrated and felt that the officer should have waited, given a description of the suspect's vehicle, and then allowed others on the detail to close in. The surveillance was terminated. Eventually, we observed a matching vehicle near an isolated residence and arrested the operator as he attempted to ignite the home.

Sometimes it is part of God's plan for us to wait. Psalm 37:7 says, "Be still before the Lord and wait patiently for Him." Since God wants to be included in all our decisions, we should begin each day by asking Him, "What is it that You have planned for me today? Please direct my steps and help me to wait upon You." Waiting upon the Lord requires patience, one of the God-given "fruits" of the Holy Spirit. It is a fruit that is more evident in some than in others, but it is one that we can endeavor to develop. Hebrews 6:12 tells us not "...to become lazy, but to imitate those who through faith and patience inherit what has been promised." Colossians 3:12 suggests that we can make conscious choices about our behavior just as we do about our clothing: "...clothe yourselves with compassion, kindness, humility, gentleness and patience."

"Sometimes God lets you be in a situation that only He can fix so that you see that He is the One who fixes it." Tony Evans, pastor/author

Proverbs 15:18, Romans 12:12, 1 Thessalonians 5:14

GOOD AND EVIL

Some of the most popular movies of all time are about good vs. evil. From the earlier successes of *Superman* and *Batman* to the ongoing *Star Wars* saga, most people enjoy cheering on the good guys. Our society is made up of those who attempt to be good and those who choose evil. This is nothing new and reflects human behavior reported in historic documents and the Bible. On the job, we often must focus on those who are intent on doing evil because it is our responsibility to try to right the wrongs. We frequently interact with people who refuse to obey both the laws of God and the laws of man. However, in today's society, it seems that more and more people are disgruntled, dissatisfied, angry, bitter, and violent. This is evidenced by the growing number of shootings around the country, not only toward those in law enforcement, but also randomly at large crowds, and even at children in schools.

In reality, the fight between good and evil is a battle we all must face to some extent. However, without the atoning blood of Christ, none of us is innocent of sin; we all stand guilty. Romans 3:10 says, "There is no one righteous, not even one." In Romans 3:12, we are reminded, "All have turned away, they have together become worthless; there is no one who does good, not even one." Thankfully, God loves us enough to have provided a way out. We can find great peace in knowing that our salvation, our eternity, is not based on being good, although that should be our desire and goal. Because Christ has fully paid for those times when we are disobedient and sin against Him, His sacrifice on the cross allows us to live victoriously.

"God's love for me, for you, and for the world was settled at the cross."
Andy Stanley, pastor/author

Isaiah 53:5, John 3:16, 1 John 1:9

THE LAW

As I reported to the PA State Police Academy to begin my long months of training, as much as I wanted to join the ranks of those in law enforcement, I was very apprehensive about what lay ahead and wondered whether or not I would be able to endure the demanding requirements. During the first week, several cadets had decided that it was more than they could handle, and it was not an unfamiliar sight to see someone walking toward the front door with suitcase in hand. On a cold December day, my family traveled to Hershey, PA to witness my graduation and swearing in as a PA State Trooper. The many months of studying and the rigorous and sometimes grueling training had finally come to fruition. As I looked at the pride and love in their faces, I was overwhelmed by the great responsibility that I had assumed when I took the oath to uphold and enforce the federal and state laws. That ceremony caused me to consider the magnitude of that promise.

As important as man's laws are, God's laws are far more significant. In the Old Testament, the Israelites were required to follow the laws which regulated their behavior. Often, that required providing sacrifices that would cleanse them before a just and holy God. At Christ's coming, The New Covenant (promise) changed it all. Christians no longer were required to follow the intricate laws of the Old Testament because a new and final sacrifice had been provided. Jesus, who was sinless, willingly went to the cross and suffered a cruel and vicious death. In doing so, He took away the penalty of death that we, unquestionably, deserve for our sins. When we get to heaven and stand before the judgment seat, Jesus, our advocate, will say to a holy God that we are not guilty because at Calvary, He had taken the rap that we deserve. God's grace is more than sufficient for each of us who willingly accepts Him as our Lord and Savior.

"God doesn't give laws for our pleasure. He gives them for our protection."
Max Lucado, author

Romans 7:8, Galatians 3:25, 1 John 2:1-2

STRENGTH

I first met Colonel John Schafer when he was a trooper who had just transferred to troop headquarters. What first impressed me was his Herculean physique. As I spent time with him, he introduced me to the rigorous routine that he endured to achieve his impressive stature (though it never had quite the same results for me). Of the many things required of those on the job, being strong is one of them--strong both physically and emotionally. We know that many who are incarcerated, especially for a considerable amount of time, spend long hours each day working out and strengthening their bodies. If those in law enforcement lose sight of the need to do the same, encountering someone who has become physically strong and is now back on the street could present a significant threat to us.

Believers have another source of strength that protects us and encourages our spiritual health as well. The Bible is replete with verses of encouragement for those who believe in Christ and who realize that our strength comes from God. 2 Chronicles 16:9, "For the eyes of the Lord range throughout the earth to strengthen those whose hearts are fully committed to Him." Psalm 18:32, "It is God who arms me with strength and keeps my way secure." Psalm 37:39 tells us, "The salvation of the righteous comes from the Lord; He is their stronghold in time of trouble." Psalm 18:32, "It is God who arms me with strength..."

"In all my perplexities and distresses, the Bible has never failed to give me light and strength." Robert E. Lee, American military officer

Psalm 21:1, Isaiah 41:10, Philippians 4:13

TAKE HEART

Protecting those we serve, investigating criminal activities, bringing those to justice who have violated the law, and preserving the peace: these are not simple tasks. Add to the list our family responsibilities and commitments we make to the church we attend or to the organizations we belong to. Mix in the endless national and international situations that make up the tumultuous world we live in, and it is no wonder that at times we need to pursue peace. We can consciously do this by meditating on Scripture and reaching out to the Lord. There have been and continue to be times when even in my frustration, I did not consciously reach out to God. I even have thought, at times, that my lack of peace was just something I had to work out on my own. Yet, if I turn things over to the Lord, He always gives me the peace I need.

On the night of the Last Supper, Jesus knew that the disciples would be overcome by fear when the Roman soldiers came for Him. In John 16:33, He foretold some of what was to happen afterward so that they would have courage. "I have told you these things, so in Me you may have perfect peace. In this world, you will have trouble. But take heart. I have overcome the world." Even while Paul was imprisoned for sharing the gospel of Christ, he was reaching out to encourage fellow laborers to find not only peace, but also joy in the midst of treacherous times: "Rejoice in the Lord always. I will say it again; Rejoice! Let your gentleness be evident to all. The Lord is near. Do not be anxious about anything, but in everything, by prayer and petition, with thanksgiving, present your requests to God. And the peace of God, which transcends all understanding, will guard your hearts and your minds in Christ Jesus." Philippians 4:4-7.

"No circumstance is so big that He cannot control it." Jerry Bridges, author

Isaiah 26:3, Galatians 5:22-23, Colossians 3:15

PUBLIC SERVANTS

Early in my training at the PA State Police Academy, I began to learn about ways to serve those in need or distress who were looking for help. In my first weeks on the job, I often heard people refer to me as a "public servant" in a demeaning way. This usually happened during routine traffic stops for speeding when they were quick to say, "What about all those others who are going faster than I was? Are you blind?" At such times, I often wanted to look closer to see if there might be additional violations that I could tack on to the original speeding charge, and, of course, I no longer considered giving them any break because of their disrespectful attitude. However, even in confrontations with obnoxious people, we are still there to serve. The same people who are quick to be critical of us often forget that when they are in a difficult or dangerous situation, we are the first ones they seek for help. Most of us chose the law enforcement profession because of our desire to serve others, and we do not seek to make their lives more stressful.

We who are Believers have an even higher responsibility in serving. That is in our service to God. Jesus set the example when He was here on Earth. Philippians 2:5-7 says, "Your attitude should be the same as that of Christ Jesus: Who, being in very nature God, did not consider equality with God something to be grasped, but made Himself nothing, taking the very nature of a servant, being made in human likeness." We always need to be aware of the opportunities around us to serve. Then, ask God for His wisdom and direction to serve in a Christ-like way.

"Duty is ours. Results are God's."
John Quincy Adams, 6th President of the United States

Matthew 25:42-45, Galatians 5:13-14, Hebrews 6:10

HELP IS ON THE WAY

We are often dependent on others during any given shift. Back in the 1930's, the means of transportation for the Pennsylvania Highway Patrol was an Indian motorcycle. Since the bikes obviously had no radios, the officers had to pay close attention to the businesses of local merchants that had telephones. A call from the barracks notified the business owner to put out a flag, hopefully to be noticed by a passing trooper who then called in. The response time for any officer was unpredictable, and in most circumstances, backup was impossible. Even in a more modern environment with significantly improved communications, the need for help may develop from an on-going, escalating, and dangerous incident, but help may not be immediately available. Sometimes when we respond to a call, we realize that the situation has worsened since it was initially reported, and now it has the potential to turn tragic quickly. Many of us had to make a call-in for backup after responding to a crash that was reported as a relatively minor incident, but we found that it involved multiple vehicles, significant injuries, and, perhaps, even fatalities.

Our families and loved ones may also come to us in times of need. Even though we may be reluctant to admit it, anyone's needs may be beyond our capabilities to resolve. Fortunately, God is ready and willing to help us with every one of our needs, even those that we may deem too mundane to take before the Lord. In Matthew 7:7-8, Jesus said, "Ask and it will be given unto you; seek and you will find; knock and the door will be opened to you. For everyone who asks receives, he who seeks finds; and to him who knocks, the door will be open." Isaiah 41:13 reminds us, "For I am the Lord your God, who upholds your right hand, who says to you, 'Do not fear, I will help you.'"

"You don't really know Jesus is all you need until Jesus is all you have."
Tim Keller, pastor/author

Matthew 7:11, Mark 11:24, James 4:3

STRESSED

When we are feeling physically and mentally well, we feel strong enough to handle just about anything. This sense of well-being can allow us to work a double shift and then go out to play a game of baseball with co-workers. However, our battery is not always fully charged. The schedule that I most disliked was two double-backs: 3:00-11:00 PM, out again at 7:00 AM-3:00 PM, and return at midnight to 8:00 AM, to be repeated once again at 3:00 PM that afternoon. In addition to such physical stresses of the job, we are also exposed to many emotionally draining issues. We witness the loss of life, the abuse of children and the elderly, the taking of one's own life, the devastation from addiction. Even putting together an intricate investigation involving many perpetrators and witnesses, the gathering of crucial evidence, the ultimate filing of criminal complaints, and the accurate preparation of reports can be exhausting. We know that a successful conclusion with justice being accomplished is most dependent upon what we have done before we even enter into the courtroom, and that adds weight to our load.

During these times, as we seek to regain our strength, God's word provides us insight and direction. Psalm 119:28 addresses the solution, "My soul is weary with sorrow; strengthen me according to Your word." Psalm 62:5-6 directs us, "Find rest, O my soul, in God alone; my hope comes from Him. He alone is my rock and salvation; He is my fortress; I will not be shaken." Psalm 18:32-33 reminds us, "It is God who arms me with strength and makes my way perfect. He makes my feet like the feet of a deer; He enables me to stand on the heights."

"You must learn to let go. Release the stress. You were never in control of it anyway."
Steve Maraboli, author/motivational speaker

Isaiah 40:29-31, James 1:2-4, 1 Peter 5:7

OVERWHELMED

My first assignment on the job was in patrol. At the end of my shift, I handed in reports based on the activities of the day, hung up the keys to the patrol car, and went home. I thought very little about the job until reporting for my next shift. When an opportunity became available to move into another area of police work, I welcomed the change. I knew that working in the detective bureau would bring new experiences, and I believed that I was up for the challenge. After several weeks, I began to wonder if I had made the right decision. Frequently, at the end of a long shift which had exceeded my regular tour, I knew that I still had to report all that had occurred that day before leaving. While off-duty and trying to relax at home, I had to think about plans for the next shift which might include interviews, proper submission of evidence, the filing of criminal complaints, seeking search warrants, and the apprehension of the perpetrator whom I suspected of committing the crime that I had been investigating. While I traveled from one site to another, I often reflected on my new position and realized that it was far more demanding and draining than I had anticipated.

If we take our eyes off ourselves and focus on God, we can consider each day as one that God has designed specifically for us. Then, our outlook during tough times will improve. God has already seen what we will be going through, and He is available to help us if we call out to Him. Realizing that God has created the day should cause us to enter into it with grateful anticipation. Psalm 118:24, "This is the day which the Lord hath made; let us rejoice and be glad in it."(KJV). Psalm 145:1-2, says, "I will exalt You, my God the King; I will praise Your name forever and ever. Every day I will praise You and extol Your name forever and ever."

"Stop looking for the path of least resistance and start running down the path of greatest glory to God and good to others because that is what Jesus, the real man, did." Mark Driscoll, author

Psalm 94:18-19, Romans 12:11-12, 1Thessalonians 5:16-18

THE HIGH ROAD

As much as we seek to maintain peace, order, and positive interactions with the people we work with as well as with others in society, sometimes, it does not seem to be possible. When we encounter problems with our co-workers, it is especially frustrating. We know how to deal with unreasonable people in the community, but we expect that those we work with every day, those we depend on, would not be a source of contention. At the start of each shift, I eagerly checked the roster to see who would be working with me. It was always disappointing when I saw the name of one who was known for not taking his share of the assignments. If a call from dispatch requested anyone not tied up to respond to a significant incident, this officer was always the last to arrive, probably hoping that most of the responsibilities were already covered. Fortunately, this type of person was very rare on the job because most had chosen to take the high road as they swore to do in the Call of Honor: "To me is entrusted the honor of the force."

As Christians, we are called to take the high road to heaven. Refusing to seek revenge and loving our enemies are the responses that Christ desires from us. Although this is often difficult, when we choose to obey, we know that He will be pleased; we will be blessed, and in time, we will be rewarded. Matthew 5:44-46 directs us, "But I tell you: love your enemies and pray for those who persecute you, that you may be sons of your Father in heaven...If you love those who love you, what reward will you get?" Loving people who behave as if they are our enemies is no easy task. However, when we seek out the Lord, He can keep us on the high road.

"Taking the high road is hard work--walking uphill requires strength and effort. Anyone can take the low road--walking downhill is easy."
Rachel St. John-Gilbert, author

Colossians 3:1-2, Ephesians 4:32, 1 Peter 2:20

HARDNESS

After some time on the job, and often after witnessing horrific scenes of death, I realized that I had become calloused. That is not uncommon for most of us. Perhaps it is a coping mechanism because we see so much that others do not. Regardless of our experiences, certain incidents, especially those involving children, leave a lasting impression. One image that is indelibly printed in my mind occurred when I was responding to a crash where an elderly woman had been hit by a tractor trailer. Her body had been dismembered and decapitated. After the coroner arrived at the scene, he began to gather the scattered parts of the woman's body. When he came to her head, he grabbed hold of her long, grey hair and walked down the highway with the head dangling from his hand.

In our spiritual walk, likewise, we have to be alert that we do not become hardened. This can happen to any Believer, but our experiences on the job may cause us to become more susceptible than most. After facing a difficult situation, it is not uncommon to ask, "Where was the Lord through all of this?" In Psalm 51:10, when David was pleading for forgiveness and renewal, he knew that his heart attitude had to change: "Create in me a pure heart, O God, and renew a steadfast spirit within me." Jesus affirmed His desire to heal us as He indicates that we have to make a conscious decision to turn to Him: "For this people's heart has become calloused; they hardly hear with their ears, and they have closed their eyes. Otherwise they might see with their eyes, hear with their ears, understand with their hearts and turn, and I would heal them." Matthew 13:15.

"The Lord watches over us every moment of every day. He is there---and He cares---about every step and every breath."
Dillon Burroughs, author or co-author of 30+ faith-based books

Exodus 8:15-32, Ephesians 4:18, James 1:22-24

CHANGED

On the job, we come across so many people who have their minds set on doing things that are wrong, destructive, violent, and illegal. Consequently, we may begin to stereotype people based on first encounters. I have sometimes said, "I will see him again. He will never change." At other times, I assumed how people were going to behave and wrongly expected them to exhibit a combative attitude because I had "seen this type before." My assumption about a large number of scruffy-looking guys riding motorcycles was that many of them probably had criminal records or were wanted. Instead, they were combat veterans engaged in a charity drive for a handicapped-accessible home for a wounded warrior. Because we have been disappointed so many times with empty promises from those who do not follow society's rules and laws, we are hesitant to have much faith that they will change. Sadly, this often is true, and a pattern of recidivism begins. However, at times I was pleasantly surprised when my assessment of a suspicious person turned out to be unfounded. Instead, this was someone that I would have liked to get to know better.

We, as Believers, need to remember that God is in the business of changing people. Many of us have witnessed that happen, even in our own lives. God's word, along with the indwelling of the Holy Spirit, has the power to change lives. Reading and studying God's word reminds us, "For nothing is impossible with God." Luke 1:37. Although the thief on the cross acknowledged Christ as Savior only hours before he himself died, yet Christ said, "I tell you the truth; today you will be with Me in paradise." Luke 23:43. God has created everyone we come in contact with, and He will never give up on anyone. Neither should we.

"You have never looked in the eyes of someone who does not matter to God."
Bill Hybels, pastor/author

Matthew 6:33, Romans 12:2, 2 Corinthians 5:17

SLOW TO SPEAK

Because of our experiences on the job, we often find that people expect us to have all the answers. Some who approach us are desperate and consider us to be their last resort. Dr. David Jeremiah tells the following story: "It is said that on one occasion, a young man came to a great orator to be trained in oratory. In his first meeting with his famous teacher, the potential student began to talk without stopping. When the orator finally got a word in, he said, 'Young man, I will have to charge you a double fee.' 'A double fee, why is that?' 'I will have to teach you two subjects: first, how to hold your tongue and then how to use it.'" Before we speak, we have to be careful that we do not begin to believe that we have all of the answers and do not need to hear from anyone else. Sometimes, we will be surprised to find that what we thought was true is far from the actual facts.

James 1:19-20 says, "My dear brothers and sisters, take note of this: Everyone should be quick to listen, slow to speak and slow to become angry, for man's anger does not bring about the righteous life that God desires." Proverbs 29:20 reminds us, "Do you see a man who speaks in haste? There is more hope for a fool than for him." When we show genuine concern for those we are listening to, and they sense that we really want to hear what they have to say, it may show us to be different from so many around us. Then, others may be more willing to hear what we have to say, especially about the best news we could ever share: their Creator loves them very much and has a plan for them in this life and throughout eternity.

"Most people do not listen with the intent to understand; they listen with the intent to reply." Stephen Covey, author

Proverbs 10:19, Proverbs 17:28, Proverbs 18:2

ABUSE OF AUTHORITY

The first time that I stopped someone for a traffic violation and walked up to her vehicle, I sensed that she was very upset. She began to cry as I explained that she was going well over the speed limit. After I told her that I was going to have to arrest her, she cried out, "Oh, please don't. I have young children at home. They need me!" I immediately realized that she had interpreted "arrest" to mean taking her into custody and possibly being incarcerated. Fortunately, after I was able to explain the consequences in everyday terminology, she felt great relief. On another occasion, I stopped a vehicle for going through a red light. An elderly male driver said, "Good morning, officer. Have I done something wrong?" He politely gave me his license, and when I explained the violation, he said, "Oh, I am so sorry. I am not from the area; in fact, I am lost." Soon he was happily on his way with directions and a warning. After several such incidents, I realized that exercising discretion in using my authority could determine the outcome of each situation.

In Romans 12:3, Paul cautions us, "...Do not think of yourself more highly than you ought, but rather think of yourself with sober judgment, in accordance with the measure of faith God has given you." This "power" that we have on the job can quickly turn into an arrogant demeanor. Believers who are filled with pride can cause others to reject the good news of salvation that we know. Why would anyone want to be like us if we have a haughty attitude because of the power granted us in our profession? Proverbs 16:18 warns, "Pride goes before destruction, a haughty spirit before a fall." James 4:10 tells us to "Humble yourselves before the Lord, and He will lift you up."

"The key to winning is choosing to do God's will and loving others with all you've got." Lou Holtz, college and pro football coach

Proverbs 11:2, Romans 12:16, Philippians 2:3, James 4:6

ROUTINE

Anyone on the job soon realizes that even though our days can be action-packed, some of our responsibilities are routine, just as in any other profession. In some areas of the job, it is critical to follow routine procedures for safety reasons. Even when an incident initially appears to be routine, it may be far from that. An everyday car stop is common place. However, we follow the routine that we have been taught, realizing that at any of these stops, a subject may have reasons for not wanting to be identified. A seasoned officer stopped a vehicle and determined that there were outstanding warrants for the operator. He placed him under arrest, cuffed him, and placed him in the rear of the patrol car. After several minutes, the suspect pulled out a small gun that the officer had not noticed, and he shot the officer in the back of the head. After freeing himself, the perpetrator then drove away in the officer's patrol car.

In our spiritual walk, it is easy to slip into negative routines. When people first learn how to know Jesus in a personal way, they may be on fire about their new-found relationship. Often, they are eager to tell others about the peace they now have and with it the assurance of eternity in heaven. 2 Corinthians 5:17 says, "Therefore, if anyone is in Christ, he is a new creation; the old has gone, the new has come!" In contrast, other Believers become uncomfortable and find it difficult to share this information. They may be concerned that it will not be well received or that they may be ridiculed. As those intent on following Jesus, we should routinely remember that with everyone we meet, we may be the only person in their lifetime who will ever have the opportunity to show them the way to Christ.

"God has a plan, and it should be our goal to live out that plan to the best of our knowledge and ability." Charles Stanley, pastor/author

Matthew 24:42-43, Mark 13:33-34, 2 Timothy 1:9

STANDING ALONE

After receiving information from my repeatedly reliable informant, we conducted a successful raid and arrested several high-level drug dealers. On the day of the trial, the defense attorney for one of the defendants requested the judge to order me to reveal the identity of my source. When this informant had agreed to provide information about on-going drug activity, I gave him my word that his identity would never be revealed, knowing that if I broke that promise, his life would be in jeopardy. As the court was about to adjourn for lunch, the judge called the prosecuting attorney to the bench. The judge said that if I did not release the name of the informant after lunch, I would be held in contempt of court and be immediately incarcerated. I did not have lunch that day, for I felt an overwhelming sense that I was now standing alone.

Jesus was willing to stand alone in a situation of much greater magnitude and everlasting significance when He told the Father that He would go to the cross on behalf of all in His creation to pay the penalty that we deserve for our sinfulness. What depths of loneliness Christ must have felt as He carried the cross, knowing that He soon would be nailed to it. Yet, even as Jesus hung on the cross, His compassion for mankind never wavered. Among His last words, Jesus said, "Father forgive them; for they know not what they do." Luke 23:34. About 700 years before the crucifixion, Isaiah prophesied: "But He was pierced for our transgressions, He was crushed for our iniquities; the punishment that brought us peace was upon Him, and by His wounds we are healed." Isaiah 53:5. In John 19:30, Jesus, alone on the cross, proclaimed, "It is finished." as He completed His work on Earth.

"Love was compressed for all history in that lonely figure on the cross, who said that He could call down angels at any moment on a rescue mission but chose not to--because of us. At Calvary, God accepted His own unbreakable terms of justice." Philip Yancey, author

Isaiah 53:3-5, Luke 23:33, John 19: 28-30

PRIORITIES

As children, we usually learn the importance of keeping things in order. If we are haphazard about this, our lives can become so scattered that we accomplish little, and what we do is often not done well. During each shift, a call from dispatch may quickly take priority over what we had planned to do that day. A sense of urgency always accompanied a call that directed me to an "accident with injuries." When I arrived at a site where there were multiple injuries, I had to quickly prioritize and attend first to the obviously more seriously injured victims. Often, after I determined that a victim was dead, I had to quickly move past that fact and look for someone that I could help. During those times when it was impossible for me to give aid because of the nature of the injuries, the lack of medical equipment at hand, or the need for professional medical knowledge, the ambulance always seemed to be taking too long to arrive. I often wondered if the first responders were involved in another incident and if they, too, had to prioritize their calls.

The best way to ensure that we will make proper decisions in a timely manner during our shift is to start each day by calling out to the Lord and asking Him to direct our path and help us to prioritize. He will do so and also provide peace along the way. In Genesis 1:31, God established an order to everything, and when He completed the creation of Earth, "God saw all that He had made, and it was very good." 1 Corinthians 14:33 says that "God is not a God of disorder but of peace." James 3:17 tells us, "But the wisdom that comes from heaven is first of all pure; then peace-loving, considerate, submissive, full of mercy and good fruit, impartial and sincere." When we seek an orderly plan and prioritize our responsibilities with wisdom from above, we can rest in knowing: "…in all things, God works for the good of those who love Him." Romans 8:28.

"By failing to prepare, we prepare to fail." Benjamin Franklin, statesman/scientist/inventor

Matthew 6:19, Luke 12:29-31, Romans 12:2

GOOD INFORMATION

Much of our daily work in law enforcement is dependent upon getting good information, though sometimes we receive inaccurate information. An eyewitness to a crime can provide valuable information which leads to solving a case. Yet, the weakest information sometimes comes from an "eyewitness" who, in the heat of the moment, became confused about what he or she actually saw. Others deliberately provide untrue information in an effort to deceive us about their involvement in an incident. Gathering accurate statements and discovering valuable evidence are critical in our work. At times, we have to rely on tips from confidential informants, most of whom have been involved in or continue to be involved in criminal activity. They become trustworthy only when their information is validated.

Dr. James Kennedy's book, *Why I Believe,* provides extensive examples of archeological evidence and historical secular documents which authenticate the Bible. One dramatic account tells of the atheist archaeologist, Sir William Ramsey, Ph.D., who spent decades attempting to undermine the Bible. However, after careful examination of the book of Acts, he could not refute any details. Soon, he revealed that he had become a Christian! 2 Timothy 3:16 assures that the Bible is eternal and inerrant: "All Scripture is God-breathed..." God's word **never** changes. 2 Peter 1:20-21 explains, "Above all, you must understand that **no** prophecy of Scripture came about by the prophet's own interpretation. For prophecy never had its origin in the will of man, but men spoke from God as they were carried along by the Holy Spirit."

"Looking for a word from the Lord? Believe that He has already spoken and read what He has already written." Mark Driscol, pastor/author

Psalm 119:142, Luke 24:44-48, Revelation 22:18-19

DIFFERENT

On my first undercover assignment, I was very apprehensive about fitting in with those from whom I needed to get information about illegal activity or perhaps even purchase stolen guns, drugs, or other contraband. I knew that if I acted differently from those I would be spending time with, some might begin to question who I really was. When we are on the job, we encounter many people who are crude, vile, and coarse; sometimes they are among those we work with. Some believe that our persona on the job must be one of toughness, and coarse language goes with that. When we hear inappropriate language so regularly, we can become accustomed to it and even start using it ourselves. Because it is so commonplace in our society, those who guard their tongues are soon recognized as being different. Since our choice of words may be one of the first signs that others recognize as making us different, we may then have credibility when we witness for Christ.

Believers really do not have an option about the way we talk. 2 Corinthians 5:17 enthusiastically exclaims, "Therefore, if anyone is in Christ, he is a new creation; the old has gone, the new has come!" Romans 12:2 cautions, "Do not conform any longer to the pattern of this world, but be transformed by the renewing of your mind. Then you will be able to test and approve what God's will is--His good, pleasing and perfect will." James reminds us in 3:10, "Out of the same mouth comes praise and cursing. My brothers, this should not be." Being different may cause our co-workers to avoid discussing our beliefs with them. Interestingly, however, when they are going through difficult times, they may come to us in "private" and ask for our advice, even wanting us to pray for them.

"You have no idea the number of people that God may want to influence through you."
Andy Stanley, pastor/author

Psalm 1:1, Proverbs 12:2, Matthew 15:10-11

BEWARE

When we learn of a violent person who is wanted by a law enforcement agency and may be in the area, bulletins often go out describing the suspect and calling for people to beware. Our society continues to be more violent all the time, and we have to be aware not only of foreign terrorists but of homegrown terrorists as well. While interacting with so many people each day on the job, I often told them to be careful, cautious, and alert. Because I had investigated so many burglaries, I learned where property owners may be vulnerable, so I shared ways to better secure a home or business with the victims. I have also taught classes to women on risk awareness and assessment and to children on the dangers that they, too, may encounter.

Believers also need to be aware that when we seek to do what is right, based on the biblical principles that we follow, the evil one is not pleased and will constantly attack us in the hope that we will fall and fail. The Bible issues numerous alerts to us about various situations that we may face while it also reminds us of the power that we have to overcome such attacks and circumstances. Through the presence of the Holy Spirit, who lives within us, God provides us with all the wisdom and strength that we need. 1 John 4:4 reassures us, "You, dear children, are from God and have overcome them, because the One who is in you [the Holy Spirit] is greater than the one who is in the world." [Satan].

"I have held many things in my hands, and have lost them all; but when I have placed them in God's hands, that I still possess." Martin Luther, leader of the Protestant Reformation

1 Samuel 2:9, Psalm 12:1-7, Matthew 10:17, Philippians 3:2

THE REAL TRUTH

During a home burglary investigation of a residence owned by a wealthy, elderly couple, the perpetrators had assaulted the husband when he refused to open a safe. When I developed a person of interest and called her to the barracks for an interview, she adamantly denied any involvement in the crime. I said to her, "I am sure then that you are willing to take a polygraph. She seemed uneasy but eventually agreed to take the test. The examiner put the attachments on this woman who now appeared worried. After several questions, the examiner said, "This machine is never wrong, and you are being deceptive." Breaking down, she blurted out, "I was with my boyfriend, but I had no idea he was going to hurt that old man." Although the polygraph cannot be used in court, it was still effective in proving the real truth.

Some scholars have dedicated much of their lives trying to prove the inaccuracy of the Bible. However, after extensive study, many recognized that the facts of God's word are infallible. Believers know that there are absolutes, and they are found in the Bible. We also know that God's word is inerrant, and that is why we believe as we do. God Himself provides a way to test the authenticity of prophecies in Deuteronomy 18:18, 22: "I will raise up for them a prophet like you from among their brothers; I will put my words in his mouth, and he will tell them everything I command him... If what a prophet proclaims in the name of the Lord does not take place or come true, that is a message the Lord has not spoken." Dr. James Kennedy noted in *Why I Believe,* that more than 2,000 specific and detailed prophesies in the Old Testament alone have already come to fruition. He said, "Predictions are also promises. I believe that God gave us more than two thousand predictions in order that we may learn to believe His promises."

"The Bible has stood the test of time because it is divinely inspired by Almighty God, written in ink that cannot be erased by any man, religion, or belief system."
Billy Graham, evangelist/author

Psalm 53:1, Isaiah 46:9-10, 1 Thessalonians 5:20-21

LIGHTEN UP

When the daily stresses of the job wear us down and we feel beaten up and discouraged, it is a good time to step back, relax, and enjoy the less serious things in life. As members of the State Police Rodeo team, we met in May of each year to begin practicing prior to traveling throughout the state to perform. One of the trick riders, known for his sense of humor, had purchased a small donkey which he thought would be a great mascot for our team. At the end of the summer, he faced the task of finding a home for his four-legged friend. As he left the PA State Police Academy and headed home with the top down on his convertible, the donkey sat in the back seat. When he reached the toll gate on the turnpike, the attendant almost fell out of the booth when she saw the trooper's donkey sitting calmly in the back and enjoying the balmy weather. Maintaining a straight face, the trooper did not acknowledge that anything was out of the ordinary. However, after he drove through the tollgate, he bellowed like his donkey as he recalled the woman's astonished gaze.

Some may think that living a Christian life must be serious, boring, and without fun. However, nothing in God's word indicates that we are to live like that. In fact, the word "laughter" appears several times in the Bible. God may have a sense of humor as well. In Genesis 17:17, God told Abraham that his ninety-year-old, childless wife, Sarah, was going to give birth to a son. In disbelief, "Abraham fell facedown; he laughed." Later in Genesis 18:12, when Sarah heard the news, "Sarah laughed to herself as she thought, 'After I am worn out and my master is old, [about 100 years] will I now have this pleasure?'" Perhaps upon hearing this news at their age, laughing was all they could do. At any rate, Psalm 33:1 tells us that joy should be a part of our lives, "Sing joyfully to the Lord, you righteous; it is fitting for the upright to praise Him."

"A day without laughter is a day wasted." Charlie Chaplin, actor/comedian

Psalm 118:24, Psalm 126:2-3, Proverbs 15:13

THE ENEMY

Recent newspaper headlines have been filled with reports of the ever-increasing attacks on officers: a sheriff putting gas in his patrol car was shot to death while he stood at the pump; a California officer was fatally shot by a paroled gang member after a car crash; a Texas officer was shot after stopping a car for a traffic violation. In addition, we also read about extremist terrorists who have chosen to come to America to fight against all that our country stands for and take as many innocent lives as possible. Their goal is "collateral damage," attempting to murder as many as they can at one time. As "Soldiers of the Law" (PA State Police Call of Honor), we are aware that we have enemies who seek to devour us. Knowing this should cause us to be extremely vigilant and ready to defend ourselves whenever necessary.

We must not lose sight that we also have an enemy who is not visible to us in human form, but he, too, is seeking to devour and destroy us. 1 Peter 5:8-9 reminds us, "Be self-controlled and alert. Your enemy the devil prowls around like a roaring lion looking for someone to devour. Resist him, standing firm in the faith." Ephesians 6:11,16 tells us: "Put on the full armor of God so that you can take your stand against the devil's schemes…Take up the shield of faith with which you can extinguish all the flaming arrows of the evil one." Throughout life, we need to be conscious not only of those in human form who are our enemies, but also of the evil one who diligently attempts to attack us.

"Satan, like a fisher, baits his hook according to the appetite of the fish."
Thomas Adams, priest.

Ephesians 6:12-15, 2 Thessalonians 3:3, James 4:7

KEEP THE PEACE

When we consider the responsibilities that we shoulder and the lives that we impact, we should recognize that our profession is a high calling. Those who stand against crime and violence face a daunting task. Often, we are called upon to enter into volatile situations, strikes, and protests. When called to domestic disputes, we attempt to encourage spouses to make peace. Society expects us to be peacekeepers, but making peace with those we have to confront does not always go as we would like. At times, the people with whom we are engaging exhibit a high level of emotion and may act out their rage or frustration. Fortunately, some will eventually listen to us, but getting them to the point where the situation can be resolved requires great insight and wisdom on our part.

As Believers, we are also called to be peacemakers. When we enter into "battle," it is imperative that we initiate a conversation with God and ask Him for help. James 1:5-6 reassures us that He will provide us with the words to say and the way to say them: "If any of you lacks wisdom, he should ask God, who gives generously to all without finding fault, and it will be given to him. But when he asks, he must believe and not doubt, because he who doubts is like a wave of the sea, blown and tossed by the wind." In Psalm 32:8, we see that God keeps a watchful eye on us as He leads us to make the best decisions: "I will instruct you and teach you in the way you should go; I will counsel you and watch over you."

"God looked at your entire life, determined your assignment, and gave you the tools to do the job." Max Lucado, author

Ecclesiastes 2:26, Matthew 5:9, Philippians 4:6-7

STRIFE

Thinking back to the first time that I was called to testify in court about an arrest I had made, I had no idea about what was facing me. Once the jury arrived, the court crier announced the arrival of the judge as the entire courtroom stood up and the trial began. I sat in the front of the courtroom next to the prosecuting attorney. When directed to proceed to the stand to begin my testimony, I focused on being honest, accurate, and articulate in stating the details of the case. After I presented the facts of the case, the defense attorney began to cross examine me. He was brutal and did everything in his power to discredit my initial testimony. Maintaining my composure while trying not to appear to be intimidated or nervous was very stressful as I responded to the caustic inquisition by the defense attorney. Court appearances are just one of the many areas in law enforcement that can create significant stress. As we face each day, our job demands that we remain in control, provide necessary assistance when called upon, and often to think quickly in dangerous situations. As we face these challenges, we may begin to feel overwhelmed. When this happens, we can become less productive, difficult to be around, and even unable to focus.

Help is on the way when we redirect this tension and call upon God, for He will supply our every need. Isaiah 26:3-4 tells us that trusting in the Lord is the key to reducing strife, "You will keep in perfect peace him whose mind is steadfast, because he trusts in You. Trust in the Lord forever, for the Lord, the Lord, is the Rock eternal." Psalm 32:7 illustrates a safety zone where we can always find solace: "You are my hiding place; You will protect me from trouble and surround me with songs of deliverance."

"What lies behind us and what lies before us are tiny matters compared to what lies within us." Oliver Wendell Holmes. Associate Justice of the Supreme Court 1902-1932.

Psalm 37:23-24, John 14:27, Philippians 4:7

DISHARMONY

Each day on the job, we interact with people, many of whom are unreasonable. When I ran radar on a busy highway, many drivers that I stopped demanded to know why I did not stop the car in front of them. Sometimes after I stopped a driver, walked to his car window, and asked for his license and registration, he would say, "What for?" Such a reaction was a signal that the remainder of our conversation was not going to go well. Early on the job, I determined that if I ever attempted to physically subdue an unruly person, I had to be certain that I was able to win the physical confrontation that would erupt. Consequently, I used words first as my most powerful weapon. That weapon is also important as we find, perhaps surprisingly, that other difficult people may be some with whom we regularly work. Although we may not see eye to eye today, disharmony among officers is dangerous, for tomorrow, that officer may be our backup.

Psalm 133:1 tells us, "How good and pleasant it is when brothers live together in unity!" In the ideal world, we should expect fellow Believers to be in harmony all the time. However, in our humanness, we all are likely to be offensive to each other from time to time. Loving one another, however, no matter how difficult it may be, is not optional. 1 John 4:11-12 tells us of the benefits we will reap when we show the love of Christ to others: "Dear friends, since God so loved us, we also ought to love one another. No one has ever seen God; but if we love one another, God lives in us and His love is made complete in us."

"God teaches us to love by putting some unlovely people around us. It takes no character to love people who are lovely and loving to you." Rick Warren, pastor/author

John 13:34-35, 2 Corinthians 13:14, 1 John 2:10

FITTING IN

Most often, people want to fit in. This desire starts early when children leave the security of their home and parents and go to school. They want to make friends and fit in. When families move to a new town or state, both the kids and the parents want to fit in and make new friends. When I walked through the doors of the PA State Police Academy for the first time, I had no idea what was ahead of me, but I wanted to fit in. I certainly did not want to stand out because if I did, it most likely meant that I was about to be disciplined. In my first assignment in an undercover capacity, someone had vouched for me to gain entry to a private club where a large-scale gambling operation was going on each night. Although I knew nothing about gambling, my goal was to act confidently and not become noticeable while I acquired information that could lead to a search warrant. I subtly tried to fit in with others in the club. My backup would be right down the street, and if a significant problem occurred, I was to pick up a chair and throw it through the front window.

Sometimes, however, as Believers we should not fit in with others. When Jesus came to this world, He was very different. In Luke 9:23, He challenges us, "If anyone would come after Me, he must deny himself and take up his cross daily and follow Me." Paul did just that and preached in Romans 12:2: "Do not conform any longer to the pattern of this world, but be transformed by the renewing of your mind. Then you will be able to test and approve what God's will is." If we seek peace and joy in the wrong places, with the wrong people, we will never be truly satisfied. 1 John 2:15, 17 tells us, "Do not love the world or anything in the world…The world and its desires pass away, but the man who does the will of God lives forever." That does not mean we are to live with somber, sullen hearts, though. In Philippians 4:4, Paul reminds us, "Rejoice in the Lord always. I will say it again: Rejoice!"

"If I walk with the world, I can't walk with God."
Dwight L. Moody, American evangelist

Matthew 16:25-27, James 4:4, 1 John 5:18-20

LEGACY

Various stages in my career allowed me to witness firsthand the behind-the-scenes lives of millionaires and even billionaires. While some of these people thought only of their own needs and pleasures, others were generous and wanted to leave a significant legacy, signifying that their lives had made a difference in the world. A nearby hospital was the beneficiary of a gift of one hundred million dollars that allowed it to build a state-of-the-art cancer center. A local businessman has been underwriting a missionary effort in Siberia for decades. A new elementary school bears the name of the man who funded it. Although most of us will not have opportunities to leave such legacies, what we do every day on the job can make a societal difference. However, when we are gone, how significant will that be? Will anyone remember anything we have done?

The best legacy that we could have is being known for our ongoing desire to love and serve the Lord and being eager to tell the lost world about Him. If we plant the seed of salvation, water it, or have the privilege of bringing someone to the saving knowledge of Christ, that would cause the Lord to say, "Well done, good and faithful servant." Matthew 25:21. When we leave this life, Death will not sting us, but God will grant us immortality. 1 Corinthians 15:57-58 offers both assurance and encouragement to us as we continue to work out our legacy: "But thanks be to God! He gives us the victory through our Lord Jesus Christ. Therefore, my dear brothers, stand firm. Let nothing move you. Always give yourself fully to the work of the Lord, because you know that your labor in the Lord is not in vain."

"The Lord wants us to walk wisely so that we can enjoy all of the marvelous benefits that He's promised in his Word and longs to give us." Charles Stanley, pastor/author

Matthew 25:23, Romans 12:11, Hebrews 6:10-12

GUARDED

Working the 3:00 to 11:00 PM shift along with four other officers, Trooper Roberts was assigned to patrol a major highway. Soon, a radio broadcast announced that another trooper was in pursuit of a vehicle traveling at a high rate of speed, and the operator was refusing to stop. Immediately, Trooper Roberts joined the other officers in the pursuit, and they covered many miles while the suspect still refused to stop. As the suspect attempted to elude the officers, Trooper Roberts was the only officer able to stay close to the suspect vehicle. Suddenly, the driver diverged from the highway onto a secondary road, traveled a short distance, drove into a field, and then jumped out of his car. Trooper Roberts dashed out of his patrol car and began to chase the suspect on foot. Shortly, shots rang out, and Trooper Roberts was hit in the arm and then in the chest. As he fell to the ground, he returned fire and subdued the suspect. Of the five officers working that night, Trooper Roberts was the only one wearing a Kevlar vest, which physically protected his heart. Consequently, he survived the shooting and soon recovered.

We Believers need to guard our hearts both physically and spiritually. Our society constantly bombards us with things that can pull us down spiritually. Many of them are subtle, such as suggestive billboards along the roadways that we cannot avoid. Others, like television shows and movies that are overtly filled with sex and violence, we can choose not to view. The Lord offers us a source of protection that covers all things and situations, but it is up to us to implement it. Paul tells us in Philippians 4:6-7, "Do not be anxious about anything, but in everything, by prayer and petition, with thanksgiving, present your requests to God. And the peace of God, which transcends all understanding, will guard your hearts and your minds in Christ Jesus."

"God develops Christlike character in you by allowing circumstances where you're tempted to express the exact opposite quality!" Rick Warren, pastor/author

1 Samuel 16:7, Proverbs 4:23, Proverbs 27:19

ABOVE AND BEYOND

Each day as my shift began, I wondered if I would have an "out of the norm" experience. Knowing that we could be called into harm's way at any moment, we develop a sense to always be ready to go beyond our regular duties. This awareness even carries over to times when we are not on duty. One day, my wife and I were traveling on a highway when a car several vehicles ahead of us suddenly veered off the roadway, traveled down an embankment, and rolled onto its roof. Immediately pulling off the road, I jumped out of my car and raced to the vehicle. Pulling the door open and grabbing the driver, I assisted him in getting away from the car which soon burst into flames. When the situation was under control, I returned to my car and found my wife still visibly shaken. Her first words were, "Do you realize what could have happened to you?" I told her that I had not given it much thought. Often, we do not think about taking such actions because our job calls us to go above and beyond, and it becomes instinctive to do so.

The Father called Jesus to go above and beyond and sacrifice His life even for those who do not want to acknowledge Him. Because Jesus and God are One, He already knew the agony that He would soon suffer. In Mark 14:34-36, we hear His distress as He prayed in the garden, "My soul is overwhelmed with sorrow to the point of death." [v.34]. Because He lived on Earth as a human for thirty-three years, He also had human feelings as He agonized, "Abba, Father, everything is possible for You. Take this cup from me." [v.36]. Yet, He ends His prayer in total submission to God the Father and provides an example for us to follow: "Yet not what I will, but what You will." In 1 Peter 2:24, Peter, who had been with Him that night, said, "He, Himself, bore our sins in His body on the tree, so that we might die to sins and live for righteousness; by His wounds you have been healed." Let us ponder where we would be had He not done so.

"What touches His (Jesus's) heart is not how much we know but how much we love. Not how pure we are, but how passionate." Ken Gire, author

Matthew 27:30-31, Luke 9: 23-26, Romans 12:1, Hebrews 5:7-9

DECEIVED

My informant had provided details about a major drug dealer and was to take an undercover officer from another jurisdiction, a new face, to purchase drugs from him. Following his introduction, the officer could contact the dealer any time he "needed" to buy dope. After several significant purchases, we decided to make the arrest. Accompanying me to the dealer's residence, the undercover officer covered the rear of the home while I went to the front door. When the suspect answered my knock on the door, I identified myself as he attempted to slam the door shut. Then he bolted to the rear exit where he encountered the undercover officer and warned him, "The cops are here!" Flashing his badge, the officer responded, "Yeah, I know. I'm one, too." The astonished suspect then raced to the front of the house where we tackled him and tried to take him into custody as he strongly resisted. Seeing the commotion, an elderly neighbor hobbled off her porch and started beating the three of us with an umbrella. Even after we had identified ourselves, it was difficult to convince the woman that two of us were the police. As it turned out, two people were deceived that day.

The Bible repeatedly tells us to watch out for those who justify their sinful acts and try to deceive us. If we are in doubt, the truth can always be found in God's word. Psalm 12:6 tells us, "And the words of the Lord are flawless, like silver refined in a furnace of clay." Satan, the master deceiver, will never stop provoking us until we are in heaven where the door is shut to him. "No one who practices deceit shall dwell in my house." Psalm 101:7. Revelation 20:10 describes Satan's defeat: "And the devil, who deceived them, was thrown into the lake of burning sulfur, where the beast and the false prophet had been thrown. They will be tormented day and night for ever and ever."

"The greatest deception men suffer is from their own opinions."
Leonardo da Vinci, artist/scientist

Psalm 5:5-6, Romans 16:18, 2 Thessalonians 2:3

REAL PURPOSE

Often, the reality of the job does not set in until the first day when we enter the academy. When I arrived early one morning and walked through the front door of the PA State Police Academy, the demeanor of the seasoned officers, who were now going to control our lives for the next long months, was daunting. They made it very clear that we were not welcomed guests. As we began our classes, which included Criminal and Vehicle Code, Search and Seizure, Laws of Arrest, Report Preparation, Affidavits and Search Warrants, Citations and Reporting, Range Qualification, Self-Defense, First Aid, Court Preparation, and Pursuit Driving, it became evident that all of this training was meaningful and had a purpose. In the following week, it surprised me to see several cadets depart after they had endured the year-long process to be accepted into the PSP Academy. Apparently, they did not understand the purpose of the training, nor were they willing to endure it.

Because of the demanding nature of our work, it is not uncommon to lose sight of what should be most important in our lives. In Matthew 5:14-16, Jesus clearly defines what we should be doing while we are on Earth: "You are the light of the world. A city on a hill cannot be hidden. Neither do people light a lamp and put it under a bowl. Instead they put it on its stand, and it gives light to everyone in the house. In the same way, let your light shine before men, that they may see your good deeds and praise your Father in Heaven." Those we come in contact with every day must see that we have identified our real purpose.

"If you fail to discover the reason why you are on Earth, Satan and men will happily sell theirs to you." E.A. Adeboye, pastor

Mark 16:15, Ephesians 4:22-24, Philippians 2:3-5

EXPECTATIONS

After working many months in an undercover investigation of a major drug dealer and purchasing significant quantities, I was ready to make the arrest. I set up a large purchase with the dealer. John, a 6'4", 225 pounds, very physically-fit officer, was with me in this buy/bust, and his presence was reassuring. On arrival, John and I walked toward the cabin. As we approached the door, one of the suspects standing outside indicated that only I could enter. With his arm crossed and one hand inside his winter coat, John looked down at him, pushed him aside with his other hand, and walked in. After observing the drugs, I identified myself and indicated that the five suspects were under arrest. At the same time, John pulled his hand out of his coat, displaying a large .357 firearm. Taken totally by surprise and believing that we were ripping them off and then killing them, the shocked and fearful suspects pleaded to see our identification again as they kneeled on the floor with their hands behind their backs.

While we are in this world, we cannot claim that we do not know what is expected of us since God has provided a blueprint in the Bible that will keep us on track if we read and follow it. Once we accept Jesus as our Lord, our past sins are completely blotted out, and we are fully forgiven. As we continue in this life, we will never be sinless, but we will always be fully forgiven. Romans 6:23 explains that Christ saves us from the death penalty: "For the wages of sin is death, but the free gift of God is eternal life in Christ Jesus our Lord." Accepting the gift of salvation with all of its benefits seems like an easy decision, but it is one that some do not choose. Eventually, they will face unexpected consequences.

"Through salvation, our past has been forgiven, our present is given meaning, and our future is secured." Rick Warren, pastor/author

Isaiah 59:2, Jeremiah 17:9-10, 1 John 3:1-3

THE ROCK

Alcatraz, a prison off the coast of San Francisco, is called "The Rock." The nickname was given because it was extremely difficult to escape from such a place. Although I was never there, many times I had to walk up to a prison gate, turn over my firearm, and then walk through one of several iron gates that clanged as they locked behind me. Going into a prison, whether to take an accused perp that I had just arrested or to interview a prisoner, always made me uncomfortable. Especially concerning was going into a maximum-security state prison, where the worst of the worst were incarcerated, many for a very long time. As my footsteps echoed in the empty walkways, it was always on my mind that every person in each cell was there because of those in law enforcement who had done their job.

Our goal as Believers should always be to draw closer to our "Rock," Jesus, our Lord. In Psalm 62:2, we hear of the security and protection that He provides for us: "He alone is my rock and my salvation; He is my fortress; I will never be shaken." Unlike Alcatraz, our Rock is accessible. In Psalm 100:4, the Lord opens His hands and calls us to, "Enter His gates with Thanksgiving and His courts with praise." Matthew 7:24 reminds us, "Therefore everyone who hears these words of Mine and puts them into practice is like a wise man who built his house on the rock." How then should we live? "Trust in the Lord forever, for the Lord, the Lord, is the Rock eternal." Isaiah 26:4.

"Jesus is interested in a relationship with you, not a 45-minute date every Sunday morning. Make Him first in your life." Joyce Meyer, author/speaker

Psalm 18:1-3, Isaiah 17:10-11, 1 Corinthians 10:3-4

FEAR NOT

We received information from a confidential source that he was with a group who were going to pick up a large quantity of heroin. The informant described the suspects as armed and violent. Once the informant was in the suspect vehicle, we were no longer able to communicate with him. As darkness approached, the suspects went to a hotel and entered a room. Although officers could continue following them if necessary, it might become difficult to keep them in sight if they decided to move. I suggested smashing out a rear light on the suspect vehicle to ensure that we would not lose them. Knowing that the suspects might have counter-surveillance in the area to make certain that they were not being followed, I proceeded through the large parking lot. Not knowing whom I might encounter, I began to feel fearful, for my backup was a good distance away. Reaching the suspect vehicle, I quickly broke the light and retreated to the safety of my car. Then congratulations came over the radio: "Good job! You made it through the lot without being noticed…but you smashed the wrong car!"

If we do not want to admit being fearful at times, we may prefer to say that we felt anxious. Whatever we want to call it, God's word tells us how to keep calm. When the disciples did not recognize Jesus as He walked across the lake to them, they were fearful. In Matthew 14:27, Jesus said, "Take courage. It is I. Don't be afraid." Once they were settled in the boat with Jesus, their fear turned to joy. Philippians 4:6 says, "Do not be anxious about anything, but in everything, by prayer and petition, with thanksgiving, present your requests to God." It is natural for us to experience fear or anxiety, and we will. During those times, we should focus on the true source of our strength, our Lord.

The presence of fear does not mean you have no faith. Fear visits everyone. But make your fear a visitor, not a resident." Max Lucado, author

Psalm 34:4, Psalm 91:14-15, John 14:27

WHY ME?

Every cadet who entered the PA State Police Academy during my time was required not only to groom and feed the horses, but also to ride them each day. This was a tradition since the establishment of the department in 1905 when horses were the means of transportation. Since I had never ridden a horse, on the first day that I sat on the huge beast, I quickly assessed its massive proportions. On the second day, we were instructed to ride without using the stirrups. We stayed in the saddle by squeezing our legs together, putting great pressure on the horse. The next morning at the sound of the 5:00 AM alarm, I got out of bed and began to walk across the room. After taking a few steps, I was sure that I had contracted polio. Deep, dull, nagging pain from the previous equestrian drill traveled through my legs, back, and stomach--a fitting retaliation from my horse. Three months after my PSP Academy graduation, I was called back to join the State Police Rodeo team for the remainder of that summer. My first thought was, "Of all those cadets who were experienced and rode so well, why me?" Ironically, I rode not only in drills but also as a trick rider, one of the highlights of my career.

When we are going through a difficult time, we often cry out, "Why me?" Sometimes we may learn the reason, but at other times, we will not. As Believers, we need to trust that the Lord allows even difficult situations in our lives to bring us closer to Him. Jeremiah 29:11 says, "For I know the plans I have for you, declares the Lord, plans to prosper you and not harm you, plans to give you hope and a future." In 1 Peter 5:10, we find reassurance that perhaps in this life--or in the next--but ultimately, "The God of all grace who called you to His eternal glory in Christ, after you have suffered a little while, will Himself restore you and make you strong, firm and steadfast."

"Be patient. God is using today's difficulties to strengthen you for tomorrow."
Max Lucado, preacher/author

Romans 5:3-5, James 1:2-3, Revelation 21:4

GOD'S HAND

The troopers had received an alert that an escapee from a federal prison was heading toward their area. He had broken into an unoccupied house nearby to commit a burglary when a woman and her ten-year-old daughter unexpectedly arrived home. Forcing the daughter into his car, the escapee took off with her as a hostage. Several troopers had set up a road block a few miles away and saw the suspect vehicle heading toward them. Realizing that he was trapped, the suspect stopped his car and began to run toward one of the marked vehicles. With a gun in his hand, he approached the marked cruiser where one of the troopers was in the driver's seat. Holding the gun to the face of the trooper, he shot. Amazingly, the gun misfired, and the officer was saved. Troopers then subdued the escapee who was no longer a threat.

At times, not only while we are on the job but also in our off-duty lives, God intervenes on our behalf. Sometimes we do not even realize when He intervenes. At other times, however, His intervention is so obvious that we actually sense God's hand upon us or on others around us. Romans 8:28 reminds us of God's personal presence in the lives of Believers: "And we know that in all things God works for the good of those who love Him, who have been called according to His purpose." Psalm 31:15 encourages us to recognize that our lives are in the hands of our God who created us and who cares about us. "My times are in Your hands; deliver me from my enemies and from those who pursue me."

"We are so well-guarded that the only way our life can be touched with hardship is if God allows it." Charles Stanley, pastor/ author

Psalm 138:7, Isaiah 41:10, Romans 8:34

April 17

MISTAKEN IDENTITY

In Mike's patrol zone, was a bridge spanning the river from Pennsylvania to New Jersey where an old man had worked for years as the toll taker. Traffic across the bridge was light each day, and Mike often took coffee to the lonely, old man who was always glad to see him. One day while Mike was at the barracks, dispatch received a call that a local bank had just been robbed. Mike's sergeant, a crusty, gruff old-timer, told him to grab a rifle and follow him. Searching for the suspect vehicle, the sergeant drove down the highway and eventually to the bridge. The old man peered into the passenger seat and said hello to Mike, asking how he was. Being on a mission and annoyed by the small talk, the sergeant took out his picture identification. Addressing the old man, he said, "I am with the state police. The local bank was just robbed, and an armed subject is in the area." Mike noticed that the old man became upset and trembled as the sergeant continued, "I want you to be on the lookout for him." The old man stammered, "Yes, sir. I certainly will." Then looking down at the sergeant's ID and thinking it was a picture of the wanted armed robber, he said, "He certainly is an ugly guy, isn't he?" The sergeant drove off in disgust.

Believers, know that when we get to Heaven, there will be no mistake about our identity. Having forgiven us of all sins, Jesus, our Lord and Savior, will call us by name as He welcomes us into His Kingdom for eternity. As we wait for that day, 1 Peter 1:3-5 reminds us to praise God, for "In His great mercy, He has given us new birth into a living hope through the resurrection of Jesus Christ from the dead, and into an inheritance that can never perish, spoil or fade – kept in heaven for you, who through faith are shielded by God's power until the coming of the salvation that is ready to be revealed in the last time."

"To be assured of our salvation is no arrogant stoutness. It is faith. It is devotion. It is not presumption. It is God's promise."
Augustine, early Christian theologian/philosopher

Matthew 7:21, Matthew 24:42-44, Luke 22:29-30

RIGHT TO REMAIN SILENT

In our early days in the PA State Police Academy, we are taught a phrase which we must say to a suspect upon arrest beginning with: "You have the right to remain silent." It would be hard to count how many times we will say those words during our career. Our society has taken great steps to ensure that the rights of all citizens are protected, including those suspected of committing a crime. Even if we witness someone committing a crime and there is no doubt that they are responsible for the illegal act, we are still required to tell them that they do not have to talk to us or answer any questions. A critical part of the Miranda Warnings is, "Anything you say may be used against you." When the case comes to a preliminary hearing or court, the officer usually begins testifying to the fact that he gave the suspect his Miranda Warnings prior to asking any questions. Criminal cases have been thrown out for neglecting to explain a suspect's rights and then failing to adhere to whether or not they were willing to talk.

When our life in this world is over, we will face God, who knows beyond any doubt whatsoever, the gravity of our sins during our entire lifetime. We can remain silent, but nothing we could say will change the fact that we have sinned against a holy God. When we meet Him face to face, whether we remain silent or not, our entry into Heaven will **not** be based on what we might confess **then**, but on what we confess **today**. 1 John 2:1 offers some of the most comforting words in the Bible, "My dear children, I write this to you so you will not sin. But if anybody does sin, we have One who speaks to the Father in our defense--Jesus Christ, the Righteous One." Praise God that we have an advocate, Jesus, who has not only taken the punishment that we deserve, but also speaks to His Father on our behalf and does not remain silent.

"Like the thief hanging on the cross beside Jesus, we can cry out to Him in the midst of any mess or consequences we find ourselves in, whether or not we caused it."
David Jeremiah, pastor/author

Matthew 10:32, Romans 8:34, Hebrews 10:16-18

WHAT A MESS

On the job, I frequently encountered people whose lives were a complete disaster. Some of them had committed terrible crimes which caused much harm to others and, sometimes, even to themselves. Often, I thought that these people were in a huge pit because of what they had done, and they probably would never get out. Sadly, many of them had never known any better, for their behavior was similar to that of their parents, who also were in a total mess. Many had entered into bad relationships, and even when they got out, they began another with someone who was just like the one they left. When people recognize that they have been or currently are living an inappropriate lifestyle, they may also believe that there is no way that God could ever forgive them.

When Jesus went to the cross, He went in place of us to pay the penalty that we deserve for our sinfulness. He did not say to His father that His love and forgiveness were conditional or that there were some sins which He just could not forgive. On the contrary, God's word is explicit, and it says that His grace is infinite. There is no limit to the sins that He is willing to forgive. Psalm 103:12 says that their sin was gone, removed from them "as far as the east is from the west." John 19:30 tells us that when Jesus was on the cross, He said, "It is finished." The Greek word for "finish" is "tetelestai," which means "paid in full." What better gift could we ever receive?

"Whenever our lives are a mess, things are falling apart, relationships failing--Jesus is running toward us." Tim Keller, pastor/author

Daniel 9:9, Romans 12:1-2, Hebrews 10:17

THE WOLVES

Some people are openly against us and disrespect authority. They publicly show their disgust toward those who enforce the established laws of society. Some believe that they have every right to revolt angrily, demonstrate, loot, destroy, and cause injury. We have learned that several protest leaders go outside their communities and pay others to come in to create havoc and violence. The respect that was once extended toward law enforcement officers is no longer acknowledged by many in our society. Those who are recklessly and dangerously participating in unlawful acts of rebellion seek to devour us as they threaten and then carry out vicious physical attacks against us.

Believers also face a far less visible enemy that often comes in direct contact with us. That one, who is intent on causing us physical, spiritual, and emotional harm whenever possible, is Satan. He is angry with God and uses humanity to retaliate as he tries to gain power. He is out to do harm, especially to those who believe in God and desire to walk in His will. Job 1:1 tells us of a man who honored God and attempted to live a godly life: "In the Land of Uz, there lived a man whose name was Job. This man was blameless and upright; he feared God and shunned evil." Nevertheless, Job suffered physically and endured great losses as Satan sought to break him. His wife and friends mocked him for not blaming God for his misfortunes. This story of Job's faithfulness as a God-fearing man also illustrates how Satan will use others in our lives as his agents. Seeing us in our attempt to live godly lives, they may tempt us or taunt us in the hope that we will fall so that they can salve their consciences regarding their own sin. Matthew 7:15 warns us to beware of pretenders who have evil motives, "Watch out for false prophets. They come to you in sheep's clothing, but inwardly they are ferocious wolves."

"Satan can wreak havoc, but he cannot claim victory." David Jeremiah, pastor/author.

Matthew 7:22-23, John 3:20, 1 Peter 5:8

BE ON THE READY

In a movie theater, 70 people were shot by a lone-gunman, and 12 died. In an elementary school, 27 were shot by a lone-gunman, and 20 children and 6 adults died. In a nightclub, 49 people were killed, and over 50 were injured. Such tragedies continue to occur, for potential assailants are intent on exceeding the collateral damage of previous tragedies. Many such incidents appear to have been inspired by the shootings at Virginia Tech. Ironically, SWAT teams, dressed in their gear, had been practicing nearby and were able to respond within two minutes. Nevertheless, upon their arrival, 32 were dead. Lt. Colonel David Grossman, a renowned trainer of law enforcement officers on responding to shooting incidents, calls these tragedies "active murders," for death was intended. When we on the job hear of these horrific incidents or see the footage captured at the scene, we begin to think about the ways that we might respond to similar incidents. We are jolted back to the realization that our roles in society require us to be ready every moment.

Believers should be prepared to provide comfort to those who may be involved in the horrific incidents that we see. We may interact with the victims' families for days afterwards. Pray that our Holy Spirit will give us the words to say, the way to say them, and the time to say them as we seek to comfort those who are hurting. In Philippians 1:9-10, Paul prayed for the Believers, "that your love may abound more and more in knowledge and depth of insight, so that you may be able to discern what is best and may be pure and blameless until the day of Christ." Matthew 5:13-14, 16 reminds us of our high calling and our responsibility: "You are the salt of the earth...You are the light of the world...let your light shine before men that they may see your good deeds and praise your Father in heaven."

"Seek opportunities to show you care. The smallest gestures often make the biggest difference." John Wooden, UCLA basketball coach

Matthew 25:40, 1 Corinthians 12:22-27, Hebrews 6:10-12

HE KNOWS US

When we begin our career in law enforcement, we know that we will eventually have to "cut our teeth" on a major investigation. As I was finishing a 3-11 PM shift, I pulled into the parking lot of the barracks where troopers were hurriedly exiting the building. One of the troopers, who was assigned to the evidence collection and processing unit, was loaded down with equipment as he headed to his van. When he told me that he was going to a homicide scene, I asked if I could assist on my own time since I had not yet been involved in a murder investigation. We drove to a remote area where the body of a young woman was sprawled on the ground. It was obvious that after she had been strangled, her attacker then drove a vehicle over her. Although I had witnessed death many times, none had been a homicide, and the sight was gruesome. I became disheartened to think that someone found it acceptable to take this young life, and I wondered if the person who had committed this atrocious act even knew her. As I drove home early the next morning, the image of that young, lifeless body remained vivid in my mind, and it would for many years.

This young woman was no stranger to her Creator. Although He certainly detests this kind of action from any of His creation, He allowed this to happen, and I could not understand why. While it is not uncommon to ask, "Where was God?" in such times, I make a conscious choice not to. Instead, I claim God's promises and follow the advice of Proverbs 3:5: "Trust in the Lord with all your heart, and lean not on your own understanding." I trust Him to carry out His plan, which may not be revealed until we leave this Earth. Pastor Billy Graham said, "But man rebelled against God. Man said, 'I don't need you, God.' Man took that position, and he began to suffer, and he has been dying ever since. All of our suffering and pain, including death, is a result of our rebellion against God. Physical death is just the death of the body, but the spirit lives on. If your spirit is separated from God for eternity, it will be lost forever."

Genesis 3:6-7, John 16:33, Romans 6:23, 1 Corinthians 13:12

THE WRONG ANSWER

One of the most challenging aspects of our job is determining what may be partially true, what is totally false, and what the real truth is. Many people give such an intricate, well-developed account that we realize their story may, in fact, be true. When others answer to an authority figure, they feel that they must be careful not to provide too much information or be totally honest. Still others are obviously trying to be deceptive. While interacting with those who had addictions and claimed to be serious about "getting clean," it was always apparent when they were continuing to use drugs. When informants got into my car, I always asked them immediately if they had done any drugs that day. Although their response was always, "No," within a few minutes, many of them were nodding off.

Believers know that Satan continues to have power over the human race, and he is eager to try to deceive those who seriously attempt to follow Christ. It is really nothing new, for it began back in the Garden of Eden as recorded in Genesis 3:1, 4-5: "Now the serpent was more crafty than any of the wild animals the Lord God had made." When the woman explained to him that they had been told not to eat fruit from a particular tree, for they would die, the serpent [Satan] said, "You will surely not die. For God knows that when you eat of it your eyes will be opened, and you will be like God, knowing good and evil." Satan was wrong then, and he still is to this day.

"Unless Believers appreciate their own weakness, that is, know how incompetent they are in themselves to encounter the supernatural, they shall be deceived."
Watchman Nee, persecuted Chinese-Christian /author/church leader

Genesis 3:6-8, Matthew 6:13, 2 Corinthians 11:3, Ephesians 6:11

EXERCISING AUTHORITY

Although news headlines sometimes announce yet another incident where an officer misused his/her authority, we can be heartened to know that the percentage of such episodes is relatively low. We certainly cannot condone such behavior, but we can offset some of its negative impact by consciously striving to gain the respect of the public when we interact. When I worked on the Vice Unit, I frequently arrested women for prostitution. After being arraigned, they were either released on bail or incarcerated. More than once, the women then thanked me. The first time that happened, I was so taken by surprise that I asked the woman how she could say that. She replied, "Because you treated me with respect even though I broke the law."

The Ultimate Authority, our Lord, holds Believers responsible to be different from the world both on and off the job. Romans 12:2 says, "Do not conform any longer to the pattern of this world, but be transformed by the renewing of your mind." That can become easier if we ask the Lord for discernment as well as patience. Being proud and boastful and abusing the authority behind the badge will never allow us to tell the good news of the saving power of Jesus with any credibility. I Peter 2:9 tells us, "But you are a chosen people, a royal priesthood, a holy nation, a people belonging to God that you may declare the praise of Him who called you out of darkness into His wonderful light."

"It is impossible to serve God without serving one another." Alistair Begg, pastor

Psalm 96:3, Matthew 24:14, Revelation 14:6-7

PREPARED

Even though our days can be action-packed, some routine tasks also come with the job. One of my most unfulfilling responsibilities was having to complete the endless number of reports that had to be filed after every shift. In other areas of our jobs, however, following the established practices is critical to ensure that we and others will be safe. Several officers were injured or killed after stopping a motorist and approaching the driver's window, exposing themselves to passing traffic. Consequently, a new procedure was instituted which requires officers to approach a stopped vehicle on the passenger's side, thereby shielding them from approaching traffic. Since we make car stops so frequently, we can easily get lax; however, following a designated procedure helps to ensure that we will be prepared should a situation threaten our safety.

In our spiritual walk, we often establish some routines, such as not missing our daily devotional time, and that can be good. However, if we just go through the motions of reading a few Bible verses and perhaps a devotional but do not seek a personal conversation with the Lord or call out to Him for direction, or spend time in thanksgiving, we will miss the benefits that He wants to provide for us. Many of us know Believers who routinely and openly witness to others, but we all are called to that practice. We may be the only one in a person's life who will tell them about the peace and forgiveness available through Christ. In 2 Timothy 1:8, when Paul was in prison, he wrote to Timothy to encourage him to be bold in his testimony: "So do not be ashamed to testify about our Lord, or ashamed of me, his prisoner." The person that we witness to today could be the very last person that the Lord is waiting for before He returns. That should certainly encourage us to be bold about our faith.

"The people who make a difference are not the ones with the credentials, but the ones with concern." Max Lucado, author

Matthew 9:37-38, Matthew 24:14, 1 Peter 3:15

FINISH STRONG

Throughout life, we reach milestones that signal the end to what we had been doing. Life changes significantly after we graduate high school and/or college. It changes even more dramatically after we graduate from the police academy. As we pass through the ranks, many of us know that retirement will be our last major career milestone. Disappointingly, most of us have observed some on the job who checked out years before they actually retired. They put in just enough effort to get by, and some even try to dodge assignments. Many spend a good deal of time talking about when they will be able to retire while they are only midway in their career. Not only are they wishing their lives away, but they also are not finding satisfaction and worth in their profession, for their hearts are no longer in their work. Others who have to pick up the slack can become resentful and concerned that they may someday need to depend on that disengaged officer for backup.

Because of our faith, we have been called to set ourselves apart, not only in our spiritual walk, but also in our secular life. We should want to be remembered as a Christian who made an effort to witness, to love, and to do whatever we could for others until our last breath. 1Corinthians 9:24-27 says, "Do you not know that in a race all the runners run, but only one gets the prize? Run in such a way as to get the prize. Everyone who competes in the games goes into strict training. They do it to get a crown that will not last; but we do it to get a crown that will last forever. Therefore I do not run like a man who runs aimlessly; I do not fight like a man beating the air. No, I beat my body and make it my slave so that after I have preached to others, I myself will not be disqualified for the prize." If you are reading this page, you have been blessed with another day–to do something for Him! "This is the day the Lord has made; let us rejoice and be glad in it." Psalm 118:24.

"Every job is a self-portrait of the person who does it. Autograph your work with excellence." Ted Key, writer/cartoonist

Ephesians 6:7, 2 Timothy 4:7, Hebrews 12:1

WHERE AM I?

Many rookies are often under the impression that it is not wise to ask questions because they may appear to be unprepared. Whenever I went to a new station, I wanted to learn the area as quickly as possible, but I tried to do so without asking questions of others. Many times, I got lost. After taking a new assignment in the detective bureau, I soon realized that often I did not have either the experience or the knowledge to proceed with a particular investigation. As I sat with the seasoned investigators in the large office that we shared, I came to realize that I was part of a team, and I did not have to solve things on my own. Their experience and their willingness to advise me whenever I was lost and asked for help resulted in solved cases and some gratifying friendships.

In our Christian walk, we will face times when we wonder where we are supposed go next. We may have significant decisions that must be made about financial responsibilities, care for elderly parents, college choices for our kids, or whether a costly purchase is necessary. Sometimes, I never even thought to call out to the Lord, thinking that He really did not want to hear from me regarding such aspects of my life. Since then, I have learned that nothing is so insignificant that it cannot be brought before Him. At times, it amazes me (and I know that it should not) that when I do include the Lord in my search for an answer, in His time, He does provide, so often in a way far better than I could have imagined. Unless we have asked of the Lord and feel His total peace, our solution may be empty, inappropriate, and even disastrous. "Surely you desire truth in the inner parts; you teach me wisdom in the inmost place." Psalm 51:6.

"Our prayers may be awkward. Our attempts may be feeble. But some of the power of prayer is in the One who hears it and not in the one who says it. Our prayers do make a difference." Max Lucado, pastor/author

Proverbs 15:29, Matthew 7:7, James 5:16

ORDERLY

With the investigation of serial homicides comes both a degree of anticipation as well as a sense of desperation. FBI agents and profilers, Roy Hazelwood, John Douglas and Robert Ressler, compiled a list of factors that help identify whether a killer was organized or disorganized. Gathered from evidence at the crime scene, these factors include: the position of the body by the killer, signs of cannibalism or mutilation, and evidence of sexual acts committed. The classification scheme describes organized criminals as antisocial, psychopathic, lacking remorse, but knowing right from wrong. They are likely to be of above-average intelligence, attractive, personable, married, employed, cunning and controlled, and **orderly**.

Christians are encouraged to be orderly in a far more positive way. The first example of order in Scripture occurs when God created the universe in a precise, orderly way. In *Why I Believe,* Dr. James Kennedy cites noted scientists who offer amazing details about God's handiwork. For example, if the Earth were either 10% larger or 10% smaller, it could not support life; if the Earth were closer to the sun, we could not survive; if we were farther away, we would freeze. Many Biblical references address the value of being orderly. If we are seeking to follow God's word, we must not pick and choose only the precepts that we want to follow. Paul tells us in 1 Corinthians 14:33, "For God is not a God of disorder but of peace." In 1 Corinthians 14:40, he further explains, "But everything should be done in a fitting and orderly way." The Lord knew that conducting our lives in an orderly manner will give us a sense of peace in our everyday activities and thereby allow us to live a more productive life.

"What can be more foolish than to think that all this rare fabric of heaven and Earth could come by chance when all the skill of art is not able to make an oyster?"
Jeremy Taylor, 17th century British author/bishop

Genesis 1:1-31

DESPAIR

A call from dispatch directed me to a residence several miles away. When I walked up to the partially open door, I saw a woman standing inside and sobbing uncontrollably. Unable to explain the reason for her call, she pointed to a door leading to the basement. As I slowly walked down the steps, I found a middle-aged man hanging from the rafters and frothing from the mouth. Within a few seconds, another officer arrived, and we cut the rope tied around the victim's neck. He was no longer alive. After the coroner was called and family members began to gather, I asked for permission to search the home, hoping to find some explanation for this act of desperation. Why had he felt that death was his only recourse? Upon opening the closet in the main bedroom, I was surprised to find all of his belongings in perfect order: shoes shined and neatly placed beside each other, clothes meticulously hanging on the rack, items carefully stacked on shelves. My continued search revealed that all those things that he cared for, tools, equipment, personal items, were neatly in place. My search ended without finding anything that would answer questions not only for me, but also for the wife whom he had left behind.

We, as Believers, need to remember that we will encounter many who appear to have their lives in order, but the outward appearance does not always give indication of inner turmoil. We who are seeking to walk closely with the Lord will experience times of uncertainty, frustration, disappointment, even despair. We were never promised that the Christian life would be easy. However, even in the darkest times, we can cling to the knowledge that our Lord is in total control as 2 Corinthians 4:8-9 reminds us, "We are hard pressed on every side, but not crushed; perplexed, but not in despair; persecuted, but not abandoned; struck down, but not destroyed."

"Now God be praised, that to believing souls gives light in darkness, comfort in despair."
William Shakespeare

Psalm 43:5, Colossians 3:2, 1 Peter 5:7

REVERENCE DESERVED

At one time, I was assigned to a court-approved wiretap of organized crime, targeting several members of a large crime family. The conversations of the mob members that we intercepted and recorded always began with, "Be careful; they (the police) may have ears." Then they continued the conversations which implicated themselves and others in the family. One day, we intercepted a call and learned that a meeting was going to be held in another state, and high-ranking members of the mob would be attending. We conducted a surveillance as they arrived at a well-known casino where members gathered to watch a boxing match. Cameras located around the large facility captured many interesting interactions. One especially revealing incident occurred when the underlings walked meekly into the room and greeted the crime boss by reverently kissing his ring as he pompously perched on a large chair.

Those of us with a faith in God know that only He deserves our reverence. Our Creator, God the Father, loves each one of us enough to have created us in His own image. In love, He sent His Son, Jesus Christ, to pay an undeserved penalty for **our** sins. Out of loving concern for us, He sent the Holy Spirit to comfort, empower, and guide us while we travel on Earth. The essence of His all-encompassing unselfish love for us appears in John 3:16: "For God so **loved** the world that He **gave** His one and **only** Son, that whoever believes in Him shall not perish but have eternal life." He alone deserves our honor, devotion, and praise. Our response should be loving praise such as Psalm 34:1,3 describes: "I will extol the Lord at all times; His praise will always be on my lips...Glorify the Lord with me; let us exalt His name together."

"Man was created to praise, reverence, and serve God, our Lord."
St. Ignatius, 16th century priest

Nehemiah 1:11, Psalm 5:7, John 15:9, Hebrews 1:3, 1 John 5:5

THIEVES

The elderly couple had a pleasant afternoon shopping together and enjoying each other's company. Talking about their dinner plans, they stood in shock as they opened their front door to find their orderly home in total disarray. Drawers hung open, and items had been strewn throughout the house. I was called to their residence, and as they began to describe their missing possessions, the wife started to sob. Tears ran down her wrinkled face as she recalled the sentimental value of the things that she and her husband had gathered over a lifetime. Ultimately, I was able to arrest the person responsible, a drug addict, who had stolen to feed his habit. He had already sold the couple's possessions, so there was not much comfort for the couple to learn that the suspect had been caught. A few years later, at the age of 30, he died as a consequence of ingesting methamphetamine for many years.

As we acquire our own possessions, we may think that these "things" will not only solve our problems, but also make us feel better. God's word, however, reminds us of what real treasures are. Matthew 6:19-21 says, "Do not store up for yourselves treasures on earth, where moth and rust destroy, and where thieves break in and steal. But store up for yourselves treasure in Heaven, where moth and rust do not destroy and where thieves do not break in and steal. For where your treasure is, there your heart will be also." The apostle Paul learned what was of real value in life: "I know what it is to be in need, and I know what it is to have plenty. I have learned the secret of being content in any and every situation, whether well-fed or hungry, whether living in plenty or in want. I can do everything through Him who gives me strength." Philippians 4:12-13.

"Security only comes from relating to that which is anchored in eternity. Jesus said that we have eternal life and that no one can snatch us out of His hands."
Neil T. Anderson, author

Psalm 34:10, Matthew 6:31, Matthew 7:11, Luke 12:24

BY WHAT AUTHORITY

When I was in the PA State Police Academy, I felt that the only thing that I had authority over was my assigned horse. However, one morning as I began to groom him, he pinned me next to the wall with his powerful body. It took a seasoned instructor some time to extract me from this demeaning position. Early in our training at the PSP Academy, we learn that our authority comes from laws and statutes adopted through local, state, and federal legislation. These laws are consistent and very infrequently change. A certain amount of authority has been vested in us as law enforcement officers. At times, when we act to enforce the laws that we have sworn to uphold, some think that we were responsible for establishing these laws. Therefore, they argue that their compliance should be optional.

We learn in God's word that the greatest authority comes from Him. Romans 13:1-3 says, "Everyone must submit himself to the governing authorities, for there is no authority except that which God has established. The authorities that exist have been established by God. Consequently, he who rebels against the authority is rebelling against what God has instituted, and those who do so will bring judgment on themselves. For rulers hold no terror for those who do right, but for those who do wrong. Do you want to be free from fear of the one in authority? Then do what is right and He will commend you." We, then, are really doing God's work, authorized by Him. That should encourage us not to take what we do for granted.

"Don't bother to give God instructions, just report for duty."
Corrie ten Boom, author

2 Chronicles 20:6, Romans 13:1-5, Hebrews 13:1

CALLED BY NAME

The accused is seated next to his attorney at the defense table. Potential jurors are escorted into the courtroom. As the judge announces that the voir dire is about to begin, many in the jury box appear uneasy. When the judge says that if any potential jurors have reasons why they should not be selected, this is the time to make that known. Some have valid hardships, while others offer lame excuses: "I'm afraid that I will not be able to stay awake; my grandfather was a police officer, so I may be prejudiced; I don't have a car and can't get here." This has been a highly-publicized crime, and the selected jurors could be required to hear a case that could last many days, even months. As the names in the jury pool are announced, some jurors become very apprehensive, dreading the possibility that their name may be called next.

For Christians, there will come a time when the calling of our names will be far more significant than being called to be a juror. When we leave this world and appear before the Lord in Heaven, we will wait for Him to call out our name that has been written in the Lamb's Book of Life. We will feel excitement, not apprehension, for we know that we have been chosen and accepted as a result of our prior commitment to follow Jesus as our Lord and Savior. What greater words could we ever hear than those of the Lord welcoming us into His home? "He will wipe every tear from their eyes. There will be no more death or mourning or crying or pain, for the old order of things has passed away." Revelation 21:4.

"What surprises me most about God is that the Creator of the Universe should want a relationship with me." Rick Warren, pastor/author

John 14:1-3, Galatians 3:29, Hebrews 11:16

IN THE DARKNESS

Whenever I was working shifts that occurred during the hours of darkness, a gnawing apprehension always hovered over me. I knew that the night hours shielded evil-doers who lurked in the darkness. In fact, statistics show that often those who are intent on committing criminal acts desire to do so during those times when it is more difficult to be detected. Conducting a search in the dark for someone wanted for committing a crime is not only difficult, but often dangerous. Likewise, a search for someone who may be lost may be called off during the hours of darkness, as it could put the searchers at risk.

A great deal of darkness exists in our world today–even in the daylight hours. We are often called upon to deal with the evil, as many who choose to live in the darkness inflict pain and sadness on others in society. We have to be aware that because of what we experience, we, too, can be pulled toward the dark side, like a moth to a flame. Satan will entice and encourage us to explore and embrace the darkness. Fortunately, we have the most powerful resource Who will help us to move toward the light and that which is good. 2 Corinthians 4:6 tells us, "For God, who said, 'Let light shine out of the darkness,' made His light shine in our hearts to give us the light of the knowledge of the glory of God in the face of Christ."

"The fundamental principle of Christianity is to be what God is, and He is Light."
John Hagee, pastor/author

Psalm 43:3, John 1:3-5, Matthew 5:16

ON THE ALERT

Very few professions require one to be on a constant state of alert as law enforcement. We have come to realize that around every corner, danger may be present. Today in our society, some are actively making an effort to inflict personal attacks against police officers. Frequently these attacks are random and without any provocation or any previous contact. Such was the case of a local sheriff who stopped to fill up his cruiser as he began his evening shift. A deranged citizen pulled into the gas station and opened fire on the officer, killing him instantly. Even at the national level in our country, the threat level changes, and we are warned to be on the alert for terrorist activities that threaten our society.

Some threats may be easier to see than the constant, sometimes subtle attacks from Satan. Although he has often been depicted as merely a mischievous culprit wearing a red suit and carrying a pitch fork, we must remember that he is real, and he is powerful. In 1 Peter 5:8, Peter commands us: "Be self-controlled and alert. Your enemy the devil prowls around like a roaring lion looking for someone to devour." In v.9, Peter tells us that not only do we have the power to withstand his attacks, but how to do so: "Resist him, standing firm in the faith, because you know that your brothers throughout the world are undergoing the same kind of suffering." Satan likes nothing more than to see a Believer stumble and succumb to sin. Just as we strap on our vest before starting our shift, we can consciously equip ourselves daily for protection from evil. "Put on the full armor of God so that you can take your stand against the devil's schemes. For our struggle is not against flesh and blood, but against the rulers, against the authorities, against the powers of this dark world and against the spiritual forces of evil in the heavenly realms." Ephesians 6:11-12.

"Whenever God calls us to a task, He will equip us and enable us to complete that task."
Michael Youssef, pastor/author

Luke 10:19, 1 Corinthians 16:13, 1 Peter 5:8

PARDONED

Thinking back on my time in the PA State Police Academy, I soon learned that we were going to be pushed to the max. That meant that things that were so insignificant, like leaning against the wall, could result in some type of penalty. I can vividly recall both the classes and the long nights of studying as we learned about the Criminal and Vehicle Codes. Understanding these Codes is essential for us, for they are the foundation for our criminal justice system. These Codes often provide for a range of punishment depending on the gravity of the offense. Those who violate the laws and are eventually cited or arrested will have to pay some type of penalty, whether a fine or even incarceration. Taking the life of another may result in one receiving the most severe judgement of all: the death penalty.

When we consider our sins toward a perfect and holy God, we, too, deserve a penalty. "All have sinned and fall short of the glory of God." Romans 3:23. Not one of us is sinless, regardless of how well we may try to live. So what about our most deserved penalty? After all, in our eyes, some sins seem much more grievous than others. However, different from a court of law that eventually determines our guilt and the subsequent penalty we must pay, we have an advocate who will be there with us, Jesus Christ. John 3:16 reminds us of the best news we could ever receive: "For God so loved the world that He gave His only Son, that whoever believes in Him shall not perish but have eternal life." When we stand before our Creator, Jesus will say in essence, "Yes, this child of mine has sinned, but he is pardoned because I already paid the penalty that he deserves by shedding my blood on the cross for him." The charges will not be reduced; not even a period of probation will be required. We will be pardoned, and **all** the charges will be dropped.

"God doesn't owe us anything–yet in His grace, He still gives us good things."
Billy Graham, evangelist

Romans 6:23, 1 Corinthians 6:20, 1Peter 2:24

TRIALS

Testifying at trials becomes a common part of our experiences in the law enforcement profession. As we seek justice and are called upon to enforce the law, we encounter some who are unwilling to obey not only the laws of man, but also the laws of God. Once apprehended for their lawless deeds, they are quick to seek their day in court in an attempt to prove their innocence. Although we, as Believers, seek to lead godly lives and live within the laws that we are called to uphold, we, too, face trials of many kinds. Some are not necessarily caused by our disobedience. Sometimes our trial is the stress of the job, the unreasonable people that we may work with from time to time, or even difficult supervisors. In our personal lives, we face family difficulties, economic struggles, significant illnesses, the deaths of family and friends, and even burnout.

It is easy for us to question why God allows these trials to happen when we are seeking to walk in His will. We must never forget that when we accepted Jesus as our Lord and Savior, we were not guaranteed a trial-free life. Even Jesus faced a trial for charges that He did not commit. "Consider it pure joy, my brothers, whenever you face trials of many kinds, because you know that the testing of your faith develops perseverance. Perseverance must finish its work so that you may be mature and complete, not lacking anything." James 1:2-4

"God has a right to interrupt your life. He is Lord. When you accepted Him as Lord, you gave Him the right to help Himself to your life anytime He wants."
Henry Blackaby, author

John 16:33, Romans 5:3, 1 Peter 4:12-13

PUZZLE PIECES

One of the most challenging but also the most interesting parts of law enforcement is attempting to solve a crime. Evidence is not always easy to put together and often comes in bits and pieces. Like a big puzzle, when one piece fits together with another, solving the crime becomes a greater possibility. DNA was first used to aid in a criminal investigation in 1986 as a result of breakthroughs in molecular biology. It not only convicted a perpetrator of a crime, but also exonerated someone falsely accused. When a woman's body was found alongside an interstate highway, the investigation ultimately did not reveal who she was, and she was listed as "Jane Doe." Recently, as cold-cases were being reviewed, her body was exhumed, and DNA evidence was gathered. After the exhumation, a man came forward, suspecting that the victim might be his aunt. As the only living family member, he provided DNA samples which were found to be a one-in-400 billion match. The DNA provided a piece to the puzzle and some closure for this family, and the investigation continues.

Believers know that absolutely no more evidence is needed to prove that God exists; that He sent His Son, Jesus, to the cross to take the punishment we deserve for our sins; and that Jesus rose from the grave and now waits with His Father in Heaven for all who trust in His promise. The proof to these truths can be found in the inerrant word of God. So much evidence is available in prophecies that have been fulfilled and in facts that are irrefutable. For someone who does not believe these truths, the best way to be absolutely sure before rejecting them totally is to put all the puzzle pieces together. Our eternity depends on it.

"Coming together is a beginning; keeping together is progress; working together is success."
Henry Ford, industrialist/businessman

Ephesians 2:8-9, Romans 3:23-28, Romans 8:34

THE BATTLE

Every day on the job, we battle forces of evil. Some are very evident as we witness abuse of the elderly, child pornography, physically brutal attacks, and the taking of human life. Some people seem to place no value on human life. They will kill over a parking space or a pair of new sneakers or murder those who have a different religious belief, ethnic background, or race. As the battle rages, we can begin to believe that very little good exists in the world. Our daily efforts to right the wrongs and take a stand against those who seek evil and corruption can become wearisome. On some days, we may feel that we do not have the strength to go on for the sake of justice. This is exacerbated during those times when we know that someone we have charged and know is guilty may be set free. Since Satan especially detests our relationship with Christ, he is poised to invade our lives, wear us down, and attack.

However, as followers of Christ, we know that we have a power available to us that others do not. Our strength comes from above. God's word says in Ephesians 6:12, "For our struggle is not against flesh and blood, but against the rulers, against the authorities, against the powers of this dark world, and against the spiritual forces of evil in heavenly realms." Paul explains how we can live a holy life by focusing our desires and thoughts on Christ: "Since, then, you have been raised with Christ, set your hearts on things above, where Christ is seated at the right hand of God. Set your minds on things above, not on earthly things. For you died, and your life is now hidden with Christ in God." Colossians 3:1-3.

"With God, life is an endless hope. Without God, life is a hopeless end."
Bill Bright, evangelist

Psalm 27:1, Romans 12:1-2, 1 Timothy 6:12

IS THERE ANY PEACE?

We received information that demonstrators were going to protest the Vietnam War at a rally in a huge park nearby. The main antagonist at this rally was Abbie Hoffman, a political and social activist, anarchist, and revolutionary, who co-founded the Youth International Party, "Yippies." He had previously been arrested for conspiracy and inciting a riot. The protests that he was involved in often led to violent confrontations because he incited the crowd, most of whom were "high." LSD was the drug of choice in that era. Several of us, working undercover and looking as scruffy as those we were trying to infiltrate, mingled with the crowd. Uniformed officers in riot gear were ready to converge on the group if necessary. Eventually, Hoffman was arrested for attempting to sell $36,000 worth of cocaine. Especially during civil disputes and demonstrations where rioting often occurs, officers become more vulnerable. Even when I was called to restore peace in domestic disturbances, many situations were already out of control. While responding officers must face dangerous circumstances in attempts to restore peace, unfortunately, the resolutions may not be permanent.

Throughout life, we will also face times when we find ourselves struggling with our own inner peace. Since we are more aware than most of perils and discord all around us, it is easy for us to become discouraged and wonder if there is any peace in our society. Especially in these times when many are confrontational with those on the job, it is imperative for us to remember that our true source, the only source, for real peace is our Lord and Savior. "You will keep in perfect peace him whose mind is steadfast, because he trusts in You." Isaiah 26:3. "Cast all your anxiety on Him because He cares for you." 1 Peter 5:7. Imagine how much easier our jobs would be if more people accepted the peace that the Lord freely offers.

"No circumstance is so big that **He** cannot control it." Jerry Bridges, author

Isaiah 26:3, John 14:27, Romans 5:1, Philippians 4:6-7

LOOK!

In this world, there will always be those who do not believe in God. Others are not sure, but they hope that He is there. Still others have absolutely no doubt that God exists. However, even those who profess to be followers of Christ may ponder the concept of God at times because our human minds are too limited to fully grasp His magnificence. We in law enforcement certainly are not immune and may, in fact, be more susceptible to such thoughts because we are often exposed to the depravity of life. During times when we see the sinfulness of man in their willful acts of violence and destruction or the tragedies caused by earthquakes, tornadoes, and floods, we may say, "Where is God?" Psalm 19:1 tells us of the glorious proof of His presence every day as we look up toward Him, "The heavens declare the glory of God; the skies proclaim the work of His hands."

This magnificent universe
You created for me.
Each night the firmament of heaven
You allow me to see.
The stars and the moon
You put into place.
The galaxies in each system -
You created time and space
I want to cherish Your work,
Your presence each day.
Holy Spirit when I doubt,
encourage me, I pray.

rfg

Psalm 103:11, Psalm 108:3-5, Psalm 121:1-2

BE WISE

While I was on the job, very few days were devoid of activity, anxious moments, and difficult decisions, requiring me to be in a state of readiness. In retrospect, the outcome of some situations could have been better if I had made a different choice. Several years ago, George J. Thompson, Ph.D., a former professor and police officer, wrote *Verbal Judo, the Gentle Art of Persuasion.* Through his experiences, he learned the hard way that verbal persuasion was far better than a physical confrontation: "Verbal Judo is a philosophy that can show you how to be better prepared in every verbal encounter: How to listen and speak more effectively; how to engage people through empathy (the most powerful word in the English language); how to avoid the most common conversational disasters; how, instead, to have a proven, easily remembered strategy that will allow you to successfully communicate your point of view and take the upper hand in most disputes." Unfortunately, I did not read this book early in my career. If I had, I could have avoided many confrontations, some of which caused me significant pain.

Being wise and making wise decisions should not be a new concept for Believers. Anyone who reads God's word, knows that it says much about wisdom. "The way of a fool seems right to him, but a wise man listens to advice." Proverbs 12:15. The Bible also mentions consequences many faced in Old Testament times when they chose foolish ways. If we really want to make wise decisions, both on and off the job, we must not hesitate to call out to the One who will provide wisdom. "If any of you lacks wisdom, you should ask God, who gives generously to all without finding fault, and it will be given you." James 1:5.

"Smart men walked on the moon, daring men walked on the ocean floor, but wise men walk with God." Leonard Ravenhill, evangelist/author

Proverbs 2:1-6, Romans 1:21-23, Colossians 2:2-3

TRUTH SETS US FREE

I received a call from a city vice officer with whom I had worked closely on many cases. He told me that a well-known heroin dealer, Joe Webster, had just been murdered, and he shared some of the known details. Shortly afterward, I contacted Sally, an informant that I knew bought drugs from Joe on a regular basis. When we met, she revealed that she was already aware that Joe was dead, and she appeared to be upset. However, after I told her that her fingerprints had been found in Joe's house and that she would soon be brought in for questioning, her demeanor quickly turned to fear. When I explained that she could be considered an accomplice, she quickly revealed all the circumstances of the incident. She said that she had accompanied Dennis, another drug dealer, to Joe's home. His sole intent was to rip off Joe, not only of his drugs, but also of any cash he had. Dennis was subsequently arrested, and based on Sally's testimony in court, he was convicted of homicide, but no charges were filed against her.

On any day on the job, we can expect to encounter people that we know are not telling us the truth. Our responsibility as Believers is not to follow their example, but to be continually seeking the truth found in God's word and then living accordingly. "The Lord detests lying lips, but He delights in men who are truthful." Proverbs 12:22. In 2 Timothy 2:15, Paul says, "Do your best to present yourself to God as one approved, a workman who does not need to be ashamed and who correctly handles the word of truth." In 3 John 3-4, John was joyful to learn of Believers who walked their talk: "It gave me great joy to have some brothers come and tell about your faithfulness to the truth and how you continue to walk in the truth. I have no greater joy than to hear that my children are walking in the truth."

"Where I found truth, there found I my God, who is Truth itself." St. Augustine

John 14:6, Ephesians 4:14-15, Philippians 4:8

FALLEN WORLD

Many times, I have wondered why God allowed the events of a certain day to occur. Why did that teenager feel compelled to hang himself in his bedroom for his mother to discover? Why are some elderly people brutally beaten by those who are supposed to be caregivers? Why were Egyptian Christians blindfolded, forced on their knees, and beheaded? Why do terrible things happen to those who appeared to be basically good? Amidst all of the evil, poverty, perversion, and despair that we see all around us while serving as police officers, we have to make a greater conscious effort not to become discouraged. Because of our God-given free choice, which most of us would not be willing to give up, the human race is allowed to make decisions, even those that are sinful, inappropriate, or hard for others to understand.

Even as Christians, who have the promise of eternity in Heaven, we can allow the world to consume us and get us off track. We can forget that Satan never stops attacking those who have a strong faith and desire to live a Christ-like life. He considers it a great reward when he can cause a Believer to stumble and fall. During those times of discouragement, we cannot lose sight that each day was created and ordained by God. Psalm 118:24 tells us, "This is the day the Lord has made; let us rejoice and be glad in it." On some days, it is easier to rejoice than on others. However, when we remember that God makes all days, it will help us to keep things in perspective and be glad in them.

"If you look at the world, you'll be distressed. If you look within, you'll be depressed. If you look at God, you'll be at rest." Corrie ten Boom, author

Genesis 6:5-6, Galatians 5:17-18, 1 John 2:15-16

PAYING THE PRICE

Each year on this day, known as Peace Officers Memorial Day, our country recognizes and honors those who have paid the ultimate price in the law enforcement profession. In 2017, 128 federal, state, and local law enforcement officers died in the line of duty. In 2016, sixty-four police officers in the United States were killed in firearm-related incidents. Of those, twenty-one were ambush-style shootings. As Christians, we should take time each **day** to recall the sacrifice that was made for every person in God's creation, as Jesus went to the cross for us.

What adequate penalty could pay the price
to set the captive free?
Only the precious blood of Christ
Shed that day at Calvary.

He took the weight of my sin,
He who was sinless and pure,
On a stark wooden cross
in pain I will never endure.

The shame should be mine;
the pain should be, too.
But He made a promise:
nothing else need I do.

Why did He make
such a choice for me
when before creation He knew
how sinful I'd be?

Help me remember:
Christ chose to die for me
when He poured out His love
on Calvary's tree.

His unconditional love
is mine to embrace.
He offered it freely
so that I will see His face.

rfg

NEEDY

The job description of the necessary qualities for those in law enforcement could read in part: ability to assist those in distress; compassionate and caring toward others in need; able to act quickly, especially for those whose lives may be in danger; willing to provide words of comfort to those who are struggling. Fulfilling those responsibilities consumes much of our time on the job. However, our obligations do not end there. We also have families and friends who, from time to time, are in need of our time and attention. In addition, we, too, have needs, some of which we are not able to fulfill on our own. Consequently, we sometimes find ourselves thinking, "I just need a break!"

An old hymn, says, "I need Thee, Oh, I need Thee; every hour, I need Thee." Imagine how different our lives would be if our awareness of Christ permeated each hour of our existence. "I call to the Lord, who is worthy of praise, and I am saved from my enemies." Psalm 18:3. Our Lord never takes time off. He is never too busy to listen to our prayers and petitions. He actually wants us to call out to Him. Psalm 4:3 assures us, "Know that the Lord has set apart the godly for Himself; the Lord will hear when I call to Him." He knows that when we are weak and in need and reach out to Him, we are showing our dependence upon Him and our desire to walk in His will. When others see the true source of our strength, wisdom, and peace, they, too, may want the same.

"You're a soul made by God, for God, and made to need God, which means you were not made to be self-sufficient." Dallas Willard, author

Isaiah 58:11, Mathew 6:8, Philippians 4:19

MY WAY

Since we are in a position of authority in the law enforcement profession, we are often required to take control. However, we must be careful that we do not always expect to have things done our way just because we have such authority. Sometimes when I came home after my shift, a decision had to be made with my family. Too often, I reacted by jumping right in and telling the others how the situation had to be handled. In reality, I did not have all the answers, and many times, the issue would have been better resolved if I had considered what others thought the course of action should be.

In our Christian walk, God has given us free will, and for our well-being, it is important that we make the right choices. Most importantly, our choices must be consistent with His word and His will. When our decisions align with His thoughts and His ways, they will bring us peace and joy in this world. Isaiah 55:8-9 tells us, "For My thoughts are not your thoughts, neither are your ways My ways," declares the Lord. "As the heavens are higher than the earth, so are My ways higher than your ways and My thoughts than your thoughts."

"Learn to commit every situation to God and trust Him for the outcome."
Billy Graham, evangelist/author

John 14:26, Romans 8:26-27, 2 Timothy 1:13-14

THE SHIELD

When the trooper graduated from the PA State Police Academy, his family observed the highlight of that day as he was rewarded with his shiny, gold badge, a symbol of all that he had worked for and all that was yet to come as a trooper. Years later, he was given an opportunity that was perhaps even more rewarding. He proudly walked across the ceremonial stage to hand his son his own badge as he graduated from the PA State Police Academy. Upon graduation, all officers carry and display a badge, or as some departments call them, a shield, to represent their authority. Officers who fail to uphold the oath of office to serve the community with honesty and integrity typically must turn in their badge.

God's word has several examples that refer to a shield, but the shield that God provides is not a shiny piece of metal. His shield is the strength and protection of the Lord which He gives to all who believe in Him. Psalm 28:7 says, "The Lord is my strength and my shield; my heart trusts in Him, and I am helped." Psalm 3:3-4 says, "But You are a shield about me, Oh Lord; You bestow glory on me and lift up my head. To the Lord I cry aloud, and He answers me from His holy hill." The shield that the Lord provides to those who know and trust Him is much more significant and represents far more power than the tangible shield which we carry.

"Prayer is a shield to the soul." John Bunyan, 17th century English preacher/author

2 Chronicles 20:15-17, Psalm 7:10, Jeremiah 46:3

GUILTY OR INNOCENT

During a trial, after I presented all the facts and the evidence, both tangible and circumstantial, the next phase was often the most difficult. After all the testimony was presented and the jurors were excused to the deliberating room, they now had to determine the fate of the perpetrator. I had committed many days to solving a crime, interacting with the victims, making the arrest, and then preparing the case for trial. Often, I had to wait many hours, sometimes a day or more for the jury or the judge to determine the penalty for the crime that had been committed. Since I often interacted with victims and their families, I saw the personal effects of the crime and the pain that it caused. In most situations, the crime will have changed the life of the victim forever. Often it had a rippling effect on the families of both the victim and the accused. Looking at the far-reaching impact of the crime, I wanted to see justice served in a fair but significant way.

Whenever we acknowledge our sin, we recognize that we are deserving of the maximum penalty. Thankfully, we serve a compassionate God who is willing to provide complete forgiveness because of the sacrifice Jesus made for us on the cross. Furthermore, He exhibits the qualities that we need to emulate as we offer forgiveness to those who have hurt us. Psalm 103:8-10 says, "The Lord is compassionate and gracious, slow to anger, abounding in love. He will not always accuse, nor will He harbor His anger forever; He does not treat us as our sins deserve or repay us according to our iniquities."

"Forgiveness is unlocking the door to set someone free and realizing you were the prisoner." Max Lucado, author/preacher.

1 Corinthians 6:20, Romans 6: 17-18, 1 John 4:10

PERFECT

After receiving information from a confidential source, I obtained a search warrant for the home of a high-level bookmaker. His information indicated that this was an extensive gambling operation with mob connections. Significant amounts of money were being illegally garnered each week. In addition, those who were placing bets and not paying on their losses were being threatened, often physically. On the day of the carefully designed raid, five officers trudged through the snow and approached the back door. After identifying ourselves and not receiving a response, we heard commotion inside the home. Forcing the door open, the first officer entered the kitchen with his snow-covered shoes, immediately fell on his back, and slid across the floor. The following officer did likewise, as did the remaining three. We then realized that the floor had recently been waxed, and the snow on our shoes turned our perfectly planned entry into a disaster. By the time we reached the other rooms, much of the evidence had been destroyed in a large barrel of water where rice paper now floated on the surface.

Likewise, in our spiritual life, when we attempt to be perfect, we will soon find that it is impossible. In our time on Earth, we will never be perfect. Romans 3:23 tells us, "For all have sinned and fall short of the glory of God." 2 Corinthians 5:21 says, "God made Him who had no sin to be sin for us, so that in Him we might become the righteousness of God." Upon close reflection, we should recognize that even our best and most sincere efforts on this side of Heaven will never be perfect.

"God's words to man, found in scripture, are complete, lacking for nothing; they cannot be improved upon. There is nothing missing, nothing God forgot to include that we need for faith and practice in the Christian life." Now that's perfect!
 David Jeremiah, pastor/author

Ecclesiastes 7:20, Isaiah 64:6, Hebrew 10: 11-14

THINK ON YOUR FEET

Prior to joining the law enforcement profession, I did not always think and respond as quickly as I needed to in many situations. Being able to assess a situation rapidly and respond appropriately are crucial skills in this profession, and we often employ them to protect not only ourselves, but also others around us. These skills are especially valuable when we have to testify in court. In one of my earliest "big" cases, I carefully conducted an investigation and spent a great deal of time in preparation before appearing in court. I met with the district attorney, and we discussed the case at length. Nevertheless, during my time of testimony, the sitting judge asked a question that we had not anticipated. Fortunately, I redeemed myself because I was able to respond logically and calmly. We were even able to secure a winning decision from the court. Being able to "think on our feet" is also useful beyond the job.

Our walk as Believers should be different from the lives of those who do not know Christ and choose not to conform to God's will. It should not be uncommon for others around us to recognize that something makes us different. They may then wonder why we have a certain peace, joy, and assurance. If they are seeking and ask us about the way we live, we must be ready to explain how Christ directs our lives. "But in your hearts set apart Christ as Lord. Always be prepared to give an answer to everyone who asks you to give the reason for the hope that you have. But do this with gentleness and respect." 1 Peter 3:15. We may get only one chance to explain our case, and we need to have enough knowledge and the ability to present it in a way that makes us believable.

"The goal of our sanctification [to be set apart for God] is that we place Christ on display in the way we love others." Larry Crab, author

John 1:3, John 3:16, John 10:10, Romans 6:22-23

MEANINGLESS

Some experiences on the job give us a great sense of accomplishment. Solving a major case, restoring hope to someone in despair, or helping others to get their lives back in order can be exhilarating. As important as all that is, we must be careful not to chase after things in life that have no lasting value. When we realize that the things we have spent our lives acquiring do not satisfy us anymore, we will begin to feel an emptiness inside. That expensive car no longer gives us a thrill. The "forever home" that we worked so hard to acquire has lost much of its appeal. As a young man, King Solomon had a close relationship with the Lord, and He became the wisest and richest king in history. However, he turned to earthly pleasures and away from a godly life. In his old age, he realized that success and earthly things and pleasures often lead to sin, do not last forever, and have no eternal value. In Ecclesiastes 1:2, Solomon proclaimed that without God, "Meaningless, meaningless…Utterly meaningless. Everything is meaningless."

Fortunately, Solomon shared his understanding of life's purpose in Ecclesiastes 12:13, "Fear God and keep His commandments, for this is the whole duty of man." In essence, the defining purpose of our lives should be to love God with all of our being. We also must be loving to others around us as we live a life that exemplifies a close walk with the Lord. The good news of salvation is something that we cannot and must not keep to ourselves. As we prepare for our life in Heaven for eternity, we need to remember that the best is yet to come.

"If our identity is in our work, rather than Christ, success will go to our heads, and failure will go to our hearts." Tim Keller, pastor/author

Joshua 1:7, Isaiah 40:28-31, 2 Timothy 3:16-17

OUT OF TIME

Early one winter morning, as I headed toward the barracks for the start of my shift, I quickly realized that the roadway was treacherous. Throughout the night, it had been snowing, and now drivers were having a difficult time staying on the road. After I went out on patrol, a call from dispatch directed me to a rural area, the location of an apparent car accident. I arrived to find several people standing at the edge of a frozen pond with a gaping hole in the ice. The township supervisor was just arriving as well and told me that several days ago, the township had constructed a berm just before the pond to prevent anyone from sliding into it. As witnesses then described the vehicle that was now submerged in the pond, the supervisor realized that it was his wife's car. The scuba team had been dispatched, and I could do nothing but wait next to the pond. Staring at the hole in the ice, the supervisor stood next to me and began to sob as minutes seemed like hours. I felt completely helpless. I could do nothing but cling to the hope that at any moment the woman would be able to free herself and suddenly emerge to the surface... but to no avail.

Evangelist Billy Graham once said, "Our days are numbered. One of the primary goals of our lives should be to prepare for our last day." Those in law enforcement have a deeper understanding of the old saying, "Life is Fragile," for we witness the loss of life regularly, often feeling that it is untimely. For Believers, our awareness of how quickly a life can be lost should also cause us to realize the urgency to tell others how they can receive the gift of eternal life. We know that when our life is over, we will, in fact, spend it someplace. Great peace comes by knowing without a doubt that it will be in Heaven with Jesus for Eternity.

"Did you wake up feeling fragile? Read the Bible 'til you find a promise strong enough to carry you through the day." John Piper, pastor/author

John 10:28-30, Romans 6:23, 2 Corinthians 4:17-18, 1 Peter 5:10

EVIDENCE

Officers regularly face the need to have infallible evidence in order to solve a crime. When a business establishment has been burglarized, we process the scene to see if fingerprints, blood, or anything foreign to the owner of the business, and possibly belonging to the perpetrator, was left behind. We check any interior or exterior cameras to determine if the suspects might have been captured on tape. We canvas the neighborhood or other establishments in close proximity in the hope that someone may have observed something unusual or seen a vehicle in the vicinity around the time of the crime. Even when a body is discovered, and the cause of death is not immediately apparent, it is always treated as if foul play may have occurred. Evidence can then be used to determine if a person is either guilty or innocent of a crime.

Because evidence is so important in the work of those in law enforcement, we may be more likely to seek proof in other areas of our life, including our faith. As Believers, our faith is based on the evidence we find within the Bible. How can we then be sure of the infallibility of God's word? Dr. James Kennedy, in his book, *Why I Believe,* observes that, "The evidence for the resurrection of Jesus Christ has been examined more carefully than the evidence for any other fact in history." Citing prophesies in both the Old and New Testaments, he presents evidence of the exactness and the reliability of the Biblical prophecies that is impossible to refute. Interestingly, some of the greatest scholars who conducted lengthy investigations to prove the inaccuracy of the Bible found that they were wrong and, consequently, accepted the saving knowledge of Jesus Christ. The evidence is available and too important for us not to test it. Our eternal destination is at stake.

"The exquisite order displayed by our scientific understanding of the physical world calls for the Divine." Vera Kistiakowsky, MIT physicist

Isaiah 40:8, 2 Timothy 3:16, Revelation 22:18-19

FAITHFULNESS

For those who have been in a canine unit or just observed an officer with a canine "partner," the faithful bond between the two is most apparent. K-9 officers know that regardless of the circumstances or dangers before them, they can depend on their furry partner to respond and perform as trained, while always protecting the handler. Often, a canine will be sent into a building where an armed suspect has escaped, and the canine does not survive the assignment, but his partner does. In 1931, Pennsylvania State Police Sergeant Timothy McCarthy was attempting to serve a warrant at a home when he was shot by the suspect. His K-9, "Omar," prevented the suspect from escaping the home but suffered several bullet wounds during the fracas. When the action was curtailed, Omar ran outside of the home to find McCarthy, who was lying on the ground, dead from his injuries. Omar lay down beside McCarthy, not allowing anyone to approach his partner until he knew it was okay to do so.

We can find comfort in knowing that we have a Creator who is far more faithful than we could ever imagine or hope for. Think about how He loved Peter after he had denied knowing Christ three times in a day. Ponder how He lovingly responded to Thomas who refused to believe that Christ was resurrected until he later saw Him face to face. He wants to care for us through all of our experiences this side of heaven and then afterwards into eternity. "For great is His love toward us, and the faithfulness of the Lord endures forever." Psalm 117:2.

"We need a Shepherd to care for us, and we have one. One who knows us by name."
 Max Lucado, author

Nehemiah 9:6, Isaiah 45:18, Revelation 4:11

WHY LISTEN?

When we are the first responder to an incident, it seems to be our nature to want to step right in and resolve the issue. Fortunately, I learned early the importance of listening so that I fully understood the situation that faced me when I arrived at a scene, whether it was a vehicular accident, a potential crime scene, or a dispute between several individuals. What I heard determined the way that I would proceed. When I was called to a hit and run crash, the distraught, elderly woman blurted out, "I was just hit from behind. The driver who failed to stop was driving a yellow sports car. You have to find him!" As I stood at the side of the road, I saw a vehicle a short distance ahead parked on the berm. A young man was walking toward us. He said, "I saw the accident happen. The old man, driving an old, full-sized, dark-colored car, appeared to be disoriented as he pulled around this woman's car and continued down the highway. I have a partial registration number of his car." Although attentive listening can be difficult to practice in the midst of turmoil, it can be critical because witnesses or suspects may not always provide the same version of the "facts."

Some of us have a tendency not to listen as carefully as we should to the direction that the Lord has for us. In both professional and personal situations, I, too, often felt that I was most capable of handling the issue and did not need to seek advice. As a result, I sometimes made things more difficult for myself, and the resolution took much longer to accomplish. James 1:19, 22 outlines an appropriate way to respond to all situations: "My dear brothers, take note of this: Everyone should be quick to listen, slow to speak and slow to become angry...Do not merely listen to the word, and so deceive yourselves. Do what it says."

"Everyone has something to teach you if you are humble enough to listen."
Mark Driscoll, pastor/author

Proverbs 2:1-5, Mark 4:9, Hebrews 2:1-3

THE POWER OF WORDS

The detective was dispatched to a residence and advised that a possible shooting had taken place. As he cautiously approached the home and looked through the open front door, he observed a middle-aged woman calmly sitting at her kitchen table. When the detective walked in, the woman motioned toward a room in the rear of the residence. Upon entering it, he saw a man sitting back in a recliner and wearing a white tee shirt with a red bullseye drawn on the shirt. In the middle of the target was a bullet hole with blood oozing out. It was immediately obvious that the man was no longer alive. When the detective walked back into the kitchen, the woman said, "He has been arguing with me all day. I couldn't take it anymore."

Many people struggle with difficult issues that can be physical, emotional, and even spiritual. In law enforcement, we come in contact with so many people who are obviously distraught, and we cannot even imagine what has happened in their lives that causes them to do what they do. We do know that they have not been able to find the answer to true peace. At these times, we who believe should remember that the words we say to someone when we interact with them may be just what they need to hear. Our words may even prevent them from doing something traumatic. We know that genuine peace comes only from knowing and trusting the Lord and being able to call out to Him to ask for wisdom and direction. We need to be able to reflect the peace that we have and offer comfort when we can.

"Kindness is the language which the deaf can hear and the blind can see."
Mark Twain, author

Colossians 3:15, Hebrews 12:14, 1 Peter 5:7

PERSPECTIVE

Because we see many horrific situations in our profession, we may develop a tendency to believe that in certain circumstances, nothing is going to change. Upon obtaining a search warrant for a residence occupied by a young woman and her one-year-old son, I went to the home with other officers. My informant said that the woman was selling methamphetamine and was also a user. As I approached the open door, I could see a woman who appeared to be asleep on the sofa. Entering the home, we saw the unattended one-year-old boy wandering around the room. The woman had obviously crashed after remaining awake for many days from ingesting the drug that she frequently sold. The innocent baby was filthy, and his unchanged diaper sagged down to his bruised knees. Cockroaches had infested the kitchen, and empty baby bottles were strewn among remnants of stale food. I wanted to scoop up this little guy and take him to a clean home and loving family.

Many people live in deplorable conditions, are undernourished, and are facing lives of abject poverty. We have chosen our profession because we believe that in some way, we can make a difference, not only in individual lives, but in society in general. When we realize that often we do not have the ability to do all that we would like to, we cannot allow discouragement to overtake us. Instead of feeling defeated, we can share the good news of the saving knowledge of Jesus Christ. In reality, that is the best information that we can pass on to others. It may not change their living conditions or their status in society or heal them physically, but that news can give them the peace to endure. If they can realize that this time on Earth is temporary and fleeting and that the best is yet to come--an eternity free from all the struggles--it may be just what they need today to encourage them and give them the strength to carry on. In Matthew 11:28 Jesus said, "Come to me, all you who are weary and burdened, and I will give you rest."

"Preach the Gospel at all times, and, if necessary, open your mouth."
Francis of Assisi, founder of Franciscan Order of Monks

Colossians 1:11, Hebrews 10:36, James 1:2-5

IMPROVEMENTS

One of the most troublesome situations in law enforcement occurs when an officer has to intervene in a situation to stop a person who has already taken or is intent on taking another's life. For years, the investigation of shootings by police was handled poorly. After an incident occurred, a supervisor would arrive at the scene and immediately request the officer's firearm. Although this was done for evidentiary reasons, it left the officer with an empty holster, something very obvious to bystanders, and it suggested that the officer might be guilty. The supervisor then directed the officer to sit in the back of a police vehicle, the place usually occupied by arrested criminals. Transported to the station, the officer immediately underwent an interrogation. Most likely, the officer would soon begin to second guess his decision. Even after an absolutely "clean" shooting, many officers left the job because of the way the investigation was conducted. Fortunately, these old procedures have been replaced with more sensitive protocol.

None of us is born without sin, and even when we get to the age of understanding, it may take many years before we accept Jesus as our Lord and Savior. If we eventually and sincerely do choose to become a Christian, there will be a change in the way we live, talk, and care about others. For some, this change can take a considerable amount of time before the results are obvious. Even when we believe that our lives have changed, we still may slide backwards and into our old sinful habits. Satan knows when we are weak, and he never sleeps as he is always trying to change us back to our old, sinful nature. The good news is that God is all-powerful, and He never stops forgiving, regardless of how often we fall. 2 Peter 3:9 reminds us, "The Lord is not slow in keeping His promise, as some understand slowness. He is patient with you, not wanting anyone to perish, but everyone to come to repentance."

"Whenever God is blessing, we can expect the devil to be opposing."
Greg Laurie, pastor/author

Numbers 23:19, Jeremiah 29:11, Malachi 3:6-7

THE REAL DIFFERENCE

During my first day on the job, I realized that people looked at me as being different. When I drove down the highway in a marked patrol vehicle, I soon noticed that others naturally turned and closely observed all that I did. When I arrived at the scene of an incident, as soon as people observed me in uniform stepping out of the patrol car, their conversations stopped, and they waited to see how I was going to handle the situation. Even when I was off-duty and at a gathering, especially with people that I did not know, when they learned that I was in the law enforcement profession, most wanted to hear what I had to say. It probably was not because they all agreed with what we generally stand for, but because they were curious about what the job entails, the dangers that may be associated with it, and any significant cases that I was willing to talk about.

If we make it known that we are members of the body of Christ, people may also want to know what it is like to be a Christian. Although they may not believe what we do, they may ask why we believe and act as we do. Since we are called upon to be different, it is important to behave in a way that glorifies Christ, with the hope that it might cause others to want what we have. Colossians 3:5-8 cautions us, "Put to death, therefore, whatever belongs to your earthly nature: sexual immorality, impurity, lust, evil desires and greed, which is idolatry...You used to walk in these ways, in the life you once lived. But now you must rid yourselves of all such things as these: anger, rage, malice, slander, and filthy language from your lips." Once we accept Jesus as our Lord and Savior as a free gift to all who want to receive it, we become a "Christian," and then have the responsibility to uphold the image-- just as we are to uphold our image in law enforcement.

"Be careful how you live. You may be the only Bible some person ever reads."
William J. Toms, British writer

Jeremiah 29:11, Romans 8:28, Ephesians 2:10

HIGHEST PRIORITY

Since the range of responsibilities in our profession is so broad, more often than not, our days can be a whirlwind. We might start the day by serving a search warrant for stolen property and end the shift by searching for an elderly man who wandered away from his home. When officers in large cities report for duty, it is not unusual to find that incidents have already backed up and are waiting for an available officer to respond, but life-threatening incidents must take precedence. Although much of our daily work requires immediate action, when a homicide occurs, time is most crucial, for evidence can be lost if too much time elapses. Because it is common for us to be pulled in so many different directions, we can find it difficult to prioritize our calls.

It is also easy to become enveloped in our daily on-the-job activities even when we are off-duty. When we allow our job to consume us, we not only shortchange our family, but we are also more likely to fail to commune with the living God whom we serve. In reality, if we were to go to Him first, He would help us to make sense out of the confusion. Then, we would clearly know the next step to take. Matthew 6:33-34 directs us, "But seek first His kingdom and His righteousness, and all these things will be given to you as well. Therefore, do not worry about tomorrow, for tomorrow will worry about itself. Each day has enough trouble of its own."

"You're a soul made by God, for God, and made to need God, which means you were not made to be self-sufficient." Dallas Willard, author

Ecclesiastes 2:11, Mark 8:36-37, John 10:10

ASSUMPTIONS

In 2005, the Pennsylvania State Police celebrated 100 years of service to the Commonwealth of Pennsylvania. At that time, an oral history project was established to interview retirees for information about the department that had never been recorded. As a volunteer interviewer, I learned that Donald Cutting had joined the State Highway Patrol in 1937. Traveling to his home in quest of an interview, I assumed that my trip was probably a waste of time, for this former Major probably would not have much recall of incidents that had occurred sixty-eight years prior. After entering his home, I was escorted to a corner of the room where a white-haired gentleman was sitting. Within minutes, I knew that this former Major, now ninety years of age, probably had a better memory than I did. During many future meetings, he provided fascinating details about his law enforcement experience, so I always looked forward to our next interview. Since a Centennial Celebration commemorating the department's milestone was to be held, I invited the Major to attend. A week prior to the gala, I called to see if he were ready. "I sure am. I went out and bought a new suit," he said happily. At age 90, he assumed that nothing would keep him from attending.

Often, we Believers assume that most people around us, especially those on the job, probably would not want to hear about our faith, the promise of an eternity in heaven, and the peace that we have. In fact, many of us were blessed to become recipients of the Good News because someone did not make that general assumption. However, we should also be cautious not to force our faith on others, for that would almost guarantee that they will not want to hear about what we believe. In Matthew 5:16, Jesus commissions us to, "...Let your light shine before men, that they may see your good deeds and praise your Father in heaven." The best "good deed" we could carry out would be to assume that people are in need of the Lord and then show them how easily He can be found.

"The way we live often speaks far louder than our words." Billy Graham, evangelist

Matthew 24:12-14, Romans 1:16, 1 Peter 3:15

REWARDS

Some incidents on the job were impossible for me to resolve. In one such case, the adult son of the owners of a successful business chain had been found murdered in his car. Even after many months of exploring the best resources and techniques available, including extensive gathering and examination of forensic evidence, eyewitness reports, and surveillance tapes, it was still impossible to identify the perpetrator. Although the family offered a significant reward for the capture and successful prosecution of the person who had taken their son's life, the perpetrator was never found. It is still difficult for me to accept the fact that someone in our society can take another life and not be caught and held accountable.

We Believers may sometimes doubt the assurance of an eventual and perfect reward from Christ. We need to remember that Satan is the author of those doubts, for he wants us to be unsure. Dr. Charles Stanley, pastor and author says, "There are only three options open to God as sinners stand in His courtroom. He must condemn them, compromise His own righteousness to receive them just the way they are, or He can change them into righteous people. If He can exercise the third option, then He can announce them righteous, which is justification." Evidence of the third option is reiterated throughout God's word. Paul tells us in Hebrews 10:35, "So do not throw away your confidence; it will be richly rewarded." In Matthew 5:12, Jesus, Himself, said, "Rejoice and be glad, because great is your reward in heaven..."

"The Bible tells us that Jesus Christ came to do three things. He came to have my past forgiven, you get a purpose of living, and a home in heaven."
Rick Warren, pastor/author

Matthew 16:27, 1 Corinthians 2:9, James 1:12

BAD DAYS

During our career in law enforcement, we regularly witness the depravity of man. Whether it is violent acts, rioting and looting, the ever-increasing war on police, loss of life at the hands of a vicious person, abuse of children, sexual abuse, or chemical addiction, it can have a powerful and negative effect on us. I well remember times when having to deal with such instances really began to pull me down. Then I started thinking that there were more bad days than good ones, and the downward spiral accelerated. It was often difficult for me to move on past the mental images that constantly replayed in my mind. By allowing myself to focus on negative feelings, it became more difficult to recognize those things for which I should be thankful.

If we desire to walk in God's will, we are commanded to give thanks for **all** things. Sometimes that is not easy, but if we develop a plan of attack, we can overcome Satan's arrows. First, we should recognize that a negative mindset pleases Satan. Next, accept that we will all experience difficulties as a part of life, some more so than others. Then, start each day by finding at least one thing to be thankful for, and be mindful to look for even little reasons to thank God throughout the day. The more time we give to thank Him, the less time we are available to be open to Satan's attacks. In 1 Thessalonians 5:16-18, Paul reminds us of the process which will help us to regain control: "**Be** joyful always; **Pray** continually; **Give** thanks in **All** circumstances; for this is the will of God in Christ Jesus for you."

"Be patient. God is using today's difficulties to strengthen you for tomorrow." Max Lucado, preacher/author

Psalm 106:5, Ephesians 5:20, Colossians 3:15-17

BUILDING CHARACTER

Shortly after coming on the job, I began to understand that what we do demands a great deal of perseverance. To find the truth often requires many tedious hours to fully determine what is fact and what is not. At times, I even considered giving up on a case because it was so physically and emotionally draining, and I was not making any headway. In hindsight, if I had turned those times over to the Lord and remembered that in everything I do, He allows the consequences and the results, I would have had greater peace and not become so discouraged. During those difficult and long investigations, when I stayed the course and persevered, I always received great satisfaction at a successful conclusion.

I also found that situations in my Christian walk likewise required perseverance. If I am not walking closely with the Lord, it will not matter how much effort I exert. He is always our source of wisdom, strength, and perseverance. If we need to be reminded of His presence and availability, it can be found in His word, through His creation, and from godly people. Despite the trials, we must be steadfast and understand that He does not allow anything in our lives to happen which He has not already approved. The apostle Paul endured beatings, shipwreck, imprisonment, and countless other sufferings, situations that anyone would choose to avoid. Yet, he recognized the value in experiencing them, for his character and his relationship with the Lord grew because of them. In Romans 5:3-5, he teaches us, "Not only so, but we also rejoice in our sufferings, because we know that suffering produces perseverance; perseverance, character; and character, hope. And hope does not disappoint us, because God has poured out His love into our hearts by the Holy Spirit, whom He has given us."

"Problems patiently endured will work for our spiritual perfecting."
A.W. Tozer, pastor/author

Galatians 6:9, James 1:12, Revelation 3:10

VIGILANT

Few professions require one to be constantly on the alert as law enforcement does. Once we join this profession, being vigilant becomes ingrained in our behavior, for we realize that around every corner, danger may be present. While we are on the job and out in public, a concern which we often have is that someone we had previously arrested might recognize us and then decide to take revenge. Even at the national level, the threat level changes at times, and we are warned to be on the alert for terrorist activity. The threat is no longer just across the ocean, but also right here in the homeland as unprovoked acts of violence toward police officers are at an all-time high.

Often these external threats are more obvious than the constant, sometimes subtle attacks from Satan. However, we must remember that he is real, and we have to be vigilant to withstand his attacks. He likes nothing more than to see a Believer stumble and succumb to his sinful temptations. Proverbs 24:19-20 encourages us to be steadfast: "Do not fret because of evil men or be envious of the wicked, for the evil man has no further hope, and the lamp of the wicked will be snuffed out." In Romans 12:9, Paul taught that Christians must make a concerted effort to live a godly life: "Love must be sincere. Hate what is evil; cling to what is good."

"It's Satan's delight to tell me that once he's got me, he will keep me. But at that moment, I can go back to God. And I know that if I confess my sins, God is faithful and just to forgive me."
Alan Redpath, pastor/author

Ephesians 6:11, James 4:7, 1 Peter 5:8

DON'T WASTE TIME

Our profession often requires us to make decisions quickly. We do not have the opportunity to "meet and discuss," or valuable time may be wasted. One day, a number of us were called to a large manufacturing company where a significant group of striking workers had gathered outside the building. Our contingency of thirty officers was in formation and prepared to quell any violence. Shortly after the supervisor of our detail had gone inside to meet with management, the angry group moved forward to storm the building, and a dangerous situation began to unfold. The number one priority of officers is to stop potential collateral damage and quickly move people to an area out of harm's way. I made a quick decision and directed the officers to move forward toward the agitated group; consequently, we were able to maintain control. Especially when we encounter a difficult situation, we should realize that an immediate, intelligent response is critical.

Pastor David Jeremiah tells us that when we seek to be in God's will in every area of our lives, we need to stop from time to time and take inventory of what is really important, what is of eternal value. Technology in its many forms often lures us into wasting many precious hours. We may allow it to invade our lives as we feel compelled to watch each playoff game, check each text message, or answer each call, often interrupting conversations we are having with "live" people. To be consistent in our spiritual walk, we must take time reflecting on and determining how God would want us to spend our days. Since we have a limited number of days in this life, whether we are on the job or pursuing our everyday activities, we should be careful not to waste that time. "Show me, O Lord, my life's end and the number of my days; let me know how fleeting is my life." Psalm 39:4.

"Short as time is, we make it still shorter by the careless waste of time."
Victor Hugo, French author.

Psalms 90:12, Ecclesiastes 3:1, Ephesians 5:15-17

DIFFICULT PEOPLE

One evening shift while I sat in the crime room reviewing reports on what appeared to be a wave of burglaries in our area, the Lieutenant called me to his office. He began to complain that I had not developed suspects, that no one had been identified as being responsible for the residential burglaries, and that victims were upset that nothing was being done. After his harangue, I walked back to my office and obtained a file that I had been working on. It included all the crimes in a specific area, the MO which was consistent, and the fact that I had even been conducting surveillances. When I returned to the Lieutenant's office and presented this evidence, he blew off my efforts, and it was obvious that I needed to be the scapegoat. Although we do not expect to have difficult times with those we work with, we will never see eye to eye with everyone in all situations.

In our personal lives, as well, we may be confronted by family and friends who might disappoint us. It is most difficult when accusations are made that are truly unjustified, and we wonder why God allows such things. We must remember that when we accepted Jesus as Lord and Savior, we were never promised a trial-free life. Sometimes, when we are walking closely with the Lord, we have more difficulties because Satan is so eager to attack. Jesus, Himself, faced a trial for a crime that He did not commit. James 1:2-4 tells us, "Dear brothers, is your life full of difficulties and temptations? Then be happy, for when the way is rough, your patience has a chance to grow. So let it grow and don't try to squirm out of your problems. For when your patience is finally in full bloom, then you will be ready for anything, strong in character, full and complete." (The Living Bible).

"God never promises to remove us from struggles. He does promise, however, to change the way we look at them." Max Lucado, author

Matthew 5:44-45, Luke 6:27-29, Romans 12:12

I CAN'T SEE THE ANSWER

People sometimes turn toward those in law enforcement to enforce the laws, keep them safe, and fix things. Often, we are able to accomplish all of those things. In other situations, we just do not have the answer or know the way to resolve the problem. When a report comes to dispatch that a person is about to take his or her life, a feeling of desperation comes over the officers who respond, for they know that time is of the essence. Upon arriving at the location where a distraught person is precariously perched on the wall of a bridge, high above the ground below, the officers make immediate attempts to talk to this subject. Most times, this person has already made the decision and is not willing to listen to the pleading officers. When that person takes the final plunge, we tend to second guess our words, anxiously wondering if we could have said or done something differently.

If we call out to the Lord at the start of each day, asking for wisdom and discernment, He is there and will hear us. The Bible has many examples of Believers who were walking in faith, but when they faced difficult circumstances, some began to question God's direction. Still, they continued to follow in faith. When Moses and the Israelites left Egypt and were on the banks of the Red Sea facing the vast body of water, the Egyptian army was close on their heels. Although the outcome appeared bleak, there was no turning back, so they marched to the sea. God parted the waters and brought them safely to the other side. Most of us have faced a seemingly impossible situation which is unexpectedly resolved, but the outcome was not what we were looking for. That is the time to remember that even when a situation does not provide what we believe would be a better conclusion, God has been and always will be in control. He sees the answer. "Now faith is being sure of what we hope for and certain of what we do not see." Hebrews 11:1.

"It often takes the darkness of a storm to show us the light of God's presence."
Tony Evans, pastor/author

Psalm 56:3, Proverbs 16:3, Isaiah 43:2

SILENT WITNESS

A young Amish man had been murdered, and his body was found in our jurisdiction. After an extensive investigation over many months, I was able to arrest the perpetrator. As I interviewed him, I asked why he had taken this young life. He hesitated briefly and said flippantly, "I have no idea. He seemed like a really nice guy." This random, senseless act against someone not even known by this killer appalled me. On the day of the trial, as I entered the courtroom, at least fifty Amish men and women, all dressed in black, quietly walked in and sat down together. Knowing that these peaceful, non-violent people were a powerful witness against his client, the defense attorney was outraged at their presence. However, in spite of his objections, the trial continued, and the murderer was found guilty and sentenced to life in prison.

Through our faith, we Believers have found the true meaning of life and the way to have true peace. We often want to tell others about that, especially those who are struggling in life. However, we need to be cautious so that our enthusiasm does not become overbearing and turn them away from the knowledge that we have. Remembering to call on the Holy Spirit will give us the words to say and the right time to say them. "In the same way, the Spirit helps us in our weakness. We do not know what we ought to pray for, but the Spirit Himself intercedes for us with groans that words cannot express." Romans 8:26.

"Every believer is a witness whether he wants to be or not."
Donald Barnhouse, pastor/theologian/author

Proverbs 18:19, I John 5:15, I John 3:18

JUST ONE MISTAKE

During each shift, we never know what we may be called upon to do. At times, we respond to very tense and dangerous situations where there is little room for mistakes. The suspect entered the bank, walked over to a camera, and sprayed black paint on the lens. He was wearing gloves and a covering over his face. After he pointed a gun at the teller, he ran outside toward his vehicle. Realizing that no one was around, he pulled off his mask. An examination of an outside camera revealed not only his appearance, but also the license plate of the car he drove away. In today's society, more so than ever, we also need to be aware of our own welfare, realizing that some are intent on causing us harm. Even with that added stress, the vast majority of those on the job respond appropriately and perform their duties and responsibilities, not only within the law, but with a great deal of restraint and integrity, in spite of what those who are ill-informed may believe.

Believers are likewise held to a higher standard. We are representatives of Christ, and many are watching all that we do. Sometimes, in our humanness, we will make mistakes; we will sin. When we do, we are called upon to acknowledge this, repent, and ask for forgiveness. Although we know it is important to try not to commit the same sins again, while we live in this world that may not happen. We will continue to sin until we reach Heaven. As Christ-followers, we should be grateful that the Lord does not have a three-strike rule, but, in fact, He continues to forgive us for our sinful ways. He will forgive all and not hold us accountable for even one. That forgiveness covers not only the past and the present, but even those sins that we will commit in the future. His mercy does not give us a free pass, but it should instill in us a desire to walk closely to the Lord and follow His will. "For we are God's workmanship, created in Christ Jesus to do good works, which God prepared in advance for us to do." Ephesians 2:10.

"God will never send anyone to Hell. If a man goes to Hell, he goes by his own free choice." Billy Graham, evangelist/author

John 3:16, John 8:11, Romans 8:1

CREDIT DUE

At some point on the job, we are likely to experience a desire for recognition. This often happens when several agencies work together and solve a significant investigation, seize a large number of drugs or weapons, or capture a wanted felon. Each department wants to get the recognition which indicates that they were responsible for solving the case. Especially when a large seizure of money has been forfeited as the result of illegal activity, all the agencies involved scramble to get at least a part of it. This attitude causes a great deal of friction between agencies and results in some not wanting to work with others in the future. Sometimes, however, those involved are satisfied just to realize that the ultimate reward is that justice has been served.

There are times when Believers are able to accomplish something, and we know that the only reason for success was that the Holy Spirit provided help. Those who are unaware of or do not understand His existence, His power, or His willingness to direct us, think that we accomplished something significant on our own. For us not to say otherwise is taking credit where credit was not due. The Holy Spirit, one of the Trinity, is someone we need to turn to for help on a regular basis. When we do, He will bless our efforts. "But you will receive power when the Holy Spirit comes on you; and you will be My witnesses in Jerusalem, and in all Judea, and Samaria, and to the ends of the earth." Acts 1:8.

"When we have the Holy Spirit, we have all that is needed to be all that God desires us to be." A. Z. Tozer, pastor/author

Micah 3:8-10, Acts 2:38, Romans 8:26-27

DIFFERENT BUT SAME

I met the group of thirty at the airport. We were flying out together for a short-term mission trip in Jamaica for ten days. After boarding the plane, I went to my seat next to a guy about forty years old. After a brief introduction, we were in the air, and Pat looked at me and said, "So, what do you do?" When I told him that I was a police officer, he appeared uncomfortable but asked, "What area of work are you assigned to?" After I told him that I did drug investigations, he shifted in his seat and grimaced, almost painfully. In turn, I asked his occupation, and he told me that he worked in a factory. Then he abruptly said, "I am a recovering heroin addict." For the next ten days, we worked side by side under the blazing sun where we developed the most unlikely but very special bond. At one point, I asked Pat what had eventually caused him to stop his addiction, and he replied that he had developed a personal relationship with God who now was his source of strength. In the years that followed that trip, Pat interacted with my younger teenagers, telling them of the terrible consequences of drug use, and they came to love and trust him. Sadly, only a few years later, he died from the consequences of the drugs that had ravaged his body.

Sometimes our God takes us to those with whom we think we have absolutely nothing in common. Even though Pat and I were different in countless ways, we were both the same as we sought and sometimes struggled to walk closely with the Lord. Later, Pat became a part of a small group of struggling men that I led in a Bible study at my home for a few years. We were brothers in the Lord, and someday I know that I will join him in Heaven for eternity. Jesus said, "Whoever does God's will is my brother and sister and mother." Mark 3:35

"There is a brotherhood within the body of believers, and the Lord Jesus Christ is the common denominator. Friendship and fellowship are the legal tender among believers."
J. Vernon McGee, pastor

John 17:23, Acts 4:32, 1 Corinthians 1:10

BE STILL

While I was on the job, very few days were quiet; activity was all around me. I frequently faced moments of concern and great anxiety as I had to make critical decisions that required me to be the best that I could be. I quickly realized that wrong choices could be disastrous, even fatal. Because of the regular heightened level of activity that we are exposed to, an almost constant state of awareness becomes a way of life, both on and off the job. We can experience post-traumatic stress because of the situations that we are often exposed to. Critical, dangerous incidents may be hard to forget and leave behind. Many of us find it difficult to fully relax. Even now, whenever I go into a restaurant, I quickly scan the occupants, and when being seated, I always sit so that I can see the door. I also identify where the nearest exits are located as my family reminds me, "You're not working." Although it is wise to be watchful, we must not forget to make time for ourselves—especially during the intensely difficult times. Consciously taking time to be still and recharge the battery is essential to our overall health, even though this may be contrary to our nature.

God tells us that rest is important for His creation. Psalm 46:10 says, "Be still and know that I am God." But how do we get that peace that causes us to rest? John 14:27 tells us, "Peace I leave you; my peace I give you. I do not give to you as the world gives Do not let your hearts be troubled and do not be afraid." Peace is certainly available to us, and we can find it through Christ. His rest is deep and everlasting.

"Wherever there is stillness, there is the still, small voice, God's speaking from the whirlwind." Annie Dillard, author/poet

Proverbs 19:23, John 16:33, Mark 6:31

OPTIONS

The freedom that we often have to make decisions that we feel comfortable with is something that many in other professions cannot exercise. Sometimes on my shifts, I had the opportunity to decide on the area where I wanted to patrol or the best way to handle a call. At other times, the only decision was so clear that no options were available. If a rash of burglaries were occurring in a certain neighborhood, I knew where I needed to focus my efforts. Since many of our responses have to be very quick, the decision we make may not always be the best one. Afterwards, it will be reviewed by someone who has the advantage of taking the time to fully evaluate the circumstances. Usually, when we believe in our hearts and minds that the right decision was made, others will likely agree.

We, as Believers, also have many options when it comes to our faith. God never intended to force His will or His word upon mankind. He made us in His image and gave us free will. As a result, many people make sinful, inappropriate decisions. Someday, those who refuse to follow the way of the Lord will face judgment, and it will be too late to receive God's forgiveness. As difficult as it may be for us at times to fully understand why some would defiantly choose to walk away from God, He still loves them just as much as He loves us. It is our responsibility to do whatever we can to make a difference in their lives and at least tell them about the promise and peace that we have. "We love because He first loved us." 1 John 4:19.

"You are free to make choices. You are not free to escape the consequences."
Howard Hendricks, pastor/professor

Isaiah 41:13, Romans 8:35-39, 1 John 4:10

GOD IN ME

In law enforcement, we regularly see the worst in humanity. Consequently, we can easily become jaded and forget that these people are just a small percentage of our society. If we become cynical, it can negatively affect the way we treat others, and we will not be a reflection of the claims we make as Believers. At times, my first impression of some people is not good because of their demeanor, the way they dress, their hair, or the number and placement of their piercings and tattoos. However, after getting to know them, I realize that they are very different from what I had first thought. I became less judgmental after a personal experience when driving with my wife on a long trip through rural areas. With a full beard and long, bushy hair, necessary for my work, I was turned away from several motels in spite of their "vacancy" sign out front. We finally got a room when I realized what was happening and sent my well-dressed wife into the motel. It is important every so often to step back and ask ourselves, "Is God in me, and is it evident? Or, am I no different from the rest of society?"

1 John 4:7-8 says, "Dear friends, let us love one another, for love comes from God. Everyone who loves has been born of God and knows God. Whoever does not love does not know God, because God is love." Many may think that love is just a feeling, but it is also an action. 1 Corinthians 13:4-7 reminds us, "Love is patient, love is kind. It does not envy, it does not boast, it is not proud. It is not rude, it is not self-seeking, it is not easily angered, it keeps no record of wrongs. Love does not delight in evil but rejoices with the truth. It always protects, always trusts, always hopes, always perseveres."

"There is something fundamentally wrong with claiming to love God without a passion to love people."
Wes Stafford, past President of Compassion International

Luke 6:31, 2 Corinthians 5:17, 1 John 2:6

HOW SIGNIFICANT?

We are expected to maintain composure and control on the job, but when we have been exposed to traumatic incidents, we can become overwhelmed even during our off-duty personal lives. One sunny day during a week when the temperature had been exceptionally high, I was dispatched to a mobile home which was occupied by an elderly man. After an entire week's worth of newspapers lay untouched in front of his door, the neighbors finally concluded that perhaps something was amiss. As I opened the door, the smell emanating from his home momentarily stopped me in my tracks. When I entered, a shock wave ran through my body, jolting me as I stared at the elderly man sprawled on the floor. It was obvious that the maggots had already been at work for a considerable time. Later that night at home, I was still struggling to process the events of that day. I know that I was less than patient when one of my children complained about having a difficult day at school.

When we make a decision to walk closer with God, it is never a guarantee that our life will be easier. Neither will it lessen the difficulties we will experience. When work-related or personal problems come our way, we must determine the relevance and significance of each by presenting them to the Father in prayer. 1 Peter 5:6-7 tells us, "Humble yourselves, therefore, under God's mighty hand, that He may lift you up in due time. Cast all your anxiety on Him because He cares for you." Although we may surely remember some horrific events, disappointments, and struggles for our entire life, we would be wise to ask ourselves, "In the whole realm of eternity, how significant is this situation?" Contemplating the answer to that question can help to release us from the impact of difficult and even horrific situations.

"I cried because I had no shoes until I met a man who had no feet."
Helen Keller, author

Ecclesiastes 3:1-8, Matthew 6:33, Luke 12:34

DOES PRAYER MATTER?

While I was on the job, on many days and sometimes for weeks, the combination of professional responsibilities with family obligations caused me to feel overwhelmed. Consequently, what should have been a top priority was not, and I did not spend much time in prayer. Because prayer is optional and no one was forcing me to do it, I reasoned that I needed to deal with the time-sensitive obligations, for I could always pray later. Experience has since taught me that if this lapse happens often, we will not be in tune with God's will for our lives. Those periods of stress are precisely the time when we are most vulnerable and should be taking our prayers and petitions to the Lord. If I had not neglected praying regularly, some of the decisions that I made might have been easier, or the issues that I had to resolve could have had even better results. Because we often solve the problems of others, we may tend to forget the source of our strength, insight, and wisdom.

Prayer is talking to God, and it is important both to God and to us that we initiate conversations with Him throughout the day, not just during a time we set aside for devotions. I Thessalonians 5:17 tells us, "Pray continually." We can talk to God about anything we encounter in our daily circumstances by praising and petitioning Him. Philippians 4:6-7 clearly illustrates the positive effects of such prayers: "Do **not be anxious** about anything, but in everything, by prayer and petition, with thanksgiving, present your requests to God. And the **peace of God**, which transcends all understanding, **will guard your hearts** and **your minds** in Christ Jesus."

"The basic purpose of prayer is not to bend God's will to mine, but to mold my will into His." Timothy Keller, pastor/author

Romans 12:12, Ephesians 6:18, 1Peter 3:12

WHERE NOW?

Even in our profession where almost every day is different, at times we may lose our enthusiasm in the day-to-day operations. We may even question, "Is this where I am really supposed to be and what am I going to be doing until my last day on the job?" This is likely to happen at a time when we are overwhelmed and worn down by our responsibilities. We all know that law enforcement is a demanding profession, but those outside have no idea of the pressures that we face daily. Even though my wife of many years and I had talked openly during my time on the job, she told me that she had not realized the extent of the internal turmoil that I had experienced on the job until she began proofreading the entries for this book. Today, many in the news media often rush to judgment before all the facts have been gathered. They are quick to make negative comments and accusations about incidents that they know little about. It is easy to become discouraged, especially when we know what we may be called to do, and we willingly do it each day.

We need to remember that through those "valley" experiences, we can know if we are on the right path if we reach out to the Lord in prayer and ask Him to show us very clearly what it is that **He** wants us to do. It is also important for us to know how He speaks to His children. It may be through His word, through other godly Believers, or through the Holy Spirit who will nudge us in the way we should go. "Trust in the Lord with all your heart, and lean not on your own understanding; in all your ways acknowledge Him, and He will make your paths straight." Proverbs 3:5-6.

"Waiting for the answer to prayer is often part of the answer."
John Blanchard, evangelist/author

Psalm 9:10, Isaiah 12:2, Romans 15:13

DESERVED

With her little dog on a leash, the elderly widow closed her back door on an early spring morning and smiled as she breathed in the scent of lilacs and began her walk through the neighborhood. When she returned home, she opened the unlocked door and was violently attacked and raped by an intruder. The ER physician said he had never seen such vicious injuries before. Months later, after the jury had reached a verdict and returned from deliberation, the judge was informed and reentered the courtroom. As the verdict was about to be read, the defendant and his attorney rose. Then the jury foreman announced, "Guilty as charged." Having spent a great deal of time on the investigation, I had witnessed the physical and mental suffering of the victim. Now, as the prosecuting officer, I felt a sense of justice as I heard the verdict.

A time is coming when we, too, will stand before the judge. Because we are far from sinless, we, like so many others, could face the most serious penalty of all: banishment from heaven for eternity. However, because we are Believers in Christ, we can know with certainty that when we face the judgment seat, our Savior, our "defense attorney," will stand before God and declare us, "Not guilty." 1 John 5:11-12 assures us, "God has given us eternal life, and this life is in His Son. He who has the Son has life." Even though we are guilty of the sins as charged, sins which we have committed in our lifetime, we will not be cast into hell. Jesus willingly took the penalty we deserve when He went to the cross. Jesus, who Himself was sinless, is willing to take the rap, the penalty which should come down on us. As a result, it is as if we are sinless, and because of the sacrifice that He made for us, we will enjoy the rewards of Heaven...for Eternity!

"Justice is getting what you deserve. Mercy is not getting what you deserve. Grace is getting what you don't deserve." Stuart Briscoe, pastor, author

Psalm 32-1-3, Luke 10:20, Philippians 3:20

GOT YOUR BACK

Sometimes when criminals are transporting large quantities of drugs, they will not be in possession of firearms. Instead, they will have a backup car following with armed occupants who are willing to use any force necessary should their plans be interrupted. As much as we might like to think differently, while we are on the job, we need to recognize that sometimes we cannot complete an assignment successfully or safely on our own. Often when we are called to respond to an incident, the dispatcher will follow with, "I am sending backup." We quickly learn to be grateful when we hear that help is on the way.

At the moment when we accept Jesus as Lord and Savior, Jesus graciously deposits in Christians a backup far greater than any that could humanly be provided. In John 14:16-17, as He prepared to leave Earth, Jesus said, "And I will ask the Father, and He will give you another Counselor to be with you forever – the Spirit of Truth..." When we are rushing to a scene, it is easy to become immersed in the immediate action. However, at the same time, we should approach every call while reaching out to the Lord and asking Him to direct all that we must do. In Ephesians 5:18, Paul said, "...Be filled with the Spirit." When we are filled with the Holy Spirit, we allow Him to control and direct our lives and our actions. In addition, the Holy Spirit also provides spiritual gifts to Believers that we should tap as a further resource. Since so much of what we do in our profession is service-related, the gift of service is one we need to rely on. The gift of discernment is another critical gift that we need to implement. We should be comforted to know that the Holy Spirit equips us and is always our backup; He never gives bad advice or directs us to the wrong decisions.

"The Wizard of Oz says look inside yourself and find self. God says look inside yourself and find the Holy Spirit. The first will get you to Kansas. The latter will get you to Heaven. Take your pick." Max Lucado, pastor/author

John 16:7-15, Acts 1:8, Romans 15:13

ALL THE ANSWERS

On a Saturday morning after I had worked overtime on my 3-11 Friday shift, the nagging ringing of my phone aroused me. Having had just a few hours of sleep, I drowsily noticed that it was only 6:30 AM. Thinking that the barracks might be calling about an emergency, I answered to hear the voice of a casual acquaintance instead. Without apology, he vented about his recent encounter with a motorist who had just forced him off the road, and he wanted me to do something about it since he had written down the license plate number. My plans for a relaxed weekend of recovery and rest were not starting off well. Those in the law enforcement community are often called upon to give advice off the job. Although this can be flattering to some extent, it can be draining as well.

As Believers in Christ, we are fortunate to have a resource to turn to for answers, one which many may not know about. Unless others see that we are different in a good sense, they may never imagine that our wisdom and strength and answers come from the Lord. Hopefully, others will see that our advice to them reflects the joy and peace in our lives, and it differs from what the world offers. God is always there to answer our prayers and concerns, and He is ready to listen and respond in His time. Actually, God finds great delight when we call upon Him, follow Him, and trust Him even though we are not able to know the future. "If the Lord delights in a man's way, He makes his steps firm; though he stumble, he will not fall, for the Lord upholds him with His hand." Psalm 37:23-24.

"When we come to the end of life, the question will be, 'How much have you given?' Not, 'How much you have gotten?'" George Sweeting, pastor/author

Ecclesiastes 7:12, Proverbs 2:1-22, 1 Corinthians 3:19-20

WHERE AM I GOING?

In the late 1930's, the Pennsylvania Highway Patrol relied on various merchants in town who had a phone. An officer's mode of transportation was an Indian motorcycle, which was not equipped with a radio. The barracks would call the merchant closest to the incident, and the store owner with a phone would put a flag up outside his building so that the officer would know to stop in to get the information. Response time was very poor, and backup was almost impossible. Years later, when an officer was dispatched to a call, especially in a rural area, getting to the location was still a challenge. If it were someplace in the countryside with very few street signs, the officer either had to know the area from a prior incident or rely on the dispatcher to provide turn-by-turn instructions. Today, with in-car GPS systems and police radios, officers can usually respond in a matter of minutes.

At times, especially in our personal lives, we simply do not know what direction to take. Should we take a promotion to a station much farther from our home, based on the hope that we can later return? Should we accept an unexpected offer to work in a different division that sounds more exciting? Fortunately, we have a source better than any technology, and He will always keep us on track. The Lord is always available to provide direction, and He wants us to call out to Him. "I will instruct you and teach you in the way you should go; I will counsel you and watch over you." Psalm 32:8. Relying on the Holy Spirit for every situation in life **will** keep us on track.

"Any intelligent fool can make things bigger and more complex. It takes a touch of genius-- and a lot of courage to move in the opposite direction."
Albert Einstein, Nobel Prize winner/ theoretical physicist

Proverbs 3:5-6, Isaiah 30:21, Matthew 7:7-11

MEETING NEEDS

Frequently on the job, I connected with people who were experiencing real needs. Although some situations were easy to resolve, those who were in the midst of the turmoil could not see a solution. Other issues were complex, and it seemed almost impossible to find a resolution. Sometimes my initial response was to wonder how people could have been so reckless, careless, or clueless to get themselves into that position. Then, I had to remind myself that why something had happened was not important. In fact, I might have been the last resource they sought for help. Afterwards, if I could not help them, I always felt frustrated and even discouraged, and that happened more than a few times. Because we are often making decisions, sometimes very quickly, our response has to be appropriate. Perhaps, if the situation is one that we have dealt with before, we may soon begin to believe that there really is not much that we cannot handle.

We cannot, however, lose sight that in our humanness, we really do not have all the answers. When we get to the place where we feel that we do, pride has set in. In Proverbs 16:18, God's word cautions us of the dangers of that attitude: "Pride goes before destruction, a haughty spirit before a fall." We are blessed to have our Savior, who is available all of the time, to give us both wisdom and direction when we call upon Him. "And my God will meet all your needs according to His glorious riches in Christ Jesus." Philippians 4:19.

"Sometimes God lets you be in a situation that only He can fix so you can see that He is the one who fixes it. Relax. He's got it." Tony Evans, pastor/ author

Jeremiah 9:23, 2 Corinthians 9:8, Philippians 4:19

HOPLESSNESS

One summer evening, my partner and I were the only detectives on duty at the station. When a call from dispatch advised of a shooting on the turnpike, which was covered only by uniformed troopers and had no criminal investigators, we responded. Maneuvering around the backed-up cars was difficult, and when we arrived, a fire engine was already attempting to extinguish the blazing car. Lying in the middle of the highway was a young woman who was being attended to by several people. Nearby, a man in handcuffs stood next to a uniformed trooper. An off-duty surgeon leaned over the woman with a very long needle in his hand as he prepared to inject a stimulant into the ventricular chamber of her heart. The man in handcuffs had already admitted that he and his girlfriend had been fighting and that he had shot her. Firemen on the scene later indicated that several gasoline containers were in the car, so this act appeared to have been planned. When I asked the suspect if he wanted to say anything more, he snapped, "No. Let your forensic guys figure it out."

On the job, we are often exposed to acts committed by others that cause us to wonder why they acted as they did. Certainly, they must have believed at the time that there was no other way, no alternative. At such times, I often thought that if they had only discovered the real hope and peace that is available to them, perhaps their involvement in a tragic situation would not have happened. 2 Corinthians 1:3-4 encourages us to share our peace with those around us: "Praise be to the God and Father of our Lord Jesus Christ, the Father of compassion and the God of all comfort, Who comforts us in all our troubles, so that we can comfort those in any trouble with the comfort we ourselves have received from God."

"If we see Him as our loving Heavenly Father, we'll understand He has the best possible plan for our life, even if the path is, for a time, through troubled waters." Andy Stanley, pastor/author

Joshua 1:9, Psalm 31:24, Isaiah 40:31

SOME THINGS NEVER CHANGE

As we look over the history of law enforcement and consider the ways that techniques and procedures in our profession have changed, we may conclude that eventually, everything changes. In 1809, plaster of Paris was used to make the first shoe impression left at the scene of a crime. In 1912, the first swing handcuffs were developed. In the early 1920s, the two-way radio communication system was initiated. In the 1950s, the New Orleans Police Department established an arrest and warrant data base. In 1960, the first computer-aided dispatch system was developed by the St. Louis PD, and in 1967, the 911 emergency response system became available. Also in that year, the FBI developed the NCIC, National Crime Information Center. In 1971, the development of Kevlar vests as well as night-time vision equipment helped to provide further safety to members of our profession. In 1973, NASA provided us with the first electronic stun gun. In 1976, the FBI advanced the use of fingerprint examination by developing an automated fingerprint identification system. In 1995, DNA evidence was determined to be indisputable.

As much as law enforcement welcomed these changes, we know that, thankfully, some things never change. In Genesis 9:12-16, we read that God created the rainbow to remind us of His everlasting covenant not to cover the Earth in destructive water again. In Revelation 21:6, God refers to Himself as the unchanging, "the Alpha and Omega, the Beginning and the End." Isaiah 40:8 reminds us, "The grass withers, the flowers fall, but the word of our God stands forever." His covenant is to the very end, for God is eternal. "Jesus Christ is the same yesterday and today and forever." Hebrews 13:8.

"Though you have changed a thousand times, He has NOT changed once."
Charles Spurgeon, preacher/author

Psalm 119:89-90, Psalm 33:11, Malachi 3:6

WOW I'M GOOD!

Many people have a difficult time remaining unchanged after receiving accolades, a promotion, or other public recognition. When a trooper received a call that he was being promoted and was being transferred to another troop, he sought out several men who had been mentors to him. One, a Captain that he had previously worked for, was soon to retire, and the Trooper did not know when he would see him again. When he walked into the Captain's office, he wanted him to know that he appreciated his willingness to mentor him over the past couple of years. He said, "It is men like you who have made the department what it is today." The Captain replied, "I appreciate your comments, but I learned many years ago, it is men like you on the job, the officers on the street each day, that form this department. I am glad you are getting a well-deserved promotion." The humility of both of these men was refreshing, especially when pride so often abounds.

A noted quote of St. Augustine tells us, "It was pride that changed angels into devils; it is humility that makes men as angels." God surely knew that His creation would have difficulty remaining humble. More than 50 specific verses and numerous illustrations in the Bible caution against pride. Proverbs 16:5 uses a strong verb to describe how despicable the proud are to God: "The Lord **detests** all the proud of heart. Be sure of this: They will not go unpunished." Proverbs 29:23 reveals that the viewpoint of God can be the exact opposite of man's: "A man's pride brings him low, but a man of lowly spirit gains honor." James 4:10 illustrates that we can avoid pride as He encourages us to make a better choice: "Humble yourselves before the Lord, and He will lift you up."

"When God measures a man, He puts the tape around the heart not the head."
Howard Hendricks, pastor/professor

2 Chronicles 26:16, Psalm 10:4, Isaiah 2:10-11

ILLUSION

Charlie and Melanie had been living together in a small apartment for about a year. One day, Charlie began to use methamphetamine, and as his personality soon began to change, their lives together started to unravel. As Charlie continued using his new drug, he began to stay awake for long periods of time, and he fell under the illusion that the drug was helping him to accomplish a great deal. In reality, he accomplished very little. Soon he began getting very aggressive with Melanie to the point of physically attacking her. With growing concern, she tried to talk to Charlie, but in his mind, nothing had changed in either his behavior or attitude toward her. One morning, Melanie was awakened to find Charlie standing over her and pointing a rifle at her head. As he yelled, "I have to kill you," he pulled the trigger. Click...The gun misfired, and Melanie was able to escape from the house.

From time to time, people develop invalid perceptions. Many have misconceptions about those who have a strong Christian faith. Some have likened our relationship with the Lord to those needing a crutch or an iron lung. Others are under the illusion that Jesus was just a good person or, at the most, a prophet, but certainly not the Son of God. Those of us who have accepted the power and peace that come from a relationship with Him know the real truth. His word is infallible, and though it can be proven beyond a reasonable doubt, some still choose not to believe in Him. Disbelief in our God has not changed in over two thousand years. "Even after Jesus had done all these miraculous signs in their presence, they still would not believe in Him." John 12:37.

"There is a reason why life can feel empty: Man was created with a yearning that God alone is able to satisfy." Charles Stanley, pastor/author

Psalm 33:4-7, Isaiah 40:28-31, Romans 1:18-20

EXEMPLARY

If we are honest with ourselves, almost all will admit that we have had times when we failed to some degree to meet our own personal standards. Most often, that is a private matter that we try to work through to avoid repeating. However, some failures of those in law enforcement become known to the public, for often the media rushes in and sometimes exploits such situations to attract viewers. When we joined various departments, whether federal, state, county, or local, we were required to pledge that we would uphold the honor of our department. During our career, we must make every effort to keep our behavior exemplary. The citizens whom we serve expect us to be beyond reproach. We have a tremendous responsibility, for often when we fail in a significant personal way, we may also fail the Law Enforcement community. When failures by a few on the job become public, they will also negatively impact those who carry the badge now, as well as former members of law enforcement.

In our Christian walk, we know that it is impossible to be perfect. Psalm 86:11-12 can be turned into a brief prayer to help us through the times when we feel weak: "Teach me Your way, O Lord, and I will walk in Your truth; give me an undivided heart that I may fear Your name. I will praise You, O Lord my God, with all my heart." Our creator is fully aware of our weakness, but even when we fail in our spiritual walk, His love for us remains unshaken. "Though the mountains be shaken and the hills be removed, yet My unfailing love for you will not be shaken nor My covenant of peace be removed." Isaiah 54:10.

"People are watching the way we act, more than they are listening to what we say."
Max Lucado, author

Psalm 107:8, Jeremiah 31:3, Romans 5:8-9

JUST WAIT

At 2 AM, my phone rattled me from a deep sleep, and I answered to hear Terri tell me that a significant amount of heroin was coming into the area. She had provided information to me for well over a year, and her tips were always accurate. She said that I should not move on this until mid-afternoon the following day. At 12 noon, I gathered several officers to assist in the raid, and after an hour, they became restless and urged me not to wait longer. I succumbed to their complaints, and we proceeded to the house. Although we conducted a thorough search, we were frustrated to find nothing other than scales, baggies, and other tools of drug trafficking. In the early evening, Terri called to tell me that I had entered too early, for the main supplier had not yet returned to the residence. He later told Terri, "That was a close one. I was delivering a kilo, and after the cops came, I got a call about the raid."

As Believers, we know that the answers we want in life do not always occur according to our timing. Experience teaches us that when we seek to walk in the Lord's will, He will show us the direction to take. When the answers do not come as quickly as we would like, that is the time to exhibit the trust in God that we say we have. Waiting tests our faith and allows us to silently show others how we trust in Him. This discipline will eventually bring about the best result, even if it is not what we had expected. "But as for me, I watch in hope for the Lord, I wait for God my Savior; my God will hear me." Micah 7:7.

"Teach us, O Lord, the discipline of patience, for to wait is often harder than to work." Peter Marshall, pastor/U.S. Senate Chaplin

Psalm 130:5-6, Romans 12:12, 2 Peter 3:9

DEATH PENALTY

The ultimate sentence in our judicial system is the penalty of death. Several years ago, a gentle Mennonite man, who drove truck for a living, was shot and killed in the back of his empty trailer for no apparent reason. The perpetrator soon began using the victim's credit cards, and after we traced his transactions, he was captured a few weeks later in a distant state. Eventually, the perpetrator had his day in court where he chose to have a judge rather than a jury determine his destiny. After testifying against him, I was relieved that my role in the case was over. As I waited to hear the verdict, I could not imagine having to stand before a judge who could sentence him to the death penalty for this senseless crime.

As we think about such situations that we have witnessed many times, it is inconceivable that someone would step forward and, regardless of the facts, say, "Let this guilty person go free. I will take the penalty this person deserves for his wrongdoing." Yet, that is exactly what our Lord has done for each of us by going to the cross and paying the penalty that we deserve. Sometimes, it is hard to fathom that we have to do nothing besides acknowledging Christ as our Savior, believing that His death paid the price in full for our acquittal. In gratitude and obedience, we will then seek to live a life following Christ's leading as we anticipate our eternity in Heaven with Him. "He Himself bore our sins in His body on the tree, so that we might die to sins and live for righteousness; by His wounds you have been healed." 1 Peter 2:24.

"When we sin and mess up our lives, we find that God doesn't go off and leave us. He enters into our trouble and saves us." Eugene Peterson, pastor/author

John 15:12-14, Romans 8:32, Ephesians 5:1-2

DEADLINES

Everyone on the job knows that we are constantly challenged with deadlines. While some are self-imposed, others are not. Early on, I was in a situation where many pending investigations with initial and supplemental reports needed to be completed. Having scheduled a weeklong vacation with my family, I had to make a difficult decision. Knowing that meeting deadlines was crucial to any investigation, I chose to stay home and send my family ahead of me with the hope that I could finish my reports and catch up with them at the end of the week. When I went in to tell the sergeant that I was going to be working the following week, he looked surprised and said, "Did you forget? You are on vacation next week." I told him that I did remember, but in clear conscience, I could not ignore the deadlines that I felt I must meet. His look of surprise told me that he was pleased. This decision strengthened my relationship with him, for he knew that I was serious about the job.

Believers know that when we enter our heavenly home for eternity, there will no longer be any deadlines. We should find great peace in this promise of eternity. Although we do not know when we will spend our last day in this world, we do know that the deadline for our life has already been set by the Lord. This awareness should cause us to have concern for those who do not know Jesus as Lord. Tomorrow may be too late to share the good news about how easy it is to receive the promise of Heaven for eternity. Jesus said, "The harvest is plentiful, but the workers are few." Matthew 9:37.

"Don't worry about having the right words; worry more about having the right heart. It's not eloquence He seeks, just honesty." Max Lucado, author

Luke 12:12, Romans 1:16, 1 Peter 3:15

CLOSE CALL

Frank and his undercover team went into a nightclub after getting information that drug trafficking was occurring there. The concern in such situations is always that a member of the team may be identified as a cop. Since it is important not to draw attention to any member, Tom decided to blend in by asking a woman to dance. After several minutes on the dance floor, the gun that Tom had concealed in the small of his back dropped out of his pants, hitting the floor and firing a round. Tom then went over to Frank to tell him that he thought he had been shot, and they calmly walked to the men's room where they learned that the bullet had grazed Tom's buttocks. Although it was, indeed, a close call, Tom did not require any medical attention. However, from that time on, he wore the bullet on a chain around his neck to remind him how quickly things can happen which could have life-changing consequences.

On the job, we will always face situations which could instantly change our lives. In addition to being continually aware and alert, we have a resource whom we can always call upon to put a hedge of protection around us during times of need. "I will say of the Lord, 'He is my refuge and my fortress, my God, in whom I trust.' Surely He will save you from the fowler's snare and from the deadly pestilence. He will cover you with His feathers, and under His wings you will find refuge." Psalm 91:2-4.

"A God wise enough to create me and the world I live in is wise enough to watch out for me." Philip Yancey, author

Psalm 5:11-12, John 10:10, 2 Thessalonians 3:3

REGRETS

It is hard to believe that anyone can go through life without some regrets. Frank Sinatra sang, "Regrets, I had a few, too few to mention." He also claimed that in living his life, "I did it my way." Some of us may have more regrets than others, and some of those regrets may be relatively insignificant. I surely have had my share and still do, including saying things that I should not have but also not saying something that I should have. Some that we work with regularly may be going through difficult times without showing it outwardly. Early in my career, a trooper who was working the same shift as I was, took his own life before his tour of duty was over. So many people that I came in contact with had many serious problems and lacked peace. I now regret that I did not share with them the peace that comes from a close walk with God.

We Believers certainly should not claim to live our lives "my way." In a critical incident, we need to consider how to be a comfort to those suffering. When we are assigned an investigation, we need to do a thorough job as if we were doing it for the Lord. Even when we know that someone has done something wrong, we need to treat that person fairly and appropriately. We should be Christ-like in all out interactions so that we will not regret disappointing our God. However, any regrets can be washed away with our sins because of the cross where Jesus provided full and perfect forgiveness. Our rap sheet has been expunged. His grace is all we need. "Let us then approach the throne of grace with confidence, so that we may receive mercy and find grace to help us in our time of need." Hebrews 4:16.

"Jesus doesn't avoid those who mess up. Jesus runs to those who mess up."
Matt Chandler, pastor/author

Matthew 7:13-14, Romans 11:6, Ephesians 2:8

FREEDOM

Frequently, we hear people say, "Freedom is not free." Often at great cost to themselves, the many men and women who willingly serve put themselves in harm's way to ensure the freedom that we enjoy in America. This is especially true when our armed forces are engaged in skirmishes around the world. Some suffer traumatic injuries, both physically and mentally, while serving our country and come home dramatically changed. Others pay the ultimate price and do not return home alive. These heroes include our police officers who suffer career-ending injuries or die in the line of duty. Data reveals that in 2017, 128 officers died in the line of duty: 44 murdered by firearms, 7 beaten, 1 stabbed; 47 died from traffic-related or other causes including a helicopter crash, drownings, boating incidents, cardiac events, and illnesses related to the 9/11 rescue and recovery efforts. In addition, 5 territorial officers, 5 federal officers, 3 tribal officers, and 2 university officers were also killed. On average, the officers left behind two children and families and friends to suffer as well.

Much of what we do on the job is done to ensure peace and tranquility as we seek to provide a safe and secure community where all can express their freedom. Many times, this requires personal sacrifices. However, the ultimate sacrifice was that made by Jesus on the cross when He took the penalty that we deserve for our sins and freed us for eternity. As Believers, we know where true freedom is found, but for those who do not know Him, their pursuit of freedom and happiness is never satisfied. "But now that you have been set free from sin and have become slaves of God, the benefit you reap leads to holiness, and the result is eternal life. For the wages of sin is death, but the gift of God is eternal life in Christ Jesus our Lord." Romans 6:22-23.

"I wish we would all remember that being American is not about the freedom; it is about those who gave it to us." Mike Huckabee, statesman/pastor/author

Psalm 119:43-45, John 15:13, Hebrews 9:28

BEYOND A DOUBT

When I joined the detective bureau, I quickly realized that the arrests that I made could have a significant impact on someone's life. They often resulted in incarceration, large fines, and a lifetime criminal record, so I needed to be precise in investigating and then reporting the incidents. Some cases were complex and took many days or even months to investigate thoroughly in order to insure an accurate conclusion. I knew that my work would be carefully examined by both prosecuting and defense attorneys, the judge, and, at times, a jury. My goal was to leave no doubt in my reports and in my testimony so that justice would prevail.

Believers have a similar responsibility; that is to be able to defend our faith. If we cannot, we lose all credibility, and we may be viewed as one having a blind faith. We know that the Bible is the infallible word of God, and there is so much supporting evidence that we can present. Although we know that the Bible is inerrant, others, especially those in law enforcement, will want more than our word. If only one statement in God's word were found to be in error, many would doubt the accuracy of God's word. 1 Peter 3:15 tells us, "But in your hearts set apart Christ as Lord. Always be prepared to give an answer to everyone who asks you to give the reason for the hope that you have."

"Even though the Bible is an ancient document, every person in every situation in every society that's ever existed can find in this book things that endure forever. Here's a book that never needs another edition. It never needs to be edited, never has to be updated, is never out of date or obsolete. It speaks to us as pointedly and directly as it ever has to anyone since it was written."
John MacArthur, pastor/author

Psalm 33:4, John 17:17, 2 Timothy 2:15

BE PREPARED

After Ralph finished a late-night shift, he stopped to eat at a local tavern. As he sat next to a middle-aged patron at the bar, the man struck up a conversation and asked Ralph what he did for a living. He answered, "Just about anything to make money." The man then asked, "Does that include illegal?" Ralph said, "Yes." The man then revealed that he had recently learned about a wealthy owner of a real estate company who had a safe filled with cash in her home. He wanted to burglarize the home, but he needed help. After Ralph told him that he was good at making entry and had burglarized many homes, they agreed to meet the next night. Contact was made with the owner who provided a key and agreed to be away the following night. That night, Ralph met with his new "partner" and told him to wait in the car while he entered through the back door. Once inside, he motioned to his partner to come in. As the man walked down a dark hallway, I emerged from a room with a shotgun leveled at his head and told him that he was under arrest. Stunned and speechless, he was obviously unprepared for what had just happened. Being prepared is probably the most important aspect of our job.

Biblical prophecy is very specific about the events that will occur before this world ends. At one point, Christ will take Believers to heaven with Him in "the Rapture." After studying prophecies of the signs preceding that event, Pastor David Jeremiah believes that they have all been fulfilled, so nothing more has to be accomplished before this happens. In Matthew 24:36, Jesus said, "No one knows about that day or hour," so we must recognize the urgency to tell those who are willing to listen about their need to be prepared and how they can do that.

"We are to wait for the coming of Christ with patience. We are to watch with anticipation. We are to work with zeal. We are to prepare with urgency. Scripture says Christ is coming when you're least expecting Him. 'Coming as a thief,' He said. Be prepared. Get ready. Prepare to meet thy God. Are you prepared?"
Billy Graham, evangelist/author

Matthew 24:42-44, Mark 13:32-33, Luke 21:34-36

TAKING OWNERSHIP

Working vice, I cruised down a city street when a young woman stepped off the curb and flagged me down. When I stopped, she walked up to my window and asked what I was looking for. I told her that I just wanted to have a good time. Confidently, she told me that she could make that happen, and she got into the car. After she said that this was going to cost me some money, she explained enough for me to place her under arrest for prostitution. Breaking into sobs, she tried to play on my emotions by justifying her lifestyle. "You just don't understand. I had no father, and I was raised by a mother who is addicted to heroin. She has just been released from prison, and we live in a motel room. We are both addicted, so I have to work the streets to support the habit. Look at what my life's been like. It's not really my fault!"

Romans 3:10 reminds us, "There is no one righteous, not even one." At first, this sounds hopeless, but verses 22-24 provide the hope. "This righteousness from God comes through faith in Jesus Christ to all who believe. There is no difference, for all have sinned and fall short of the glory of God, and are justified freely by His grace through the redemption that came by Christ Jesus." However, even though we may be Believers, we will still break God's laws. In Romans 7:18- 24, Paul, a man who had dedicated his life to Christ and suffered greatly because of that, faced the same internal battle when he wanted to do what is good but repeatedly did what is evil. When we take ownership of our sins and confess them, we can be certain that Christ will wash them away, and we will be forgiven. "He who conceals his sins does not prosper, but whoever confesses and renounces them finds mercy." Proverbs 28:13.

"But the Bible isn't mainly about you and what you should have done. It's about God and what He has done." Elyse Fitzpatrick, author

Matthew 6:33, 2 Corinthians 5:21, Hebrews 4:16

FISHING

Frank's Region 2 Drug Strike Force consisted of eight troopers who operated in several counties near a large city. They were always busy, making multiple arrests and seizing large quantities of drugs. Every month, the various regions met at headquarters to discuss operations and share experiences and new information that they had discovered during investigations. Inevitably, they bantered about the successes that one region had over another. Frank enjoyed telling the group about their arrests and seizures which always outnumbered the others. One day, after providing statistics, a trooper defensively said to Frank, "You work right outside of the city. It's like fishing in a hatchery." Frank replied, "Yeah, but you still have to go out and fish."

Because Believers have learned about the way to true peace, the promise of complete forgiveness for all of our sins, and the certainty of residency in Heaven for eternity, the Bible tells us that we are called to tell others what we know. Since this is such good news, why would we ever keep it to ourselves? Our families and our friends may not fully understand or even believe what we know to be true, so we must seize opportunities to gently share the path to salvation. The worst thing we could ever hear from someone as we prepare to stand before a holy God would be, "Why didn't you tell me?" Jesus said, "Come, follow me, and I will make you fishers of men." Matthew 4:19-20.

"What is your story? Be ready to share it." Billy Graham, evangelist/author

Luke 12:8-9, 2 Timothy 1:7-8, 1 Peter 3:15

DECEPTION

Joe White was a major drug dealer, not only in the city where he lived, but also in the communities that surrounded his home. His heroin was always of the best quality with large amounts on hand to meet everyone's needs. Joe was very sure of himself because he was not a user of drugs and therefore felt that he was always in control. A confidential informant who regularly bought from Joe told me that his home could not be penetrated. The front door was solid with a metal frame, and five sliding deadbolts securely locked it. One day, I was able to obtain a United States Postal Service uniform, and carrying several large cardboard boxes, I went to the front door. Joe called out from inside and asked who was at the door. As he peered out, he began sliding open the deadbolts. Officers immediately rushed in, and after a search, they made one of the largest drug seizures that any of us could recall. This deception was necessary in dealing with someone who was destroying lives.

In our Christian walk, we need to be on guard against those who are not accurately portraying the word of God. Nothing should ever be added to God's word because it is inerrant and accurate from cover to cover. Jesus said, "At that time, if anyone says to you, 'Look, here is the Christ!' or, 'There He is!' do not believe it. For false Christs and false prophets will appear and perform great signs and miracles to deceive even the elect--if that were possible." Matthew 24:23-24.

"Looking for a good word from the Lord? Believe that He has already spoken and read what He has already written." Mark Driscoll, pastor/author

Jeremiah 23:16, 2 Peter 3:3, Jude 1:17-19, Revelation 22:18-19

ACCEPTED

Frank received information that a local tavern in an adjacent city was involved in heroin trafficking. One afternoon, he and two of his officers decided to visit the bar. Going in "cold," without the assistance of an informant who is known by the community, is often difficult. When the officers walked in, almost everyone turned to look at them. As they sat at the bar and talked among themselves, it was obvious that their every move was being scrutinized. Making no inroads, they soon decided to leave. The next day, they stopped at a fish market in town and purchased a large slab of herring. Once again, they entered the tavern and sat at the bar. The same staring that occurred the day before was again obvious. Shortly, one of the officers pulled out the large wrapper of fish, took out a switchblade knife, and began cutting off pieces and offering them to his partners. As they continued to sit at the bar eating fish and drinking their beer, the ice began to break. Some of the other patrons began to converse with them as they were intrigued by these men who were so crazy to do what they had done. They were accepted. In time, they were buying heroin, which eventually led to a number of arrests.

It is not unusual for most people to want to feel accepted. We want to be respected and liked, and there is nothing inherently wrong with this. However, as Believers, we must be careful to reflect a positive difference that represents our faith. We must not compromise our walk just to be accepted by others. "Do not conform any longer to the pattern of this world, but be transformed by the renewing of your mind. Then you will be able to test and approve what God's will is --- His good, pleasing and perfect will." Romans 12:2.

"No compromise is what the whole Gospel of Jesus is all about."
Keith Green, musician

Luke 6:26, John 15:18-20, James 4:4

JUST NOT ENOUGH

During my first week in the vice unit, we received a call from a male wanting to provide information about drug trafficking. People become informants for different reasons: they have been arrested and want a break; they want to make money; they have a vendetta; or, in rare instances, they just want to do the right thing. Mike, a twenty-year-old, was upset that his girlfriend was using blue meth, and the powerful blue tablets were causing hallucinations. Many of his friends also made this their drug of choice. Mike's information allowed me to obtain search warrants for multiple locations and ultimately led to numerous arrests. Finally, one arrestee, wanting to make a deal, took me to the main source, a prosperous medical doctor who had a lucrative practice. A raid on his expensive and elaborate house revealed large quantities of blue meth as well as other illegal drugs. I could not understand why an intelligent and prosperous man who was caring for the sick was also poisoning others with life-threatening drugs.

Some people strive to obtain great wealth and many possessions under the misguided impression that "things" will eventually fill the void they feel. At a time when I provided executive protection for a high-profile billionaire, it soon became evident that although he and his extended family could buy anything, what they were missing was peace and genuine happiness. Sadly, many do not know the true source of real peace, and we should be telling them how to find it. Jesus said, "Peace I leave with you; My peace I give you. I do not give to you as the world gives. Do not let your hearts be troubled and do not be afraid." John 14:27.

"God can work peace through us only if He has worked peace in us. Those who are in the best of circumstances but without God can never find peace, but those in the worst of circumstances but with God need never lack peace."
John MacArthur, pastor/author

Psalm 23:4, Jeremiah 29:11, Philippians 4:6

IN CONTRAST

Those that we suspect are guilty of a crime and even those who have been found guilty of a crime typically want others to believe that they are innocent. Even with compelling evidence against them, they rarely are willing to admit responsibility for their actions. After I arrested a suspect for a burglary, he told me that he had never before committed a criminal act. He was so convincing that I carefully re-examined my evidence to see if I could find any discrepancies. Although I found none, I kept an open mind as I waited for lab results. Several days later, fingerprint comparisons revealed his presence in numerous homes that had also been burglarized.

As Jesus stood before the high priest of the Jews, evil men made false accusations against Him, and one struck Him in the face. Jesus then said, "If I said something wrong, testify as to what is wrong. But if I spoke the truth, why did you strike me?" John 18:23. We can mildly identify with what it is like to be unjustly accused of something that we did not do. However, it pales in comparison to the sacrifice Jesus willingly made, even for those who spoke against Him and ultimately sent Him to endure a cruel death on the cross. All of this was a part of His perfect plan for us. 2 Corinthians 5:21 tells us, "God made Him who had no sin to be sin for us, so that in Him we might become the righteousness of God." He asks only that we acknowledge Him as our Savior and try to live as He taught. Although we will fail from time to time, His gift is never taken away. We will never be on probation or have to experience a "time out," after we pass away. We who believe in Him will immediately be in His presence for eternity. "Oh, if He carried the weight of the world upon His shoulders, I know, my brother, He will carry you. I know my brother, and I know, my sister, that Jesus will carry you." Scott Wesley Brown, songwriter.

"We will all be alive somewhere, forever." David Jeremiah, pastor/author

John 10:33-38, Mark 14:53-65, 1 Peter 2:22

STAYING THE COURSE

When I entered the PA State Police Academy, it was often difficult to stay focused. Getting up each morning at 5:00 AM to start the day with a five-mile run did not help. Then reporting to clean both the horses and the stables did not make me eager to go to breakfast which was next on the schedule. Classes were a challenge, and some of the material was not stimulating. One section of the Vehicle Code pertaining to commercial motor vehicles, "Size, Weight, and Construction," made my eyelids very heavy. Any time a section began with, "A truck, a truck tractor or combination having a gross weight or actual gross weight, registered gross weight…," I knew that I was in trouble. Each day brought added responsibilities which made it difficult to stay the course. How thankful I am that I found the determination to do so!

Likewise, in our Christian walk, there are times when it is difficult to stay focused. We can lose sight of what is really important. Philippians 4:8 says, "Finally, brothers, whatever is true, whatever is noble, whatever is right, whatever is pure, whatever is lovely, whatever is admirable--if anything is excellent or praiseworthy-- think about such things." Colossians 3:2 encourages us to "Set your minds on things above, not on earthly things." Hebrews 3:1 advises, "Therefore, holy brothers, who share in the heavenly calling, fix your thoughts on Jesus, the apostle and high priest whom we confess." When we stay the course and seek the Lord's will in every area of our lives, He will make all things work together for His good. Romans 8:28.

"If God only used perfect people, nothing would get done. God will use anybody if you're available." Rick Warren, pastor/author

Proverbs 16:3, Matthew 6:34, Colossians 3:2

FACING THE STORM

In 1929, the Superintendent of the Pennsylvania State Police, Lynn G. Adams, issued a General Order requiring all members of the Department to memorize "The State Police Call of Honor," a tradition that continues today. Every cadet graduating from the PA State Police Academy must be able to recite it prior to graduation. It reads: "I am a Pennsylvania State Trooper, a soldier of the law. To me is entrusted the honor of the force. I must serve honestly, faithfully, and if need be, lay down my life as others have done before me, rather than swerve from the path of duty. It is my duty to obey the law and to enforce it without any consideration of class, color, creed, or condition. It is also my duty to be of service to anyone who may be in danger or distress and, at all times, so conduct myself that the Honor of the Force may be upheld." Only after I had graduated and was on the street did I come to realize the magnitude of this agreement.

In our humanness, sometimes we simply cannot accomplish all that society expects us to do. We have many challenges in our daily lives which, at times, can seem daunting. However, we do have a tremendous resource through Christ who will always be there to help us in accordance with His will. "You will keep in perfect peace him whose mind is steadfast, because he trusts in You. Trust in the Lord forever, for the Lord, the Lord, is the Rock eternal." Isaiah 26:3-4.

"The Bible is God's chart for you to steer by, to keep you from the bottom of the sea, and to show you where the harbor is, and how to reach it without running on rocks or bars."
Henry Ward Beecher, minister

Joshua 1:9, Matthew 21:22, Philippians 4:19

NEW APPROACH

Dennis was assigned to an investigation in a local mall where the merchants had been complaining that large groups of people were gathering together and appeared to be dealing drugs. The fact that Dennis was not from the area was a benefit, for he would not be identified as a member of law enforcement. However, it was difficult to infiltrate this group. After several days without meaningful interaction with anyone, he entered a store in the mall and purchased a box of bubble bath. Walking over to the fountain where everyone was congregating, he dumped it in. As bubbles began to spurt out of the fountain, down the sides, and onto the floor, Dennis quickly left. Upon his return the next day, several in the group came up to him to tell him how cool his prank the previous day had been. He now was one of them.

Sometimes, we are in situations where we feel led to tell others about our faith and desire to walk in the Lord's will, especially when we see those who are really struggling and have nowhere to turn. When people are experiencing a significant crisis or illness, they may be more receptive to hearing about the peace which they can have through the Lord. The approach we take to share our faith is critical, so if we call out to the Lord, He will direct us. 1 Peter 3:15 says, "But in your hearts set apart Christ as Lord. Always be prepared to give an answer to everyone who asks you to give the reason for the hope that you have."

"People pay attention when they see that God actually changes persons and sets them free. When a new Christian stands up and tells how God has revolutionized his or her life, no one dozes off. When someone is healed or released from a life-controlling bondage, everyone takes notice." Jim Cymbala, pastor

Isaiah 55:11, Matthew 5:16, Colossians 4:6

WHAT'S EXPECTED?

For the most part, when we get on the job, we quickly learn what is expected of us. However, I had not considered many situations that I would face, such as having to deliver a death notice or investigating a heinous crime against a child. Some situations would have been impossible for me to comprehend until I actually experienced them. Even when called upon to provide protection to dignitaries, we never know what to expect. When President Ronald Reagan was coming to our area years ago, the Secret Service requested our assistance in providing security. The day of his arrival was one that I will never forget. Three huge helicopters landed on the field adjacent to where he was to speak. When I asked an agent why there were three, he indicated that one was for the news media, one for the Secret Service, and the other for the President. For security purposes, no one knew which one President Reagan was on. The agents were very much on alert and extremely tense, not knowing what, if anything, to expect. Great relief was evident on the faces of all the protectors as the President later flew off unharmed.

God has given us so much, and He expects things from us as well. Believers must take the time to reflect on what He expects of us. Jesus said, "... From everyone who has been given much, much will be demanded; and from the one who has been entrusted with much, much more will be asked." Luke 12:48. As Paul sat in prison, he wrote in Philippians 1:20: "I eagerly expect and hope that I will in no way be ashamed, but will have sufficient courage so that now as always, Christ will be exalted in my body, whether by life or by death."

"I used to ask God to help me. Then I asked if I might help Him. I ended up by asking Him to do His work through me."
 J. Hudson Taylor, founder of the China Inland Mission

.

2 Corinthians 5:17, 1Timothy 2:3-4, Hebrews 13:20-21

THE MYSTERY

Many of our investigations begin like a mystery as we try to determine who was responsible for a hit-and-run accident, a burglary, an armed robbery, or a murder. Our objective is to search the scene, gather and evaluate evidence, attempt to locate eye-witnesses, and question suspects. In many cases, we are able to solve the mystery, but other cases remain unresolved. It was always very frustrating for me when a homicide investigation was conducted, but no charges could be made despite the countless hours spent, the number of officers involved, the good evidence uncovered, and even with a person of interest identified. I often asked, "How can anyone today get away with the most heinous crime of murder when we now have so many technical and forensic capabilities in law enforcement?"

Daniel 2:28 tells us there is a "God in heaven who reveals mysteries." As the Holy Spirit instructed men to write the books of the Bible, God provided the essence of what we need to know about our faith. Although some of our questions may go unanswered, that is not because there are not answers, but rather because the Lord chose to have some things remain a mystery for now. Paul recognized this when he said, "Beyond all question, the mystery of godliness is great." 1Timothy 3:16. As we grow to fully trust Him and understand that He allows what He knows is best for us, we realize that we do not need to know all the answers.

"To trust God in the light is nothing, but to trust Him in the dark --that is faith."
Charles Spurgeon, pastor/author

Matthew 13:11, 1 Corinthians 2:7, Ephesians 3:4

ANTICIPATION

On many shifts, shortly after I left the barracks to begin my tour of duty, a certain supervisor would call over the radio and tell me that I was to meet with him at the end of my shift. This was the same person whose office I had just walked past prior to leaving the building. Naturally, I never expected that he wanted to see me so that he could give me some kind of commendation, tell me how well I was doing, or give me an extra day off for working so hard. Rather, I immediately thought that I had probably messed up. Although anticipation can be either positive or negative, in these situations, I always thought about the worst possible scenario as I worked the next eight hours.

When Believers recognize what Christ has done for us by taking away all of our sins, past, present, and future, through His sacrifice on the cross, we also know that He promises us eternal life. Numerous references throughout the Bible encourage Believers to set their minds on living eternally with Christ in Heaven. Therefore, we should live out our time in this life with joyful and grateful anticipation for all that is to come. "He will swallow up death forever. The Sovereign Lord will wipe away the tears from all faces; He will remove the disgrace of His people from all the earth. The Lord has spoken. In that day they will say, 'Surely this is our God; we trusted in Him, and He saved us.'" Isaiah 25:8-9.

"There is only one way to be certain that you are on your way to Heaven, and that is through faith in Jesus." John Stange, pastor/author

Matthew 7:13, John 14:2-4, Colossians 3:1-7

THE LISTENER

Although some believe that their phones are being tapped from time to time, it is unlikely, for the procedure is very strictly governed. After an officer presents an affidavit of probable cause to a judge, which indicates that there is absolutely no other way to determine criminality without a non-consensual, court-approved wiretap, the judge may grant permission to proceed. It would take me days, sometimes weeks, to prepare an affidavit, none of which was ever less than thirty pages. I took this procedure very seriously, realizing that any impropriety on my part could result in my arrest and loss of my pension. Once permission was granted, only those who had been trained and certified could listen in. The conversations were always recorded, and if the conversation turned to personal matters, the monitor had to minimize the call; the listening ceased, and the recording stopped. After a brief time, the monitor could listen again, but only if the conversation could be deemed criminal in nature. Often, a great deal of minimizing occurred.

Those who believe in the presence and sovereignty of the Lord know that we can reach out to Him at any time. Our call never goes to voice mail. He never puts us on hold, and the line is never busy. When we call on His name, He is there to listen intently to every word we are saying. The communication line is always open, and our talk is never minimized. Regardless of our past transgressions, we do not have to wait until our life is in order before we talk with Him. In fact, He welcomes every call. "This is the confidence we have in approaching God: that if we ask anything according to His will, He hears us." 1 John 5:14.

"God speaks to those who take time to listen, and He listens to those who take time to pray."
Our Daily Bread Campus Journal

Proverbs 15:29, Mark 11:24-25, 1 Thessalonians 5:17

DOES IT REALLY MATTER?

Others often describe our work in law enforcement as exciting, daring, dangerous, and significant because our assignments can vary from Patrol, Criminal Interdiction, Criminal Investigation, Drug Strike Forces, Fugitive Apprehension Teams, Major Crime Units, SWAT, to Organized Crime, and on and on. Sometimes, our work may involve drug kingpins and Mob bosses who are arrested, incarcerated, or even murdered. During a court-approved wiretap on the phone of an Organized Crime family in a large city, I heard crime members discussing the need to "take out" members of another family and even some in their own family in an effort to move up in status. Sometimes "hits" were also demanded on people who were basically innocent but had been late in paying off a debt owed to the family.

When perpetrators are finally arrested for a significant crime, the pendulum sometimes swings dramatically in favor of those intent on breaking the law with little apparent regard for the victims left behind. In time, because of legal technicalities or weaknesses in the system, they may be set free. Since we are often the first to have contact with victims or their families, we well know that the judicial system sometimes seems to be more interested in ensuring that the perpetrator is cared for rather than in supporting the victims. Consequently, we may feel that our efforts were wasted, and discouragement can set in as we begin to question if we really are making a difference. At such times, we need to remember that if we seek God's wisdom and direction, we will ultimately experience peace. Ephesians 6:7-8 should encourage us and help us to keep our focus: "Serve wholeheartedly, as if you were serving the Lord, not man, because you know that the Lord will reward everyone for whatever good he does, whether he is slave or free."

"No matter how wicked the world scene may appear, God always has a remnant that is faithful to Him. Sometimes that remnant is small, but God is always great."
Warren Wiersbe, pastor/author

Joshua 24:15, Romans 12:11, Galatians 6:9

CARRY THE LOAD

We sometimes hear people say of their coworkers, "He never carries his share of the load." In law enforcement, we cannot always work independently, and we need to be assured that others on the job will be there for us. About 5:00 PM when I was dispatched to a crash on an interstate highway, I expected the traffic to be backed up during rush hour regardless of the number of vehicles involved in this accident. However, as I entered the on-ramp, it was immediately obvious that making it to the scene about a mile away was going to be very difficult. Edging my way along the outer lane, I often waited for stopped vehicles to pull over to the right, and I soon realized that numerous cars were involved in the accident. Upon reaching the original impact, I determined that some victims had life-threatening injuries while others were probably dead. After calling dispatch and advising them of the magnitude of this crash, I was grateful that other officers were notified immediately, and a number arrived to assist. This would become a lengthy investigation, and I was fortunate not to have to carry the load by myself.

From a spiritual perspective, Jesus was the one who carried the load for us. He was willing to go to the cross, and by doing so, He took away the penalty that we deserve for our sins. A song by The Hoppers says, "He didn't just carry the cross; He carried me." What an overwhelming perspective to think of our Savior willingly dragging that heavy, rugged cross for each one of us, willingly dying a vicious death, and thereby assuring us of a home in Heaven for eternity. Because it was His gift to us, there is nothing further that Believers can do or ever need to do to secure a place in heaven. In John 14:1-2, Jesus said, "Do not let your hearts be troubled. Trust in God; trust also in Me. In My Father's house are many rooms; if it were not so, I would have told you. I am going there to prepare a place for you."

"Those who go to Heaven ride on a pass and enter into blessings that they never earned, but all who go to hell pay their own way." John R. Rice, pastor/author

Psalm 22:14-18, Isaiah 53:5-7, Matthew 27:32-56

PRAYER POWER

Special Agent Jerry Parr, a member of the Secret Service assigned to the protection detail for President Ronald Reagan, probably never expected to make history when he entered the academy in Quantico, Virginia. On March 30, 1981, he accompanied President Reagan to a speech at the Washington Hilton Hotel. Afterwards, Parr and the President exited the building and headed toward the President's vehicle. Suddenly, shots rang out, and Parr's training and "muscle memory" kicked in. After pushing the President into the back seat of the limo, he jumped in on top of the President and told the driver to head toward the White House. Then as frothy, red blood began coming from the President's mouth, Parr realized that the President had been hit. Immediately, he redirected the driver to George Washington University Hospital. Parr's quick actions and clear thinking saved the life of the President.

In his book, *In the Secret Service: The True Story of the Man Who Saved President Reagan's Life,* Parr talks about his Christian faith and how he relied on direction from the Lord. We can only imagine that during his service of protecting high profile individuals, he must have prayed often for wisdom and guidance. All Believers have that same resource, and when we call upon the Lord for help, He will provide. Sometimes we may overlook the power of prayer, but when we do pray and see the results, we should realize that prayer is as important to us as our Kevlar vest. "If My people, who are called by My name, will humble themselves and pray and seek My face and turn from their wicked ways, then I will hear from heaven, and I will forgive their sin and heal their land." 2 Chronicles 7:14.

"One man can make a difference, and every man should try."
John F Kennedy, 35th President of the United States

Jeremiah 33:2-3, Ephesians 6:18, 1 John 5:14-15

TRAPPED

While I was driving along with two other officers to testify at a preliminary hearing, my supervisor, John, sat in the front seat of our unmarked car while Joe sat in the back. As we traveled on a busy highway, a vehicle suddenly came out of nowhere at a high rate of speed, and the operator began weaving in and out of traffic. Although we were not in uniform or in a marked car, we knew that we had to stop this vehicle before a tragedy occurred. John told me to try to get behind this car which was now at an increasing distance from us. As we approached 100 miles per hour, we still were not gaining on this driver. From a distance, we saw the operator drive onto the exit ramp where he then had to stop for vehicles in front of him. John, an imposing and fit specimen, was the first to run out of our car as I brought it to a stop. Reaching the driver's door, he forced it open and grabbed the operator by the chest in an attempt to pull him out, but he did not budge. As John continued to pull on him, the vehicle began rocking back and forth. Nearing the vehicle, I heard the obviously rattled driver yell out, "My seat belt is still on!"

On the job, we encounter many who feel trapped. After getting into terrible situations, frequently by their own doing, they often find that no one in their lives can give them the help they need. Sinking in despair, they may respond in ways that will further harm themselves and sometimes others. At these times, they may be looking for someone who can help them to change their lives and find peace. As Believers, we may be the last resource who can offer them the hope promised in His word: "No temptation has seized you except what is common to man. And, God is faithful; He will not let you be tempted beyond what you can bear. But, when you are tempted, He will also provide a way out so that you can stand up under it." 1 Corinthians 10:13.

"God will use your mess for good. We see a perfect mess; God sees a perfect chance to train, test, and teach." Max Lucado, author

John 14:27-28, Philippians 4:12-13, 1 Peter 5:10

REAL DEAL

When working in an undercover capacity that required me to infiltrate a group or to get close to a person involved in illegal activity, I experienced a great deal of pressure. My biggest concern was that someone would learn that I was in law enforcement. During one case, things were working out well, and the target of the investigation began to trust me. Soon, he was selling me drugs, and eventually, he introduced me to other dealers. When the day came to serve arrest warrants issued for a number of subjects, a team of officers assembled to bring the perps in. I chose to pick up the person who was my first contact in the investigation. When I arrived at his front door, he immediately opened it and greeted me. After I pulled out my badge and showed it to him, a broad grin spread across his face. Enthusiastically, he said, "Wow, that's really cool! Where did you get the badge? Can you get me one?"

Believers have to be careful to live in a way that would distinguish us from those who are not following Christ. Although we live in this world, we are not to be of this world, and that is not always easy. However, if we are going to show others what we are really about as a result of our desire to walk in the will of our Lord, we have to be the real deal. If others do not see us as being any different, we lose our credibility and may not be able to convince them that we do know where true peace can be found. "But you are a chosen people, a royal priesthood, a holy nation, a people belonging to God, that you may declare the praises of Him who called you out of darkness into His wonderful light." 1 Peter 2:9.

"We play to honor Jesus Christ. That's what we play for. It takes (the pressure) off our shoulders. Honestly, it makes us play harder in a sense, just understanding the humbling fact that it's not about us; it's about Him and glorifying His name."
Jordan Hicks, Philadelphia Eagles linebacker

Deuteronomy 14:2, Psalm 4:3, Romans 12:1-2

WHO IS PRAYING?

The more we see and experience the depravity of man each day on the job, the more we should recognize the need to pray, to trust Him, and to believe that He knows what is best.

Heavenly Father,

I am often called upon to respond to a situation that I may not be able to bring to a successful resolution. Please help me to know when to speak and when to listen.

> **"If any of you lacks wisdom, he should ask God, who gives generously to all without finding fault, and it will be given to him." James 1:5.**

Lord, it becomes so obvious to me that I need your wisdom all of the time. Please pour it upon me throughout the day.

> **"For the Lord gives wisdom, and from His mouth come knowledge and understanding." Proverbs 2:6.**

Jesus, my job is often physically demanding. I need strength from you.

> **"I can do everything through Him who gives me strength." Philippians 4:13.**

God, You are compassionate. Often because of what I see on the job, I become jaded. Help me to show the compassion of Christ.

> **"Therefore, as God's chosen people, holy and dearly loved, clothe yourselves with compassion, kindness, humility, gentleness, and patience." Colossians 3:12.**

My Rock, I call out to You, knowing that You not only hear me, but You also answer my prayers and petitions. Thank You for this gift.

In Christ's name, Amen.

Ephesians 6:18, James 5:13, 1 John 5:14

GOT IT ALL?

Several years ago, when I was asked to assemble a security detail for a high-profile individual and his extended family, twenty-five agents joined me in a round-the-clock protection effort. This man's wealth was evidenced by the massive estate where he and his wife resided adjacent to his 9-hole golf course. Maids, caretakers, a chauffeur, a chef, and his private jet, with pilots always on standby, were a part of their daily living. One evening, I heard the patriarch and his wife discussing what to have for dinner, and they decided on Chinese food. I expectantly waited for a vehicle to arrive shortly to deliver the food in multiple cardboard boxes. However, when a van pulled in, three Asian men exited the vehicle, placed several large woks in the driveway, and started the dinner. The life-style of this family was astonishingly different from ours, and although it seemed fascinating and alluring at first, we soon realized that most in the family were discontented and ungrateful.

For those seeking to walk in God's will, it soon becomes evident where true contentment can be found. Contrary to what many in our society believe, it is not achieved through possessions, boats, cars, extravagant travels around the world, a perfect job, or early retirement. We see so many who go through life knowing that a void is there, but not knowing how to fill it. Romans 12:2 tells us, "Do not conform any longer to the pattern of this world, but be transformed by the renewing of your mind. Then you will be able to test and approve what God's will is--His good, pleasing, and perfect will."

"You say, 'If I had a little more, I should be very satisfied.' You make a mistake. If you are not content with what you have, you would not be satisfied if it were doubled."
Charles Spurgeon, pastor/author

2 Corinthians 12:9-10, 1 Timothy 6:6-12, Hebrews 13:5

DON'T BE FOOLED

With the assistance of a confidential informant, I began buying quantities of cocaine from a street-level dealer. When he was arrested, he agreed to reveal his source, a doctor, whom he later introduced to me. Our first meeting was in a restaurant, and after reaching a deal, he slipped me three ounces of cocaine under the table. As we talked, he questioned my occupation and was amused when I told him that I was a "hit man" for an organized crime family. Later, he invited me to his home where I took a seat in a rocking chair. Unexpectedly, the gun that I had concealed in the hollow of my back slipped out of my belt and fell to the wooden floor with a loud thud. Reaching down, I casually picked it up and returned it to my belt. The doctor seemed unfazed, apparently assuming that this was standard equipment for my job. A few months later, the doctor called me, and knowing my "profession," said that he had someone he needed me to "take care of." At that point, it was obvious that I needed to conclude the investigation. Soon, the doctor was arrested and taken to the barracks where I was waiting. As I was talking with other officers, he became outraged when he noticed that I was not handcuffed as he was. Only then did he realize that he had been fooled.

Believers must be alert to those who **will** similarly attempt to mislead us, especially in regard to our faith. In 1 John 4:1-3, John cautions us, "Dear Friends, do not believe every spirit, but test the spirits to see whether they are from God, because many false prophets have gone out into the world. This is how you can recognize the spirit of God: Every spirit that acknowledges that Jesus Christ has come in the flesh is from God, but every spirit that does not acknowledge Jesus is not from God. This is the spirit of the antichrist, which you have heard is coming and even now is already in the world."

"Never adopt an attitude of indifference, for if you do, you will suffer for it. The weight will grow heavier and heavier."
Watchman Nee, Chinese Christian author/church leader

Romans 16:17-18, 2 Thessalonians 2:9-11, 2 Peter 2:1-3

THE RIGHT ANSWER

On the job, we will encounter situations where it is impossible to have all of the right answers. Working undercover, I learned of a major drug dealer in the city. When I went to his apartment, one of his men met me at the front door and ushered me to a back room. As the dealer sat at a table with scales and drug paraphernalia, another "enforcer" stood at his side. After I told him that I was there to buy heroin, he asked how long I had been using. I responded that it was for "my old lady," not me. Staring intently at me, he bellowed, "Wrong answer! Before you can leave, you have to shoot up here." Pulling out my firearm, I backed out the door. Although it was the wrong answer for the dealer, it was the right answer for me.

In the spiritual realm, when non-believers question how we can have the faith that we do, we need to be prepared to speak the truth with conviction and clarity. Many reliable sources provide scientific or historical evidence to support the validity of the Bible. In his book, *Why I Believe*, Dr. D. James Kennedy, describes God's precision in creating Earth: "If Earth were either 10% larger or 10% smaller, life would not be possible upon this planet... It is just the right distance from the sun, and thus we receive the right amount of heat and light. If it were farther away, we would freeze. If any closer, we would not be able to survive... No other planet is tilted like ours--23 degrees... If there were no tilt to the axis, the poles would accumulate large masses of ice, and the center would be intensely hot." God also physically equipped us to be able to share the gospel. Anthropologist, Sir Henry Osborn finds the human brain to be "the most marvelous and mysterious object in the whole universe," a 3.3-pound organ containing 10-15 billion neurons that can do what 500 tons of electronic equipment cannot do.

"We account the scriptures of God to be the most sublime philosophy. I find more sure marks of authenticity in the Bible than in any profane history whatsoever."
Isaac Newton, English mathematician/scientist

Hebrews 4:12, 2 Timothy 2:15, 2 Timothy 3:16

WHITER THAN SNOW

Concluding an extensive investigation, a detective in a PA coal region determined the identity of a bank robber. After obtaining a warrant for his arrest, he proceeded with several other officers to a row home where the perpetrator and his mother lived. When an elderly woman answered the door, the detective said, "I have a warrant for the arrest of your son." The woman quickly replied that he was not there. The detective then asked her if he could come in to look around, and she agreed. Finding nothing in the rooms, he went down to the dimly lit, cluttered basement. Noticing a coal bin in one corner, he shuffled through the clutter to get to it. Instinctively, he picked up a broom handle and began poking in the coal. The suspect began yelling as he climbed from under the coal. Covered in black coal dust, he was barely recognizable.

Some may believe that because of the sins in their life over many years, their souls assuredly are as black as coal, so when they eventually meet their Maker, the probability of entering heaven is very unlikely. However, the Bible tells us in 1 John 1:9, "If we confess our sins, He is faithful and just to forgive us our sins and to cleanse us from all unrighteousness." Because He chose to die on the cross for us, He forgives all of our sins, past, present, and future if we just ask. "Come now, let us reason together," says the Lord. "Though your sins are like scarlet, they shall be as white as snow." Isaiah 1:18.

"God loves us not for who we are but because of who He is." *The Philippine Star*

Psalm 103:8, Isaiah 43:25, Acts 3:19, Ephesians 2:4-5.

PASSING THE TEST

Police folklore tells of the officer who pulled over a vehicle traveling at a high rate of speed on a major highway. After asking the driver why he was speeding, the operator said that he was a magician and juggler and was running late to his performance that night. Because the officer was fascinated with juggling, he told the driver that if he would do a little juggling for him, he would not issue a ticket. Dejectedly, the driver replied that all of his equipment had been sent ahead for the show, so he had nothing to juggle. Remembering the flares in the trunk of his patrol car, the officer asked if he would juggle them. When the juggler agreed, the officer retrieved three flares, lit them, and handed them to the performer. While he was juggling, a car pulled up behind the patrol car. Slowly, a drunk got out, walked to the patrol car, opened the back door, and got in. The officer quickly walked over to ask the drunk what he was doing. He mumbled. "You might as well take me to jail, cause there's no way I can pass that test."

Some people believe that because of their past and/or current lifestyle, they would never pass the test to get into Heaven. In truth, when we face our Creator, there will be no test to determine whether we are worthy of eternal life in Heaven. One of the most well-known verses in the Bible sums up the only requirement for entry. "For God so loved the world that He gave His only begotten Son, that whoever believes in Him will **not** perish but have everlasting life." John 3:16. The apostle Paul wrote, "For by grace you have been saved through **faith**, and **not** of yourself; it is the **gift** of God, **not** of works, lest anyone should boast." Ephesians 2:8-9. That's it. Nothing more. We cannot work our way into Heaven. If we think we can, we are saying, in essence, that the price Jesus paid on the cross for our sins is not enough, and there is still something we need to do. Although in our humanness, many complicate God's plan of salvation, praise God that His plan is quite simple.

"At the end of the day, God's love for me, for you, and for the world is settled at the cross."
Andy Stanley, pastor/author

Romans 6:23, Hebrews 5:8-9, 1 Peter 2:24

PERSEVERANCE

Joining the law enforcement profession is no easy task. Sometimes the application process alone can take up to one year. Once accepted, the candidate faces the true test during the cadet classes which are typically six months long. The voluminous material to study: vehicle code, crimes code, rules of criminal procedure, rules and regulations, laws of arrest, search, and seizure; meeting physical requirements: boxing, self-defense, extended runs, water rescue; and the strict discipline can be overwhelming at times. After only two days at the PA State Police Academy, one cadet went to a staff instructor and said, "Sarge, I'm going to quit." When asked why, he said, "I didn't know that this job requires us to work swing shifts, and only now that I'm here, did I realize that I can't even go home on weekends." Obviously, this cadet did not have what it takes to enter into the law enforcement profession. He lacked perseverance.

Because we see so much negativity, injustice, abuse, broken relationships, heartaches, hatred, and death, our faith can be tested and we may backslide. After a horrific incident, such as the senseless loss of multiple lives by an active shooter, we may even think, "Where was God in the midst of this?" Since we do not have the mind of God, we cannot fully understand His purpose. However, we know that nothing happens to any of us until it first passes by Him. In John 16:33, Jesus unequivocally told us, "You **will** have suffering in this world." An important verse to remember, even though it does not answer the "Why?" question, is 1 Corinthians 13:12: "Now we see but a poor reflection as in a mirror; then we shall see face to face." Although we will face many trials in this life, when we remember that the best is yet to come in eternity, we can find peace. "Blessed is the one who perseveres under trial because, having stood the test, that person will receive the crown of life that the Lord has promised to those who love Him." James 1:12.

"This life was not intended to be the place of our perfection but the preparation for it."
Richard Baxter, theologian

Proverbs 3:5-6, Romans 5:3-4, 1 Peter 5:10-11

REPEAT OFFENDERS

One of the most discouraging situations for me in law enforcement was dealing with repeat offenders so many times. John was married and had five children by three different women. My first encounter with him was at his residence when I served a search warrant that revealed quantities of cocaine in his possession. He told me that he was unable to be employed because he had injured his back while working on a construction site, so in his mind, dealing drugs was the only way to support his family. All of his children were living with him and the mother of his most recent child. When I later revisited him with yet another warrant, it was apparent that John was upset with himself as he looked at his children while they watched strangers searching through the family belongings. He appeared to be weary of being on the wrong side of the law as he mentioned his four previous arrests. When he said that he was ready to change his lifestyle for himself and his family, I wanted to believe him.

We Believers are often similar to John, for we sin; we repent, and we are even sincere when we say to the Lord, "This time will be different." However, in our humanness, we continue to fall. From the moment of our birth, our God knew that we would continue to sin. In His perfect plan, He made a way that could absolve us of all of our sins. On the day when Believers meet their Creator, there will be no charges presented against us, for all will have been wiped clean. Romans 3:23-24 reminds us, "For all have sinned and fall short of the glory of God, and are justified freely by His grace through the redemption that came by Christ Jesus." As many times as we fail, He will remain eager to forgive, forget, and give us another chance.

"God could not remain just and ignore sin. There was a penalty to be paid. So, Christ was credited with our sin. Consequently, He suffered death in our place and in doing so paid the penalty we incurred." Charles Stanley, pastor/ author

Acts 3:19, 2 Corinthians 5:17-19, Hebrews 10:17-18

NOT ALWAYS EASY

Some of the most troubling cases we investigate involve the abuse of children, for they are so vulnerable, trusting, and usually eager to please. Typically, they are not good witnesses and often do not want to talk about what occurred. Some children have been led to believe that they did something wrong, so they are reluctant to accuse. The mother of a young girl learned that something very disturbing had happened to her daughter, and she wanted police intervention. When I entered her home, a little girl sat at the kitchen table coloring in a book, but she would not look at me. Going to the table, I began to color, while she silently looked at my work. After several minutes, I commented on the picture that she had created. In time, she became more comfortable, and we began to talk. With difficulty, she bravely related the circumstances, and a family member was ultimately arrested.

These cases are not easy for several reasons, but foremost is the knowledge that a young child will be scarred for life. Yet, even the perpetrators of the most evil of sins can be forgiven. Although that is difficult to imagine, Believers know that when Jesus suffered a horrific death on the cross for our sins, He did not exclude the sins that we consider to be the most heinous. Instead, He paid the full price for all who believe in Him--regardless of the sin--as long as we repent and sincerely and honestly request forgiveness. Isaiah 1:18 reminds us, "'Come now, let us settle the matter,' says the Lord. 'Though your sins are like scarlet, they shall be as white as snow; though they are red as crimson, they shall be like wool.'"

"Why God should choose the meanest, basest, most unworthy individuals with absolutely nothing to commend them at all to God, except their miserable, lost condition, and then exalt them to become the sons of God, members of the divine family, and use them for His glory, is beyond all reason and human understanding. Yet, that is GRACE."
M. R. DeHaan, radio Bible teacher/pastor/author

2 Corinthians 5:17, Hebrews 10:17, 1 John 1:9

SAFE HANDS

After I had received information from a confidential informant that a local club was a gathering place for many drug dealers, several in our undercover unit decided to assess the place. One of the primary concerns about going in together was whether anyone would recognize us, perhaps through a prior arrest, and blow our cover. As we entered, the band played loudly, and we all began to mingle. Suddenly, the music stopped, and the singer at the microphone said, "Attention. 'The Man' is here with us tonight. Be cool." Immediately everyone in the club began to look around the room, so we had to make a fast exit. As I was walking quickly to the door, my troublesome knee locked, and I could barely walk. One of our team members grabbed under my arm, practically dragged me out the door, and then pushed me into his car. I was in safe hands.

For those in law enforcement and for all first responders, safety, not only our own, but also that of those we work with, is paramount. At this time in my career, however, I was in the early stages of spiritual development and relied on my own instincts and training to make wise decisions. However, as my relationship with the Lord matured over the years, I readily called on Him for help, for I realized that He is ever-present, and I am always safe in the hands of God. Isaiah 41:10 reminds us, "So do not fear, for I am with you; do not be dismayed, for I am your God. I will strengthen you and help you; I will uphold you with my righteous right hand."

"If you can't fly, then run; if you can't run, then walk; if you can't walk, then crawl, but whatever you do, you have to keep moving forward."
Dr. Martin Luther King

Job 12:7-10, Psalm 31:15, Psalm 138:7

CAN'T DO IT ALONE

Today is another journey;
I wonder how prepared I will be.
Challenges, obstacles, and struggles prevail;
Lord, show me what You want me to see.

It's impossible to know what's ahead,
perhaps things totally new to me.
Lord, direct my steps through this day,
and Your presence will allow me to see.

My job is often so difficult;
so many people depend upon me.
But if I wait upon You for wisdom,
I will be all that You want me to be.

I know some will question my actions,
but I want them to see You through me.
If ultimately that is what happens,
I will be all that You want me to be.

I find it hard to slow down,
to stop, to wait, and be still.
Yet, I know in my heart if I seek You,
I will be in the center of Your will.

rfg

"Be still before the Lord and wait patiently for Him; do not fret when men succeed in their ways, when they carry out their wicked schemes." Psalm 37:5-7

CLEAR EVIDENCE

An important skill for those in law enforcement is the ability to provide compelling reasons for bringing charges against someone that we believe committed a crime. Then, we have to introduce the evidence with a conviction that is able to withstand the intense grilling of the defense attorney. Afterwards, the judge will carefully weigh the facts that we presented to ensure that the rights of the accused have not been violated. Presenting and assessing evidence is a rigorous process because the ultimate outcome could be the loss of freedom through incarceration. Fortunately, with the advent of DNA evidence and perfected fingerprint examination, someone is far less likely to be wrongly accused.

Since we may be the only carrier of the Good News to someone who does not know the saving knowledge of Jesus and may never hear about it again, we must present it with clarity and certainty. We know that the Bible is the infallible word of God, and so much evidence exists to confirm that. We can familiarize ourselves with some of the 2,000+ prophesies in the Bible that have already come to fruition, some of them hundreds of years after the prophesy was proclaimed. Archeological digs over the last century have unwittingly provided the "DNA" to confirm many details in Scripture which historians previously had refuted. 1 Peter 3:15-16 tells us, "But in your hearts set apart Christ as Lord. Always be prepared to give an answer to everyone who asks you to give the reason for the hope that you have. But do it with gentleness and respect, keeping a clear conscience, so that those who speak maliciously against your good behavior in Christ may be ashamed of their slander."

"The Bible has stood the test of time because it is divinely inspired by Almighty God, written in ink that cannot be erased by any man, religion, or belief system."
Billy Graham, evangelist

Isaiah 40:8, Ephesians 1:13-14, 2 Timothy 3:16

ON GUARD

Early in my career when I was considered a "rookie," whenever I was called to assist at a major crime scene, I was usually relegated to the lowly duty of guarding the scene. One night when I arrived at a homicide scene, two officers were already searching the area close to the body as a supervisor pulled in. He then told me that my responsibility was to ensure that no one got into the area now being cordoned off unless they were obviously a part of the major investigation. In addition, I was to document everyone entering the restricted zone. My first challenge was the news media who all wanted to get closer to the scene than was permitted. When other officers on duty, some of whom I worked with, arrived and wanted a close up, they were upset when I did not allow them entry. Soon, several higher-ranking officers arrived, and they, too, wanted a closer look. When I explained that I had been directed to guard the scene, they walked past me without hesitation as if I were invisible. I spent the remaining hours of my shift agonizing over how I would respond if my lack of control would later be questioned.

For Believers, Satan will continue to try to disrupt our walk with Christ. Those who are not attempting to live godly lives are not of much concern to the evil one, but if we are bold in our stand, Satan will be relentless in his attempt to see us fall. Often, during the times when we are closest with the Lord, Satan is most aggressively attempting to make us stumble. Throughout Scripture, we see where God put a hedge of protection around one of His own. In Psalm 91:14-15, the Lord says, "Because he loves Me, I will rescue him; I will protect him, for he acknowledges My name. He will call upon Me, and I will answer him; I will be with him in trouble, I will deliver him and honor him."

"We are at war, and the bloody battle is over our hearts. I am astounded that so few Christians see this, how little they protect their hearts. 'What's this going to do to my heart?' is a question I ask in every situation."
John Eldredge, author/counselor, lecturer

Psalm 121:7, Ephesians 6:10-18, James 4:7

CAPTURING WISDOM

When we are on the job and seeking a promotion, each department has its own procedures that officers must follow in an attempt to advance. On our force, we are required to score well on a written exam, the content of which is obtained from department regulations, the criminal and vehicle codes, search and seizure, standard operating procedures, and several textbooks on police practices--all of which are required reading. During this time of preparation, I would remove myself from family and friends and unnecessary responsibilities. At the completion of each shift, I devoted the remaining hours of the day to studying, and this rigorous routine went on for weeks. My hope was that I would remember all the material that I was reviewing. If I scored well on the written exam, I would then be interviewed by several higher-ranking officers who would fire questions to test my wisdom in resolving different incidents.

In James 1:5, God's word says, "If any of you lacks wisdom, he should ask God, who gives generously to all without finding fault, and it will be given to him." While we pray diligently for something we are earnestly seeking, we acknowledge that our loving Lord is the source for that wisdom; however, we must also trust that He knows what is in our best interests. Sometimes, we may not receive the outcome we desire if it is not in accordance with God's will. In Isaiah 55:8, the Lord declares, "For My thoughts are not your thoughts; neither are your ways My ways." Proverbs 3:7 tells us, "Do not be wise in your own eyes; fear the Lord and shun evil." When we learn to accept and grow from such disappointments, we will understand, "How much better to get wisdom than gold, to choose understanding rather than silver." Proverbs 16:16.

"Don't miss God's fingerprints all over the events, lining up people and circumstances in perfect timing to preserve His people and advance His agenda."
James Macdonald, evangelical pastor

Proverbs 19:20, Ecclesiastes 2:26, 1 Corinthians 1:25

HIDDEN DANGERS

On November 7, 2017, Trooper Ryan Seiple stopped a speeding car on a busy highway and issued a ticket to the driver. As the trooper began to leave, the driver signaled him back to his car. When the driver began asking for information that the trooper had just given him, Seiple suspected him of DUI and called for backup. Corporal Seth Kelly arrived shortly, and the driver became physical; the three got into a brawl, falling onto the highway. After extricating himself, the driver ran to his car where he retrieved a gun. Firing, he hit Cpl. Kelly three times. Nevertheless, both troopers were able to return shots as the driver raced away. Although Cpl. Kelly was critically wounded, he had the presence of mind to pull a tourniquet from his belt and apply it to his severe leg wound. Doctors later said that this action saved his life. Kelly was then airlifted to a hospital where he underwent immediate surgery and began a fight for his life. At another hospital, the driver turned himself in because he also had been shot, and within minutes, police surrounded him as he went into surgery.

In the heat of the spiritual battles in life, we, too, need presence of mind. Lurking in the shadows is the hidden danger of Satan who will try to lure us off our path. Although a surprising number of people who define themselves as Christians do not believe in Satan's existence, both Old and New Testament verses warn us of his very real efforts to derail us. 1 Peter 5:8 warns, "Your enemy the devil prowls around like a roaring lion looking for someone to devour." In John 8:44, Christ describes the very real Satan: "The devil...was a murderer from the beginning, not holding to the truth...he is a liar and the father of lies."

"There is no neutral ground in the universe; every square inch, every split second, is claimed by God and counter-claimed by Satan."
C.S. Lewis, British novelist/academic/Christian apologist

Zechariah 3:2, Matthew 16:23, I Thessalonians 2:18

HELPING OTHERS

At my first station assignment after graduating from the PA State Police Academy, all troopers were required to sleep at the barracks when they had a 3:00-11:00 PM shift followed by a 7:00 AM-3:00 PM shift. In that rural area, no one stayed up all night to answer the infrequent calls. However, someone was assigned to take incoming calls and to awaken other officers when necessary. One night, when I was quite late finishing my shift and the senior officer was already asleep, I answered a call reporting that a vehicle had hit a pedestrian. After waking the officer to say that I would respond, I left for the scene. There, the emergency responders reported that a young man lying in the middle of the highway was dead. Since I had not yet investigated a fatality, I called the barracks to relate the situation to the senior trooper who was asleep. "Kid, I never start something I can't finish," he barked and then hung up, leaving me somewhat shaken. Yet, knowing that my investigation had to be accurate, I quickly noted that the victim wore dark clothing and had crossed an unlit highway. When the complex investigation went before a Coroner's Inquest to determine the fault of the driver, I was satisfied that my investigation and testimony had revealed the truth. Eventually, the remorseful driver was exonerated.

Sometimes our acts of kindness are not appreciated or even recognized. Since I chose to take this call after an extended shift so that the senior officer could sleep, I was disheartened by his response. Yet, I knew that I had done the right thing. At such times, we need to remember that we work for our Creator. Colossians 3:23 reminds us: "Whatever you do, work heartily, as for the Lord and not for men." Our good deeds do not go unnoticed. "God is not unjust; He will not forget your work and the love you have shown Him as you have helped His people and continue to help them." Hebrews 6:10.

"The measure of a man's greatness is not the number of servants he has, but the number of people he serves." John Hagee, pastor/author

Matthew 5:16, Luke 6:28, Galatians 6:9-10

PARTNERS

In large law enforcement departments, officers often pair up during their shifts. In my department, this occurred only during the midnight-8:00 AM shift. I always felt more comfortable to know that I had constant backup during a shift when it is not uncommon for things to go bad quickly under the cover of darkness. K-9 officers have their four-legged partners, and both become dependent on and very close to each other. In many city departments, where activity is constant during the later hours, a paddy wagon is out, occupied by two officers. Their sole responsibility is to respond to locations where arrests have been made and then transport the suspects to the station for processing. In a nearby department, one of the officers had the last name Santa, and the other was named Clause. When they arrived at an incident to transport, the officers involved at the scene would say, "Here comes Santa Clause." Those being arrested and transported neither understood nor appreciated the levity brought to the situation.

When we Believers accepted Jesus as our Lord and Savior, we acquired an immediate "partner." The Holy Spirit came to be with us and in us, twenty-four/seven. The Holy Spirit will show us God's will for our lives. He convicts us when we are about to fall into sin. He translates our "groaning" into words and lays our needs at the feet of the Father. He leads us and empowers us as He provides us with peace in this world. Many of us who accepted Christ as Savior did not learn about the Holy Spirit's indwelling us until a later time. Once we understand His role, we should remember to call upon Him throughout the day. Think of the light switch on the wall. The power is there, but we have to turn it on. John 14:15-17 says, "If you love me, you will obey what I command. And I will ask the Father, and He will give you another Counselor to be with you forever--the Spirit of truth."

"It is the Holy Spirit's job to convict, God's job to judge, my job to love."
Billy Graham, evangelist/author

John 14:26, Romans 8:26-27, I Corinthians 6:19-20

DROP IT

Paying an unexpected visit to a bar that was known to be regularly frequented by drug dealers, prostitutes, and other criminals always resulted in arrests. Waiting to raid until later in the night usually meant a greater chance of success. However, the downside was that many had been drinking at the bar for several hours and now were ready to flex their "beer muscles." Since a physical confrontation was almost certain, we always had uniformed officers enter with us so there would be no question as to who we were. Upon entering the dimly-lit, smoke-filled bar packed with patrons, we usually heard the sound of firearms dropping to the floor along with drugs and any other incriminating evidence. Everyone wanted to rid themselves of anything that would determine them guilty.

In Romans 3:23, Paul tells us that in our humanness, "All have sinned and fall short of the glory of God." When this life is over and we are face to face with our Creator, it will be too late to try to rid ourselves of any sins that would determine us guilty. The best news, however, is that we can take care of that right now while we are here on Earth. When we tell Christ that we truly believe in Him and that we are sorry for our sins, past, present and future, we acknowledge that God's Son took the rap we all deserve and did it once and for all. When we ask Him to forgive us, He will do just that. It is so simple. There is nothing more that we must or can do. Why would He give us such an undeserved gift? Because He loves us. "Come now, let us reason together, says the Lord. Though your sins are like scarlet, they shall be as white as snow; though they are red as crimson, they shall be like wool." Isaiah 1:18.

"God's love for people is infinite and unconditional."
John Blanchard, preacher/apologist/author

Psalm 103:12, 2 Corinthians 5:17, 1 John 1:9

SECOND CHANCE

Preparing to serve an arrest warrant, the officer went to the individual's last known address. He walked to the back door, knocked, and identified himself, but there was no response. Seeing a light in a side window of the home, he went there and saw a television on inside. He rapped on the window and again announced his presence. After hearing shuffling inside the home, the officer returned to the back door, believing that the subject might be trying to exit. Suddenly, a man burst through the door and pointed an AK 47 at the officer. Pulling his firearm, he pointed it at the suspect and ordered him to drop the rifle. As the officer was about to shoot, the suspect then aimed toward the side of the house. After the officer gave a second command to disarm, the man dropped the rifle. When the officer subdued the suspect, he determined that this was not the person named on the warrant, and the man's rifle was not loaded. Although the officer had every right to fire upon this armed suspect, his moment of hesitation saved the man's life. The officer was profoundly affected as he later thought about what could have occurred and the fact that his actions actually gave this subject a second chance.

As people contemplate their sinfulness before a Holy God, some may wonder about the price that they may have to pay at the end of their life on this earth. They may hope that they would at least have a second chance when ultimately facing God. In contrast, Believers have the absolute assurance that the penalty for our sinfulness has already been paid. Romans 6:23: "For the wages of sin is death, but the gift of God is eternal life in Christ Jesus our Lord." How great it is to know that our final destiny is not left to chance or bargaining. Heaven awaits us!

"One of the most staggering truths of the Scriptures is to understand that we do not earn our way to heaven. Works have a place--but as a demonstration of having received God's forgiveness, not as a badge of merit of having earned it."
Ravi Zacharias, evangelist/author

John 3:16, 2 Timothy 4:18, 1 John 2:24-25

BORN TO SERVE

Former U.S. Marine Corps Lance Corporal, Matias Ferreira, lost both of his legs below the knee when he stepped on an explosive in Afghanistan. Amazingly, he recently graduated from the Suffolk County Police Academy in New York. His desire to serve, not only in the military but also in law enforcement, exemplifies his determination to continue to be of service to others. With an iron will and two titanium legs, he passed the physical training of the police department and met all of the other requirements. He is well-prepared and will not be limited in his duties in law enforcement. "I really just want to help people," said Ferreira. Almost everyone on the job will attest to the fact that they also joined their department because they wanted to serve others.

Jesus was born on Earth with the primary purpose of serving others. Mark 10:45 tells us, "For even the Son of Man did not come to be served, but to serve, and to give His life as a ransom for many." Christ set the ultimate example for all of His creation. When we do serve others for no other reason than because we care, we often realize that we are also being blessed by the experience. Yet, the greatest blessing will come on our final day on Earth. "For God so loved the world that He gave His one and only Son, that whoever believes in Him shall not perish but have eternal life." John 3:16.

"I shall pass through this world but once. Any good thing, therefore, that I can do, or any kindness that I can show to any human being, let me do it now. Let me not defer it or neglect it, for I shall not pass this way again."
Henry Drummond, evangelist/biologist/author

John 13:15-17, Romans 12:10-11, Philippians 2:3

FIX IT

Mark and Cindy have two sons and a daughter, Ben, Jacob, and Sarah. They have raised them in a God-fearing, God-honoring home. When Jacob, the oldest, entered his teenage years, his parents became concerned as they noticed changes in his behavior after he began to hang around new "friends." Since Mark has been a police officer for many years, he has seen this type of attitude-change too many times. Before long, his and Cindy's suspicions became a reality when they learned that Jacob was using drugs. During his repeated attempts at recovery, the road was never smooth. Although their son expressed remorse at times, the overwhelming power of the drugs would cause Jacob to return to a destructive life-style. Mark and Cindy knew that they were witnessing the power of Satan in their son's life, for each time that Jacob said he was now ready to go "straight," he lasted only a few days. Even when he entered a rehabilitation center, he usually stayed for only a short period. Being in law enforcement, Mark has often been able to fix difficult situations that others were experiencing, so dealing with his son's issues is very frustrating.

Although it is not uncommon during times of trial for even devout Believers to question why they are experiencing such troubling times, Mark and Cindy have never wavered from their faith in God. They are trusting that He will ultimately bring Jacob back as the son he once was. God's word often mentions that those who were seeking to walk in His will were also challenged with difficult times. Psalm 9:10 assures us, "Those who know Your name will trust in You, for You, Lord, have never forsaken those who seek You." James 1:6 reminds us, "But when you ask, you must believe and not doubt, because the one who doubts is like a wave of the sea, blown and tossed by the wind."

"If you can trust God to save you for eternity, you can trust Him to lead you for a lifetime."
David Platt, pastor/author

Joshua 1:9, Psalm 56:3-4, Philippians 4:6-7

ALL ALONE

Shortly after graduating from the PA State Police Academy and within days of arrival at my new station, a voice crackled over the public-address system and called out my name with the message, "Report to the Captain's office immediately." Wow, does that get the attention of a rookie officer! My first thought was that I obviously did something wrong, but since I had been at that station only a few days, I could not think of anything. Yet, I could not convince myself of that as the click of my heels echoed through hallways that seemed to be miles long. As I turned a corner, a seasoned officer said, "You walk in there alone, kid." (That daunting thought is as clear to me today as it was many years ago). When I reached the office, I stood at attention and saluted as the Captain continued reading a document at his desk, and my apprehension escalated. Finally, he looked up and explained that Headquarters needed additional biographical details for my file. If I had more time on the job, I would have searched for that seasoned officer and said, "He wants to see you next."

When we leave this earth and head to our home in heaven for eternity, we are going to be called before our Creator. What is most encouraging is the knowledge that we do not walk in there "alone." All those Believers who have gone before us will be there. Despite all the wrongs that we have committed, the sins of a lifetime, Jesus will speak in our behalf. He will say that we are welcomed into heaven for eternity because of His self- sacrifice for everyone who believes in Him as Lord and Savior. I wonder if that Captain or officer will be there.

"God has two dwelling places; one in heaven and the other in a meek and thankful heart." Izaak Walton, 16th century British writer/environmentalist

Matthew 10:18-20, Romans 6:23, 1 John 3:1-2

LOST BUT FOUND

Many years ago, a young trooper learned that visibly intoxicated patrons were routinely seen leaving a nearby bar. Realizing the potential dangers of such behavior, he decided to intervene. During a late-night shift after a heavy snowstorm, the trooper set up a road block at an intersection a short distance from the bar. When a vehicle stopped, the officer stuck his head in the window of the car. The smell of alcohol on the operator's breath, his slurred speech, and his glassy eyes caused the trooper to reach into the car and grab the keys out of the ignition. He looked at the operator briefly, then raised his arm and threw the keys a considerable distance where they landed somewhere in the snow. Returning to his patrol car, he drove off, believing that by the time the operator found his keys, he would be sober enough to drive home. Perhaps he would also be thankful enough for evading an arrest that he might change his drinking habits. Although this practice would certainly not be accepted today, it was effective.

When it comes to faith, many people are not certain about what to believe. Is there a God and a place called Heaven? If so, they wonder what they have to do to be accepted. They are lost. God's word is replete with the answers to those concerns. "I give them **eternal life,** and they shall **never perish**; no one will snatch them out of My hand. My Father, who has given them to Me, is greater than all; no one can snatch them out of My Father's hand. I and the Father are One." John 10:28-30. This truth needs only to be accepted by faith.

"I will not go to Heaven because I am a preacher. I am going to Heaven entirely on the merit of the work of Christ. The moment we take our last breath on Earth, we take our first in Heaven." Billy Graham, evangelist/author

Proverbs 8:35, 1 John 2:17, 1 John 5:13

LEAVE NO DOUBT

Deoxyribonucleic acid (DNA) was discovered in 1869. In the 1940s, scientists determined its role in genetic inheritance. In 1984, Dr. Alec Jeffers found that the variations in DNA were indisputably unique to each individual. After standards were established for the collection of DNA evidence, and compliance with federal standards was met, DNA became a valuable tool in law enforcement. The U.S. Department of Justice cites two early and impressive cases when it proved its value. In 1999, after New York was terrorized by 22 sexual assaults and robberies, DNA linked a male suspect to the crimes. In 2002, after a series of rapes and a murder in Philadelphia and Colorado, DNA linked the same individual to the crimes. In the ensuing years, DNA has been widely used, not only to determine the perpetrator of a crime, but also to exonerate suspects who were wrongly accused or convicted.

Ecclesiastes 3:11 tells us: "He has made everything beautiful in its time. He also set eternity in the hearts of men; yet they cannot fathom what God has done from beginning to end." Because some people "cannot fathom" the works of our mighty God, they refuse to believe that He created each one of us in His own image. Yet, modern scientists continue to prove them wrong as they present further findings about our Earth, our history, and the uniqueness of the human body. Understanding the role of DNA provides just one more piece of evidence about our amazing Creator and the elements unique to each person He created. "So God created man in His own image, in the image of God He created him; male and female, He created them." Genesis 1:27:

"What can be more foolish than to think that all this rare fabric of heaven and earth could come by chance, when all the skill of art is not able to make an oyster?" Jeremy Taylor, 17th century English theologian/author

Psalm 14:1, Psalm 19:1-4, Romans 1:20

FALL GUY

Benny had been a large-scale heroin dealer for many years. His product was always high quality, and his customer base was large. Although I had arrested him on two prior occasions, he got probation both times. Knowing that he had been in prison previously, I was frustrated that he did not draw any additional jail time. At 2:00 AM, one of my best confidential informants called to tell me that Benny was on his way back from New York City with a large quantity of heroin. I obtained a search warrant for his residence and gathered my team. Several hours later, the informant called again to tell me that Benny would be home about 11:00 AM. With search warrant in hand, I knocked at the front door as the other officers surrounded the house. When an unknown subject answered the door, I identified myself, and this male attempted to push the door closed. Forcing entry, I saw Benny heading toward the kitchen. Officers coming through the rear door grabbed Benny and several others in the residence. After our search yielded a kilo of heroin, I was confident that this time, Benny would be going to jail. As I placed him under arrest, another member of his group, someone unknown to me, said, "Everything you found belongs to me." Although I knew that was not true, I was surprised that this lackey was willing to take the rap for this high-level drug dealer.

Someday, when we leave this world, we will face our Creator. Regardless of the lifestyle we tried to lead and the good we may have accomplished, we, "All have sinned and fall short of the glory of God." Romans 3:23. However, the good news is that Jesus will be our advocate before a Holy God. Jesus will say on our behalf that He paid the full price for all of our sins. At the cross, He was willing to take the penalty that we so much deserve. "For God so loved the world that He gave His one and only Son, that whoever believes in Him shall not perish but have eternal life." John 3:16.

"It was Christ who willingly went to the cross, and it was our sins that took Him there."
Franklin Graham, evangelist

Ecclesiastes 7:20, Ephesians 5:8, 1 Peter 2:24

SIMPLE PROOF

In our attempts to determine who is responsible for the commission of a crime, we seize evidence, take statements, and look for other proof, for each investigation involves some degree of complexity to ascertain the facts. Those who question the existence of God and label themselves as "agnostics" claim that they need proof before they can accept His existence. Actually, they have to have a very strong faith to believe that He does **not** exist, for Believers can see evidence of Him at work every day. An early 20th century Bengali writer and social reformer, Rabindranath Tagore, said, "Every child comes with the message that God is not yet discouraged of man." Anyone who has witnessed the birth of a newborn baby can attest that they have all the evidence they need regarding the authenticity of God. We have proof positive.

A child is born
So innocent, so pure
Generation after generation
God's special gift for sure.
So marvelous, so precious
So beautiful to behold
Created in God's image,
What a perfect mold!
Your handwork so evident
Tiny hands, tiny feet
Generation after generation,
Your work so complete.
rfg

"A man can no more diminish God's glory by refusing to worship Him than a lunatic can put out the sun by scribbling the word, 'darkness' on the walls of his cell."
C.S. Lewis, British novelist/academic/Christian apologist

Genesis 1:26-27, Psalm 135:5-7, John 1:1-3

WHY?

Early in my career, I met John Schafer when he entered the patrol room on his first day after transferring from the West to the East. A 6'4" and 240 chiseled pounds specimen, he could not walk into a room unnoticed. As I began working with him and then for him as he climbed in rank, our friendship deepened. His work ethic was impeccable, and he had a deep sense of caring, not only for others on the job, but also for the general public. After serving a year at the rank of Major, he called me to his office to reveal that the governor had nominated him to be the next Commissioner of the Pennsylvania State Police. We who knew him and worked with and for him were ecstatic that he would soon be at the helm. On the following day, he called and asked me to meet him at the hospital. This mountain of a man slowly said, "I have just been diagnosed with cancer and have three to six months to live." That afternoon, he contacted Governor Robert Casey to tell him the news. The governor responded, "You are still my choice to lead your department. Do whatever you need to do and get better." During Schafer's swearing in, Casey said, "I want the State Police to stand for decent, honest, progressive, and forward-looking law enforcement. These are the goals John Schafer is dedicated to." Colonel Schafer died in office eight months later.

Of all the "Why's?" I asked while on the job, this was by far the most difficult to answer. Sometimes a reason for such situations may later become evident; in other cases, it may never be understood. However, if we put our full trust in the Lord, our faith will carry us through all situations. "And we know that in all things God works for the good of those who love Him, who have been called according to His purpose." Romans 8:28. Perhaps the Lord decided that John had accomplished all that he was supposed to in this life, and He needed him more in Heaven.

"Leave it all in the hands that were wounded for you." Elisabeth Elliott, author

Psalm 23:6, Proverbs 3:5-6, Jeremiah 29:11-13

THE ULTIMATE PROMOTION

Many times in my career, I faced disappointments either because something happened or did not happen the way that I thought it should. Promotion to a higher rank is a goal that most on the job would like to achieve. After many weeks of studying, I did well on the written exam and was then eligible for an oral interview. The interview board was made up of one civilian and two higher-ranking members from the department. My appointment before the interview board was scheduled immediately after lunch. Sitting across the table from the men, I soon noticed that the civilian was falling asleep. In fact, for most of my thirty-minute interview, his eyes were closed. The two officers did not observe what I was seeing, and I knew that I did not have any recourse. All of my hard work was for nothing. In the ensuing years, I scored well through the process a number of times. However, when I received the call for a promotion, the vacancy was at the farthest point from my home, and taking it would have totally disrupted my family life. I certainly did not view such circumstances as a promotion.

Sometimes our circumstances cannot change, but our attitude can, from a negative outlook to a positive one. Psalm 55:22 tells us, "Cast your cares upon the Lord and He will sustain you; He will never let the righteous fall." At a certain point in our lives, we realize that life here on Earth is temporary and fleeting. The good news, according to God's word, is that the best is still to come. When we know that our next home will be in Heaven for eternity, the disappointments that we experience in the here and now become less significant. "…And after you have suffered a little while, the God of all grace, who has called you to His eternal glory in Christ, will Himself restore, confirm, strengthen, and establish you. To Him be the dominion forever and ever. Amen" 1 Peter 5:10-11.

"There are many things that are essential to arriving at true peace of mind, and one of the most important is faith, which cannot be acquired without prayer."
John Wooden, NCAA basketball coach

Proverbs 23:17-18, Matthew 5:44, 1 Peter 5:6-7

WHERE WAS GOD?

In a Connecticut elementary school, a lone gunman snuffed out the lives of twenty children. Although it is difficult to understand why God did not intervene, a poem written afterwards provides some solace as it tenderly reminds us that God is still in control and always will be:

"Twas eleven days before Christmas, around 9:38, when 20 beautiful children stormed through heaven's gate. Their smiles were contagious, their laughter filled the air; they could hardly believe all the beauty they saw there. They were filled with such joy, they didn't know what to say. They remembered nothing of what had happened, earlier that day. 'Where are we?' asked a little girl, as quiet as a mouse. 'This is Heaven,' declared a small boy; 'we are spending Christmas in God's house.' When what to their wondering eyes did appear, but Jesus their Savior; the children gathered near. He looked at them and smiled, and they smiled just the same. Then He opened His arms and called them by name. And in that moment was joy that only Heaven can bring. Those children all flew in the arms of their King. As they lingered in the warmth of His embrace, one small girl turned and looked at Jesus's face. And as if He could read all the questions she had, He gently whispered to her, 'I'll take care of Mom and Dad.' Then He looked down on Earth, the world far below. He saw all of the hurt, sorrow, and woe. He closed His eyes, and He outstretched His hand, 'Let My power and person re-enter this land. May this country be delivered from hands of fools. I'm taking back nations. I'm taking back schools.' The children stood up without a sound. 'Come now my children, let Me show you around.' Excitement filled the space, some skipped and some ran; all displaying enthusiasm that only a small child can. And I heard Him proclaim, as He walked out of sight: 'In the midst of the darkness, I AM STILL THE LIGHT.'"

Cameo Smith, author, Mt. Wolf, Pennsylvania

Matthew 28:20, John 1:1-5, Revelation 21:3

MISPERCEPTIONS

One day, I received a call that a close friend had seriously cut his leg with a chain saw while off duty. Not knowing the extent of his injury, I immediately drove to the hospital. In the crowded emergency room, I was directed to a small cubicle where he was being assessed, and I quickly saw that the injury was significant. An intern determined that a surgeon needed to examine the injury, but he was currently in surgery. As we waited, several uniformed troopers, who were stationed with my friend, walked by, but then stopped when they recognized us. After hearing the details of this injury, they left to interview a woman in another cubicle who had just reported being raped. While we waited patiently for the surgeon, several other uniformed troopers, having learned that their comrade had been seriously injured, came into our cubicle. As eight uniformed officers gathered around us, one of the nurses walked past, looked in at the group and their friend on the table, and said to a nurse who was with her, "Wow! That guy must be a really bad dude!"

It is important, especially for Believers, to avoid a natural tendency to judge people based on their outward appearance. At times, I have rushed to judgment when I saw people who dressed differently or were covered with tattoos, had strange mannerisms, an odd-looking hair style, or numerous body piercings. Then later, I found that I wanted to spend time with or even befriend them. When we decide that we want to live a Christ-like life, it is often necessary to change the way we present our spiritual perspective so that others can see that we are different, too, but in a good way. In John 8:15, Jesus said, "You judge by human standards; I pass judgment on no one.'" In I Samuel 16:7, the Lord said to Samuel, "Do not consider his appearance or his height, for I rejected him. The Lord does not look at the things man looks at. Man looks at the outward appearance, but the Lord looks at the heart."

"Let God be the judge. Your job today is to be a witness."
Warren Wiersbe, pastor/author

Matthew 7:1-5, Luke 6:37, James 4:11-12

COUNSELOR

Several confidential sources revealed that a major bookmaking operation was running in the county. I developed an affidavit of probable cause for a non-consensual wiretap request. I knew that approval would be given if I articulated that this was the only way to determine that criminal activity was occurring. After preparing a thirty-page document, I met with a Superior Court judge who told me to wait while he read it. He asked numerous questions and then signed the order. As our team listened to conversations on the tapped phone, the significance of the criminal enterprise quickly become apparent. Previously unknown participants were identified, and three more wiretaps were approved. Forty defendants were eventually charged under RICO, Racketeer Influenced and Corrupt Organizations, a statute to combat organized crime. Since each of the defendants requested preliminary hearings, I testified for four consecutive days. Attempting to find flaws with the arrests, the defense attorneys took turns trying to discredit both the evidence and the procedure used to obtain the warrants. Their questioning was condescending, so I tried to frustrate them by responding, "I'm sorry, counselor, but I am not sure I fully understand your question. Would you please repeat it?" They eventually became aware of my tactic, but were still forced to re-phrase the question.

In this life, once we accept Jesus as our Lord, we know that we then have a righteous Counselor, the Holy Spirit, to be with us and help us on our earthly voyage. In John 14:16-17, at His resurrection into Heaven, Jesus said, "And I will ask the Father, and He will give you another Counselor to be with you forever-- the Spirit of Truth." In Romans 8:26, Paul tells us: "In the same way, the Spirit helps us in our weakness. We do not know what we ought to pray for, but the Spirit himself intercedes for us with groans that words cannot express."

"The Sprit-filled life is not a special, deluxe edition of Christianity. It is part and parcel of the total plan of God for His people." A.W. Tozer, pastor/author

Isaiah 11:2, Luke 11:13, Acts 1:8

UNPERCEIVED CHALLENGES

Riding with my Field Training Officer during my first week on the job, I felt confident that just about anything I needed to know had been drilled into my head during training at the PA State Police Academy. On day three, we were called to a multi-vehicle crash involving many injuries. As I noticed a small red convertible smashed against a large truck, I could not see the operator but thought that he or she had probably gotten out and was among the bystanders. Walking up to the driver's door, I peered in to see a male slumped in the driver's seat with his head tilted back. His mouth was wide open and filled with blood. Although his eyes remained open, even a rookie like me could tell that he was dead. In spite of the training that I had received, I quickly realized that I still had a lot to learn. When my FTO came over, he knew by the look on my face that I was struggling to process what I was witnessing. Later that night as I recalled this incident, I realized that just because I was wearing a uniform and was expected to be in control at all times, there still would be many challenges ahead for me.

When we get to the place where we make the decision to live a life pleasing to God and seek to be in His will, we may expect that life will get easier. Why not? We now have God on our side. As I confronted difficult situations over time, I began to understand that I did not need to handle or fix them on my own. Eventually, I knew with certainty that no matter what came my way, the Lord would give me direction if I just asked. "But those who hope in the Lord will renew their strength. They shall soar on wings like eagles; they will run and not grow weary, they will walk and not be faint." Isaiah 40:31.

"We are all faced with a series of great opportunities brilliantly disguised as impossible situations." Chuck Swindoll, pastor/author

Proverbs 18:10, Isaiah 43:2, John 16:33

COMMUNICATION

In my early days on the job, the importance of good equipment to communicate both to the barracks and to other officers quickly became apparent. Jim worked in vice, usually in an undercover capacity. One day, his supervisor asked if he would be willing to impersonate one who had been arrested for a crime. He would be taken to a prison where officials were trying to obtain additional evidence on a prisoner previously arrested for a homicide. Only the warden and one supervisor would know Jim's true identity. When he agreed and was taken to jail, the supervisor gave him a blanket that had a transmitter sewn into one of the corners. He told Jim that if there were any trouble, he should speak loudly, and those monitoring the conversation would come to his rescue. Jim shared a cell right next to the prisoner who had committed the murder. Being in an environment with those who had been arrested was unnerving, for Jim knew that if his identity were known, his life would be in danger. He only hoped that the monitor worked and those on the outside would be attentive and able to pick up all of his conversations anytime, day or night. Fortunately, within in a few days, the targeted prisoner befriended him and began to talk about the circumstances of the murder, incriminating himself even further.

Sometimes we Believers may wonder if God always hears us. We call out for help in all kinds of situations, but when the answer does not come quickly, we may begin to think that He did not hear us. The fact is, however, that our communication with the Lord never goes unheard. "Call to Me and I will answer you and tell you great and unsearchable things you do not know." Jeremiah 33:3. Paul encouraged the Hebrews to "...approach the throne of grace with confidence, so that we may receive mercy and find grace to help us in our time of need." Hebrews 4:16. Often we need to stop talking and wait. Psalm 46:10 tells us, "Be still and know that I am God."

"Listen if you want to be heard." John Wooden, NCAA basketball coach

Psalm 66:19-20, Psalm 145:18, 1 John 5:14-15

THANKFUL

Everyone experiences some difficult times in life, whether physical, emotional, or even spiritual. After playing sports for several years and trick riding in the State Police Rodeo for three years, these activities eventually took a physical toll on me. Fairly recently, seven major surgeries within a three-year period required me to take oxycodone and fentanyl to fight the pain. During this period, I often wondered why God was allowing me to go through this, although I also realized that there was no reason why I should not. Throughout the trial, I always felt that God was still in this. Pastor Charles Stanley says, "Believe and trust God. Only by viewing life from a biblical perspective can we understand His purposes in our trials and trust His wisdom in allowing them. Accept the situation as coming from the Lord." If we truly believe that He is working for our good, we can choose to receive each difficulty as from His loving hand, whether it was directly sent or permissively allowed. Then we can say, "Thank you." Thanking the Lord during hardships does not come easily; however, I did get to that place. Now, I continue to thank God for my journey, for I realize that there was a reason, and I try to seize each moment and dwell only on the positive.

Only by relying on the Lord can Believers go through adversity with an appreciative heart. On the job, we see many who are challenged, discouraged, and hopeless because of the difficult times they are facing. Sometimes, they are our brothers and sisters of the law. Maybe this is you. Although we may not like a situation, if we remember that God allows trials, we can confidently place our life under His authority. James 1:2-4, "Count it pure joy, my brothers, whenever you face trials of many kinds because you know that the testing of your faith develops perseverance. Perseverance must finish its work so that you may be mature and complete, not lacking anything."

"God never takes away something from your life without replacing it with something better." Billy Graham, evangelist/author

Psalm 119:71, Romans 8:35-37, I Thessalonians 5:18

WRONG WAY

Tom, John, and I came on the job about the same time and shared many light-hearted times before being transferred to other locations and assignments. When John became a major at Departmental Headquarters, the Colonel directed him to create an Internal Affairs Division to investigate complaints against our officers. Because of our long-standing friendship, he trusted Tom and me to join this new group of investigators. Although about 98% of accusations against officers were determined to be unfounded, this work would be sensitive. However, clearing innocent members was important to us, so we joined him. As expected, the work was difficult and serious, so we rarely joked or laughed. One day as we traveled to a distant area for an interview, I drove down an unfamiliar street when a car came directly at me, and I could not proceed. The operator stopped, jumped out, and screamed, "You're going the wrong way!" Wearing a business suit, I jumped out of my unmarked vehicle and yelled back, "How do you know I'm going the wrong way? You don't even know where I'm going." Quietly getting my attention, Tom said, "Bob, we're on a one- way street." Sheepishly, I got back into the car and glanced at Tom before we both burst into laughter for a very long time.

Although our goal as Christians should be to live differently, in our humanness, we often tend to go the wrong way. Even though we are Believers who are attempting to live rightly, we will fail. Yet, we can still be forgiven of any sin because of our faith in Christ. Romans 3:22-24 explains, "There is no difference, for all have sinned and fall short of the glory of God and are justified freely by His grace." 1 John 1:7-9 is filled with hope: "But if we walk in the light, as He is in the light, we have fellowship with one another, and the blood of Jesus, His Son, purifies us from all sin… If we confess our sins, He is faithful and just and will forgive us our sins and purify us from all unrighteousness."

"God loves us the way we are, but too much to leave us that way."
Leighton Ford, author

Isaiah 1:18, Ephesians 4:31-32, Colossians 3:13

HELD HOSTAGE

Dispatch received a call from a resident in a bedroom community not known for criminal activity or violence. The caller reported that her neighbor across the street was lying face-down in her own front yard. Her head was bloodied, and her body appeared lifeless. Driving down the street, responding officers saw the woman on the ground just as shots suddenly rang out. Several of the responding officers' vehicles were hit by gunfire, and emergency responders and a SWAT team were called to assist. Some nearby neighbors told an officer that a couple with two young children lived in the home. Although it was obvious that the young woman needed medical attention, it was impossible to get near her, for shots kept coming in their direction. Assuming that the children were still in the home, an officer with a bull horn called to the husband inside to let the children go. He refused to respond, and the standoff continued for several agonizing hours until a single shot resounded from inside. As officers moved closer to the house, they could hear children crying. After they forced the door open and the children ran to safety, they saw that the perpetrator had taken his life.

When we make the decision to accept Christ as our Lord and Savior and begin walking closer to the Lord, our lives are forever changed, and our sins have been forgiven for eternity. However, that does not mean that we will no longer experience difficulties. Some of our bad habits, which cause us to sin, are difficult to change. Satan will try to hold us hostage with reminders of past sins as he continues his frequent attacks. Remember that our God is greater and stronger, and He is willing to walk beside us and help us through difficult times. "Let us then approach the throne of grace with confidence so that we may receive mercy and find grace to help in time of need." Hebrews 4:16.

"Stand firm in the Lord. Stand firm and let Him fight your battles. Do not try to fight alone." Francine Rivers, author

Psalm 107:28-30, Matthew 7:7, 1 Peter 5:7

UNDER THE COVERS

Several years ago, when I required hospitalization for an illness that no local doctors could diagnose, I was transferred to a prominent city hospital known for outstanding patient care. Placed in a private room, I spent days undergoing tests. About the fourth day, I began to wonder why the attending nurses were not friendly. They entered my room, said little, did what was required, and quickly left. One, however, was always cheerful and engaged in conversation. After a few days, I told this nurse that she was the only one who was pleasant and talked to me. Closing the door, she softly said, "I can explain that, but you must assure me that this conversation will not go any further. During your admission, all your personal information was listed on your chart including that you are a state trooper. The door directly across from your room is the narcotics locker. Because your chart does not specify a diagnosis, the other nurses believe you are here to determine who goes in and out of the closet and how often and if there are any improprieties." We in law enforcement can expect to encounter many inaccurate assumptions.

We Believers are also likely to face times when others' perceptions of us are not accurate, and we will be misunderstood. If we present an attitude of superiority to others because of our confidence in Christ, they will be turned off. When we express to others that, without a doubt, we will be going to Heaven for eternity, those who know us and have seen that we continue to sin cannot imagine why we would consider ourselves to be special. We have to be very clear about humbly explaining the reason for our confidence and clarify that it is not based on assumption, but we are justified by Christ's finished work and promise to Believers. "For it is by grace you have been saved, through faith--and this not from yourselves, it is the gift of God--not by works, so no one can boast."
Ephesians 2:8-10.

"Justification is a completed fact for the believer; it is not an ongoing process."
John MacArthur, pastor/author

John 3:16, Romans 8:1, 1 John 5:13-14

PRIDE

Most of the men and women who are first responders or in the military or law enforcement wear a uniform. Even those in plain clothes usually have one "dress" uniform to be worn during special events, ceremonies, parades, and funerals. They take pride in the uniform that represents their department or branch of service. Several years ago, a chief from out of state was appointed to be the new chief of police in a large city. One of his first decisions was to change the uniform. Members of the department were very upset that they would no longer wear the uniform that had been worn for decades. Their discontentment was compounded when the new chief also changed the colors of the marked patrol vehicles. What was most discouraging to the officers, however, was that the chief took these actions without consulting or advising any current or former members of the department. This overly self-assured chief, a proud man whose main interest appeared to be in his own accomplishments, quickly alienated himself from the officers. Interestingly, he had the shortest tenure of any who had been chief and left within a few years.

For Believers, there must be no place for pride in our lives. In Luke 14:11, Christ lovingly taught, "For everyone who exalts himself will be humbled, and he who humbles himself will be exalted." We need to remember Christ's example after He got on his knees and washed the dirty feet of the apostles. If we do not show the humility and caring that is exemplified through our Lord, we are no different from others in our society who are self-serving and proud. Romans 12:16 tells us, "Live in harmony with one another. Do not be proud, but willing to associate with people of low position. Do not be conceited."

"Talent is God-given. Be humble. Fame is man-given. Be grateful. Conceit is self-given. Be careful." John Wooden, NCAA basketball coach.

John 13:12-17, Ephesians 4:1-3, James 4:6

RUNNING IN CIRCLES

People frequently seek comfort and self-worth through their accomplishments. In our profession, we may seek affirmation through a promotion, an assignment to a coveted position, the successful conclusion to an investigation, or the capture of someone responsible for a heinous crime. Early in my career, when I was like so many others, I thought that making more money, acquiring more things, and having a bigger house would allow me to "live the dream," and then I would be considered successful. Although such "better than others" possessions are not easily obtainable for many in our profession, for a few years, I was driven to acquire them. Fortunately, as I continued to interact with people that I helped each day, I began to realize that serving others, having the ability to resolve problems, and providing comfort to others became far more rewarding than anything that I could ever buy or acquire.

When we carry a desire for recognition into our spiritual lives, we may ask ourselves, "What can I do to please God?" Since He already loves us for who we are and not for what we can accomplish, we must realize that working hard is not what gets us into heaven, for Christ already paid for our entry. Yet, Ephesians 2:10 does tell us that we are "...created in Christ Jesus to do good works which God prepared in advance for us to do." However, even the smallest of our efforts should not be made to call attention to us. Instead, they should be acts of obedience that reflect God's love for humanity and our love for the Lord. Ephesians 6:7 tells us that we should work hard "....as if you were serving the Lord, not men, because you know that the Lord will reward everyone for whatever good he does." Colossians 3:17 exhorts us: "And whatever you do whether in word or deed, do it all in the name of the Lord Jesus."

"We know only too well that what we are doing is nothing more than a drop in the ocean. But if the drop were not there, the ocean would be missing something." Mother Theresa

Psalm 37:3, James 1:22, 25, 1 Peter 4:10

STOP AND REST

To this day, even though I have retired from the job, whenever I enter a shopping mall or walk into a restaurant or a venue where many people are gathered, I quickly assess the surroundings and look for anything that may be out of the ordinary. If I take a seat, I try to sit with my back to the wall where I have a view of the entrance. As Law Soldiers, we are always running toward the problem, the danger, the action, the unexpected, while others are retreating. We are constantly looking for a way to resolve a problem or a compromising situation. Once we see a need, we know that a slow response is not a choice. Sometimes, our quick response is a means of survival for us, those we work with, and others in society. Consequently, even during down time when we are not on the job, it is often difficult for us to sit and rest, for we are considering the next thing that may require our response.

God instructs us on the necessity to rest because He knows how important rest is for our overall well-being. In Genesis, God, Himself, rested on the seventh day after working for six days. Scripture also tells us that when Jesus walked in this world, He, too, sought rest when He went into a boat to escape the crowds or when He retreated in a garden to pray. If we remember to remain in Him always, He will let us know when something requires our attention. Matthew 6:33-34 reminds us, "But seek first His kingdom and His righteousness, and all these things will be given to you as well. Therefore, do not worry about tomorrow, for tomorrow will worry about itself." Although many things will compete for our attention, the Holy Spirit will direct our path. All we need to do is ask Him.

"A field that has rested gives a bountiful crop." Ovid, poet in ancient Rome

Psalm 27:13-14, Proverbs 3:5-6, Isaiah 40:30-31

I CAN DO THAT

When I served as Director of Security/Chief of Police at a local college, I noticed that a number of officers requested a change in shift if they were required to work with a certain newly hired officer. Frustrated to think that they were just not getting along or working well together, I determined to resolve any potentially ill feelings among them. However, after exploring the issue further, I learned that this man was belligerent and hotheaded, and he often behaved like a loose cannon. His behavior was detrimental to the success of investigations and was inappropriate and even unsafe, especially during sensitive assignments. After meeting with him numerous times and requiring him to seek counseling, I realized that his issues went far beyond my ability to resolve them, and eventually, he was fired. In our work, we are often called upon to make decisions that could result in dire consequences if we respond incorrectly. Because of the way God has created us, we seem to have a calling to help others when we are asked to do many things, both on and off the job, and our typical response is, "Sure, I can do that." Consequently, we can become consumed with a sense that we must successfully meet every need and do so without fault.

When facing difficult decisions, I have learned to pray for wisdom, but sometimes there is no change or further insight. Then I have to remind myself that everything is in God's hands and happens in His timing. Proverbs 3:5-6 advises us to, "Trust in the Lord with all your heart and lean not on your own understanding. In all your ways acknowledge Him, and He will make your paths straight." He created each of us with our own personalized abilities, and He will not give us anything more than we can handle. He always wants the best for those who follow Him. "Blessed is the man who finds wisdom, the man who gains understanding." Proverbs 3:13.

"If you want to grow in true wisdom, grow in knowledge of the God of the Bible."
Matt Chandler, pastor/author

Joshua 1:9, Psalm 27:14, Proverbs 20:22

GENTLENESS

Receiving a call from a female claiming that her life had been threatened, I went to her home to find a young woman whose eyes welled up as she invited me in. She shared a letter stating that her time was up and that her impending death was going to be painful. Sensing her fear, I gently asked if she had any suspicions about the author. She revealed that when she had terminated a long-term relationship with her boyfriend a few months prior, he had become very upset. Knowing the volatility of domestic incidents, I provided words of comfort and told her I would pursue this immediately. I took the letter and left. The following day, I drove by his house and grabbed his garbage at the curb. Searching the contents, I found numerous cigarette butts, so I contacted the woman to learn what brand of cigarette he smoked. Her information matched the butts that I had found, and the cigarette butts and the letter were taken to the crime lab. When the lab report indicated that DNA evidence on the butts matched the licked flap of the letter, the boyfriend was subsequently arrested and found guilty.

After reflecting on this incident, I realized that I had responded or spoken to others at times in a way that was not caring or Christ-like. If I am sincerely committed to walking with the Lord, my actions should be direct evidence of His grace and different from the behavior and language of those who do not know Jesus as Lord and Savior. Ephesians 4:24 tells us to, "…put on the new self, created to be like God in true righteousness and holiness." When we respectfully reflect the gentleness, compassion, and love of Christ, some may become intrigued by our difference and ask questions about our faith. 1 Peter 3:15 advises us, "Always be prepared to give an answer to everyone who asks you to give the reason for the hope that you have." Believers know that encounters with others do not happen by chance. God may have placed us in a particular situation to provide evidence of His redeeming love to a lost soul.

"Do you think God can be trusted? Or, do you think you need to take things into your own hands?" Andy Stanley, pastor/author

Psalm 4:3, Colossians 3:12-14, 1 Peter 2:9

A CALLING

After being accepted into the PSP Academy, I was notified to report for training and to wear a white shirt, black shoes, a black suit, a black tie, and a black hat. The sales person who helped me pick out my clothes asked, "Are you going to become a priest?" He was quite surprised when I gave my answer. Those who enter the ministry often say that they did so because they felt a calling from God. For some people, that may be a difficult concept to grasp, but many who enter the law enforcement profession can easily relate. Their career choice was also a calling, and sometimes from the time they were children, they knew that law enforcement was where they were supposed to be. Prior to entering a police force, most of us spent time imagining what the job was really like. However, not until we were among the ranks could we comprehend how consuming, discouraging, daring, dangerous, yet fulfilling the job can be. Many of us believe that very few occupations have the same demands that we face, yet we do not regret accepting the call.

Although we may be confident that our job was the right choice for us, as Believers, we also know that there is so much more to life than having a successful career. In the midst of all the darkness that we see in the world, our primary calling is to share The Good News. Acts 22:15 tells us, "For you will be a witness for Him to all men of what you have seen and heard." We should not be hesitant to tell others the best news we could ever share. "I am not ashamed of the gospel, because it is the power of God for the salvation of everyone who believes." Romans 1:16.

"Jesus Christ is the source--the only source--of meaning in life. He provides the only satisfactory explanation for why we're here and where we're going."
James Dobson, psychologist/evangelical leader/author

John 3:16, John 3:36, 1 Timothy 6:12

GOING COLD

Cold case homicide investigations are among the most challenging. The driver of a tractor-trailer, perched high in the cab of his truck, spotted a woman's lifeless body lying in a ditch adjacent to the highway. When the police arrived, the driver could provide nothing more than what they were now observing. An autopsy revealed that the woman was Caucasian, about twenty-eight years of age; she had been strangled and beaten and had been dead for at least twenty-four hours. Blood was on her clothing, and skin was under her fingernails. A request for witnesses who could anonymously shed light on this horrific crime never brought further information. The woman was eventually identified by her husband and through her dental records. When two months passed without any leads, the investigation ended, although it was not considered closed. Approximately eight years later, a detective reopened the investigation and submitted DNA evidence to more current databases. He was soon able to make an arrest based on blood evidence found on the woman's body.

As advanced forensic techniques have developed, DNA has become one of the most powerful pieces of evidence available. Although some may try to hide their identity from law enforcement, God never loses track of His children. He knows our every thought and action before we make it, including what is inappropriate or sinful. Thankfully, even when we choose not to be in His will, if we confess those sins, He is quick to forgive. Hebrews 10:17-18 brings great comfort as we understand that the price has already been paid on the cross: "Their sins and lawless acts I will remember no more." Then comes the clincher: "And where these have been forgiven, there is no longer any sacrifice for sin." There is nothing we need to do or ever could do to achieve absolute forgiveness. The full, perfect, and sufficient sacrifice by Christ does it all.

"The chaotic, confused world has no greater need than to hear the message of good news: the Gospel of Jesus Christ." Billy Graham, evangelist/author

Romans 5:8, 1 Thessalonians 4:16, Hebrews 9:12

UNEXPECTED CONSEQUENCES

Although some of our activities on each shift are routine, these are often interrupted by a significant incident or a call for assistance. Data from the National Law Enforcement Officers Memorial Fund reveals that responding to domestic calls can often go badly. Approximately 20% of the officers killed in the line of duty in the last decade were murdered while responding to domestic disputes, which usually occur at a home. However, an officer approaching what he believed was a traffic accident instead encountered a domestic, and the officer was killed. Another officer, on patrol at daybreak, observed a dead deer lying on the highway. Probably believing that it could cause an accident if left on the road, he began dragging the deer to the roadside. Then, a vehicle rounding the bend in the road struck and killed the officer.

Knowing that unexpected consequences may lead to danger or even death should cause us to remember that each day of life is sacred. Furthermore, we and those who may be left behind after the passing of a loved one can face life's uncertainties by considering the certain peace offered in God's word. In 1 Peter 3:18, we read, "For Christ died for sins once for all, the righteous for the unrighteous, to bring you to God." Romans 6:23 assures Believers of their future: "For the wages of sin is death, but the gift of God is eternal life in Christ Jesus our Lord." The apostle John describes the promised future for all Believers as he clearly tells us what we can expect: "God has given us eternal life, and this life is in His Son. He who has the Son has life; he who does not have the Son of God does not have life. I write these things to you who believe in the name of the Son of God so that you may **know** that you have eternal life." 1 John 5:11-13.

"For you who wonder if you've played too long to change, take courage from Jacob's legacy. No man is too bad for God. To transform a riverboat gambler into a man of faith would be no easy task. But for God, it was all in a night's work." Max Lucado, author

Psalm 62:1-2, John 6:39-40, Romans 10:11-13

UNDER SIEGE

Recently, some in society have been demanding police reform, often through lawless acts. Many of them jump to conclusions about incidents even before investigations have been completed. As emotions often overtake truth and restraint, the stage has been set for a war on cops. In 2015, Sheriff Deputy Darren Goforth was shot fifteen times while filling up his patrol car. In July 2016, a man ambushed and fired upon a group of police officers in Texas, killing five. In August 2017, six police officers were shot in Florida, and in Pennsylvania, two were killed and four wounded. We are experiencing one of the biggest surges in assaults and even murders of law enforcement officers in our country's history. These attacks are difficult to grasp since those in law enforcement go out each day with the intent to keep the public safe and rush to their aid in dangerous situations. In 2017, during Hurricane Harvey, veteran police officer, Sergeant Steve Perez, was like so many officers who left his home to help others. When his wife urged him to stay home, he said, "We've got work to do." Trapped in his car by the floodwaters, he drowned. Reckless demonstrators create additional stress, causing low morale for those on the job, and police departments are having a difficult time recruiting officers. Although we are not in this profession to gain recognition or praise, it is disheartening to face the antagonism and disdain, especially since the criticism is often unwarranted and inaccurate. We cannot allow such times to overwhelm us as we press on, doing what we know is right.

> "When the valley is deep, when the mountain is steep,
> When the body is weary, when we stumble and fall,
> When the choices are hard, when we're battered and scarred,
> When we've spent our resources, when we've given our all,
> In Jesus name, we press on." Lyrics from "Press On" by Selah

"God will often give you more than you can handle so you can learn to be dependent on Him rather than on yourself." Craig Groeschel, pastor/author

Psalm 118:13-14, 2 Corinthians 4:8-9, Philippians 3:14

SHIELD

Upon graduation from the PSP Academy, I received a significant symbol of this profession, a badge, which some departments refer to as a "shield." This shiny piece of metal represents our induction into an elite "brotherhood/sisterhood" which is very different from most other professions. It has great significance to us, and we carry it with us every day, both on and off duty, and often even after we retire. In many departments, when an officer is killed in the line of duty, members place a thin black band on the center of the badge, called a mourning band, in memory of their fallen comrade. It is usually worn for a thirty-day period from the date of death. On a department vehicle that displays a badge, black tape is often used in the same manner. Some officers come to think of a shield as something that could ultimately keep them from harm, but the one that we carry does not provide any assurance of that.

Because of what we are called upon to do each day, we know that at any moment we could be called into harm's way. As Believers who know our true source of safety, we should regularly call out to the Lord for His shield of protection. His word tells us that He is there to provide us all the protection that we need. Psalm 18:30 says, "As for God, His way is perfect; the word of the Lord is flawless. He is a shield for all who take refuge in Him." His protection, especially in times of our own weakness, will strengthen us and allow us to keep fighting against evil and injustice.

"The safest place in the world is in the will of God, and the safest protection in all the world is the name of God." Warren Wiersbe, pastor/author

2 Samuel 22:3-4, Psalm 91:4, 2 Thessalonians 3:3

SUPERNATURAL STRENGTH

The law enforcement profession is not for those who are weak, for there are constant physical, mental, and emotional demands. Sometimes, it was difficult to go on as I faced physical challenges almost daily. Having the stamina to push on when we feel that there is nothing left may require strength beyond our human capabilities. Arriving at the scene of a chain-reaction crash involving three vehicles and a tractor trailer, I felt anxious and helpless when I saw that the first vehicle was wedged underneath the truck. The second vehicle had crashed into the first, and the third had followed. As smoke billowed from the engine of the first car, I rushed to its occupants, knowing that the car could soon be in flames. In the front seat, a male was bleeding profusely from his head and face while a woman sat motionless in the passenger seat, and three young children screamed hysterically in the rear seat. Frantically attempting to gain entry with little success, I was relieved when a passing motorist came to my aid, and together we were able to pry the doors open.

Although physical strength on the job is critical, more important is the need to be strong in our stand for Christ in those things that we know are right. At times, that may mean being willing to be ridiculed or even persecuted for what we believe. Psalm 31:24 says, "Be strong and take heart, all you who hope in the Lord." Isaiah 40:28-29 reminds us that our Lord stands ready to help us: "Do you not know? Have you not heard? The Lord is the everlasting God, the Creator of the ends of the earth. He will not grow tired or weary, and His understanding no one can fathom. He gives strength to the weary and increases the power of the weak."

"When a man has no strength, if he leans on God, he becomes powerful."
D.L. Moody, American evangelist

Exodus 15:2, Ephesians 6:10, Philippians 4:1

LEST WE FORGET

On September 11, 2001, the terrorist attack that occurred on U.S soil took the lives of 2,996, and more than 6,000 were wounded. Seventy-one law enforcement officers along with 343 fire fighters gave up their lives while performing brave acts of heroism in an attempt to save others. The greatest number of deaths of law enforcement officers in American history occurred as a result of this single event. Those officers, firefighters, and other first responders left their homes that day, some planning on a regular tour of duty, but expecting to return home to their families. Some who were not scheduled for duty that day were called in to assist in the aftermath of this terrible tragedy. Others voluntarily rushed to help at the scene before they got the call. All of them knew that their lives were on the line. Their sacrifices were remarkable, from those who were injured to those who thereafter suffered from inhaling the poisoned air, and especially from those who paid the ultimate price.

We Believers must never forget the full and perfect sacrifice that our Lord made to reconcile the sins of the entire world for all who believe. Our sinless Savior willingly took on the pain and suffering that we deserve because He loves us. He promised that if we acknowledge Him as our Lord and Savior, on the Day of Judgment, He will declare us not guilty of our sins. While on Earth, in our humanness, we will still continue to sin, but we can find peace in knowing that the sacrifice Christ made covers past, present, and future sins. In John 14:2-3, Jesus comforted the disciples before His crucifixion as He assured them, "I am going there [to His Father's house] to prepare a place for you...and I will come back and take you to be with Me." We **will** spend eternity with Him!

"God proved His love on the Cross. When Christ hung, and bled, and died, it was as if God was saying to the world, 'I love you.'" Billy Graham, evangelist/author

Matthew 27:27-31, Hebrews 9:28, 1 Peter 2:24

POSITIVE DIFFERENCE

An elderly woman arrived home and immediately saw that the previously locked back door was open, and shattered glass covered her deck. Entering the house, she realized that someone had ransacked her home, for her possessions were strewn throughout the house. When I arrived, I thought of my grandmother as the woman sat crumpled in a chair, heartbroken and sobbing, while sentimentally describing many of her personal possessions. Evidence was gathered, and fingerprints were lifted and quickly compared. Amazingly, I made an arrest the following day, and the majority of her possessions were recovered. I could not wait to return to the woman's home to share the good news. When I saw how thrilled she was as she thanked me repeatedly, a tremendous sense of satisfaction swept over me, for I had made a difference in her life.

Such acts of kindness may lead us to think that we need to do good deeds continually to be fully accepted by our Creator. However, this dictum that we get something only if we give something is irrelevant for a Christ-follower. There is nothing that we have to do or can do to secure a place in Heaven, for Christ has fully paid the ultimate price on the cross, wiping away all of our sins. Ephesians 2:8-9 reminds us: "For it is by grace you have been saved, through faith--and this is not from yourselves, it is the gift of God—not by works, so that no one can boast." Actually, there really is something for free, and nothing can compare to this free gift of eternal life in heaven with our Lord. Believe in God. Believe in His Son, Jesus. Believe that His Son willingly came to this earth, knowing that He would suffer a cruel and vicious death. Know that He paid the full price, once and for all, for our ongoing sinfulness in this world. His message offers a real and a positive difference!

"A worker who has done a good job can boast and feel a sense of pride in the work he has accomplished. Yet all of that is contrary to grace or a gift. Grace rules out any sense of merit, and a gift does away with any sense of something earned or paid for."

T.A. McMahon, author

John 1:12, Romans 4:23-25, 1 Peter 3:18

PERCEPTIONS

The trooper received a call from dispatch that a distraught woman needed to see an officer as soon as possible. When he approached the home, a woman was at the open doorway with her cell phone in her hand. Nervously, she handed her phone to the trooper and said, "I just received this email from someone I don't even know, and it is really concerning." As he read the message: "Are you still planning on bombing the church today? Do you need any help?" the trooper was also alarmed and told the woman that he needed her phone and would begin an investigation. Returning to the barracks, he showed the message to one of the detectives. The phone was "pinged," and the address of the sender was determined. The trooper went immediately to the location and confronted a woman who exclaimed, "Oh no! I didn't mean to send that to her. I meant to send it to the pastor!" Realizing that her response still was alarming, she further explained, "Our church has cockroaches, and they were scheduled to bomb them this afternoon."

When we make a decision to accept Jesus as our Lord and Savior, we are empowered to become ambassadors for Christ. Our transformation should be perceptible to others, as described in 2 Corinthians 5:17: "If anyone is in Christ, he is a new creation; the old has gone, the new has come!" Ephesians 4:22-24 instructs us "with regard to your former way of life...put off your old self...and put on your new self, created to be like God in true righteousness and holiness." Our conversion will cause us to reflect the "fruit of the Spirit: "love, joy, peace, patience kindness, goodness, faithfulness, gentleness, and self-control." Galatians 5:22-23.

"God in His love always wills what is best for us. In His wisdom He always knows what is best, and in His sovereignty, He has the power to bring it about."
Jerry Bridges, Bible teacher/author

Psalm 51:10, Romans 12:2, Galatians 5:13-14

FULL SUPPORT

Because we repeatedly see the most violent, angry, pitiful, and selfish side of humanity, we may feel despair, anger, and doubt. Dealing with loss of life, crashes that left the occupants maimed and scarred for life, or serious harm to children often took an emotional toll on me, in spite of my belief that I was strong enough to handle anything. One day, with a search warrant in hand, I entered the apartment of a young woman who was using and dealing methamphetamine. Roaches were crawling on the walls and ceiling, and piles of dirty dishes were stacked in the sink and on tables and countertops. A young baby in a stroller wore filthy clothing and had not been changed or bathed in many days. The mother was visibly high on meth. My first concern was, "What happens to this innocent baby when her mom crashes and sleeps for days on end?" After a thorough search, evidence of use of the drug was apparent, but no product was found. As I glanced at the baby, something caused me to walk over and feel around her stroller. Numerous packages of methamphetamine were hidden there. This disturbing memory is one that I will never forget.

Often, when our brothers and sisters on the job sense that we are struggling, they come alongside us to provide needed emotional support. Such responses are critical in our profession. In addition, we Believers have an extra level of support that we can tap into and also provide to others around us. This strength comes from a close relationship with Christ and a daily walk with Him. He never walks away from us. He knows exactly what we need and wants us to call out to Him, and He is disappointed when we do not. He knows that we cannot face the challenges of life on our own and that we must depend on Him. He waits for us to call out His name. "Fear not, for I have redeemed you; I have summoned you by name; you are mine." Isaiah 43:1.

"God will not let you go. He has handcuffed Himself to you in love. And He owns the only key." Max Lucado, author/pastor

Isaiah 40:29, Ephesians 4:21-24, Philippians 4:13

WITNESS PROTECTION

At times, when those charged with significant crimes are facing a long prison term, they agree to work with law enforcement. They provide invaluable information about ongoing criminal activity, and some arrests could not be made without their help. They also testify for the prosecution against their cohorts in crimes, many of whom have been their friends for years. Michael Franzese became a member of the Colombo crime family and eventually became one of the most wealthy and powerful mob bosses in America. After numerous arrests, Franzese "rolled over" and began to work with law enforcement. Contrary to what most mob informants do, he made a risky decision and refused to go into the Witness Protection Program. In his book, *Blood Covenant,* Franzese quotes Bernie Welsh, a retired FBI organized crime expert and legendary mob hunter. Upon learning that Franzese was cooperating with law enforcement, Welch predicted, "He will get wacked." In addition, Edward McDonald, former attorney-in-charge, Organized Crime Strike Force, Eastern District of New York, said, "I wouldn't want to be in Michael Franzese's shoes. I don't think his life expectancy is very substantial."

In reality, we all need to be in a "protection" program. Because we are all terminal and will leave this temporary home in God's timing, we seek assurance that Heaven will be our destiny. That promise is secured at the moment that we acknowledge Jesus as the Son of God and ask Him to forgive our sins. "That if you confess with your mouth, 'Jesus is Lord,' and believe in your heart that God raised Him from the dead, you **will** be saved." Romans 10:9. Michael Franzese accepted Jesus as his Lord and is alive today. He considers his relationship with the Lord, to be the reason why he still lives. Because of that relationship, all of his sins have been forgiven, and he will live in Heaven for eternity.

"Saving us is the greatest and most concrete demonstration of God's love, the definitive display of His grace throughout time and eternity."
David Jeremiah, pastor/author

Psalm 32:7, Psalm 140:4, 2 Thessalonians 3:3

THE STRUGGLE

Asked to assist in an undercover operation for "ladies of the night" who had become bold on the city streets, we left in our unmarked cars. I drove a Mustang used for speed control which had a police radio. I slung my coat over the radio, attempting to conceal it. On my first trip down a city street, a woman motioned me to pull over. Entering on the passenger side, she immediately pulled the coat from the radio and asked what it was. I claimed to be a fire fighter on call, and she gave directions to a dark, deserted parking lot. After she described what I needed to hear to arrest her, I pulled out my badge and placed her under arrest. She began shouting, opened her door, and tried to get out. I clasped one handcuff around her hand as she struggled wildly, opened the door, and put both feet on the pavement. Still holding on to her with my handcuff, I straddled the radio and the seat and landed next to her. As she continued to fight, I was amazed by her strength. Eventually, I secured the second cuff on her and pulled her back into my car. After driving to the designated meeting point, I met with a vice officer from the city. Opening the passenger door, he exclaimed, "Good job! We finally got **him**!" Privately embarrassed that I had not discerned that this was a man, I did feel better to know that I was not so weak after all.

Some people mistakenly think that once they become Christians, they will not have to struggle. However, daily living can become more difficult because Satan is determined to lure us into our previous patterns of sin. Pastor David Jeremiah says, "We are being pulled in opposite directions. Our flesh is magnetized to sin. It pulls, draws, and entices us. The Holy Spirit dwelling inside Christians is magnetized to holiness. While the war within may leave us exhausted and overwhelmed, this simple truth can transform our perspective on the tension we feel: The Holy Spirit has come to set us free." Jude 1:20-21 tells us, "Build yourselves up in your most holy faith, and pray in the Holy Spirit. Keep yourselves in God's love."

John 10:10, James 4:7, 1 John 3:8

ACCOSTED

When a local plant went on strike, initially demonstrators were relatively civil. However, when fellow employees disregarded the demands of striking workers and drove past the picket line, tempers flared. We monitored the strikers closely as we drove past the plant regularly. By the third week, tempers were erupting, and strikers were blocking passage to those who wanted to enter the building. We were now a steady presence to ensure that they had a safe passage. Soon, some began breaking the law as protestors began propelling rocks and bottles at the vehicles of those attempting to work. As protestors planned to storm the plant and attempt access to the owners and those still working, we realized that time was running out, so we geared up for the confrontation. With riot helmets on, gas masks in place, shields, batons and mace in our possession, we gathered in formation. The rioters were prepared with any objects that they could carry, and they began to throw them at us. Our presence and our actions further incited the hostile protestors, and we were accosted for over one hour. As the number of protestors increased, more officers were dispatched to finally quell the disturbance.

Throughout the world today, various groups are accosted by those with different beliefs. Often these attacks by one group on another result from differing religious ideologies. Christians are frequently targets of verbal as well as physical attacks. In some countries, they are subjected to brutal beating, imprisonment, beheadings, or death by a firing squad. We need to stand firm in our faith and not be swayed by those who would attempt to keep us from speaking about what we strongly believe. Jesus said, "Blessed are you when people insult you, persecute you, and falsely say all kinds of evil against you because of Me." Matthew 5:11.

"The devil doesn't persecute those who aren't making a godly difference in the world." Paul Chappel, pastor/author

Psalm 1:1-2, 1 Peter 5:8-9, Revelation 3:5

BEING DIFFERENT

As a member of law enforcement, the first time that I put on my uniform and went out in public, I quickly realized how much I was set apart from others. It took some time before I got used to people staring at me when I got out of my car or drove down the street in a marked vehicle. One day, shortly after I had moved to the detective bureau and my uniform became a business suit, I was dispatched to a robbery in progress at a bank. Upon my arrival, several uniformed officers were also pulling in, but the suspects were no longer there. Those who were in the bank during the robbery were visibly upset as they walked toward the officers in uniform and began to blurt out details of the crime. My presence went almost unnoticed. After several minutes, the victims calmed, and one of the uniformed officers pointed at me and said that I would be conducting the investigation. I quickly realized that without a uniform, there would be times that my presence would not be noticed. Now, I was different and not identifiable as a member of law enforcement unless I chose to make myself known.

As Believers in Christ, we are set apart by the Lord as well. Sadly, however, if our lives are not different in a positive way, others may not be interested to hear about our relationship with Jesus. Philippians 1:27 says, "Whatever happens, conduct yourself in a manner worthy of the gospel of Christ." James 4:7-8 further describes how we are required to be different: "Submit yourselves, then, to God. Resist the devil, and he will flee from you. Come near to God, and He will come near to you." Although we have been set apart, it is easy to conform to the ways of the world. However, through the power we have in the presence of the Holy Spirit, we do have the strength and ability to be different. We have to make that choice daily, often, multiple times.

"God never said the journey would be easy, but He did say that the arrival would be worthwhile." Max Lucado, pastor/author

Romans 6:18, Romans 8:1-2, Ephesians 5:8-10

INTERRUPTION

When I became convicted about writing *In His Grip,* I did not realize the magnitude of this endeavor. At times, I have wondered why I had not considered a weekly devotional rather than 365 days. As this book has been evolving for well over three years, I have become more and more aware of the reality of Satan and the fact that he is doing everything he can to keep this book from going to print. Just today, as I was working on an entry, my computer froze, causing me to spend considerable time trying to remedy the problem. Finally, I realized that the only thing that I had not done was to pray. So, I began, "Heavenly Father, I come to You now..." I was not testing God because I believe that if the problem were not to be resolved for some reason, He was allowing that. When I returned to the problem computer, it was no longer frozen, and I was able to continue writing without interruption. This is not the first time such a situation has occurred during this writing. At times, when my wife (who is my editor-in-chief) and I have been working diligently toward the completion of this project, it is evident that the evil one is at work. She will call out from her adjacent office, "He's back!" and I know exactly who she is talking about. We have reached the place where we now chuckle, and we are further motivated and even more determined to press on.

"Set goals so big that unless God helps you, you will be a miserable failure."
Bill Bright, evangelist/author

"There is not a single thing that Jesus can't change, control, and conquer because He is the living Lord."
Franklin Graham, evangelist/CEO of Samaritan's Purse

"The only time my prayers are never answered is on the golf course."
Billy Graham, pastor/evangelist/author

Proverbs 15:29, Jeremiah 29:12, 1 John 5:14-15

KEVLAR

Each day on the job, the possibility exists that someone with whom we interact may try to cause us physical harm. The criminal element is often better equipped with a variety of weapons than we are. On occasion, a suspect may be wearing body armor, and some possess armor-piercing ammunition. In recent times, many people have such animosity toward law enforcement officers that they would not intervene on our behalf if they saw someone trying to attack us physically; in fact, some may even join in to inflict harm. Recently, two officers were on the edge of a busy highway, attempting to subdue a driver who had become physically aggressive. As they struggled on the ground, the assailant pulled out a gun and began firing at both officers. He struck one in unprotected areas of his body, while the other was hit in his vest. Although many drivers witnessed the initial altercation, not one person stopped to assist the officers.

We know that our spiritual safety is also under attack, for the evil one seeks to bring harm against Believers. Even those who have been spiritual leaders sometimes fall to the temptations they face. What better trophy for the evil one than to topple someone who seeks to walk in the Lord's will? In 2 Thessalonians 3:3, we are assured that, "The Lord is faithful, and He will strengthen and protect you from the evil one." However, we must also accept the responsibility to be proactive in this battle. Ephesians 6:11-18 advises us how to prepare for the spiritual battle: "Put on the full armor of God, so that you can take your stand against the devil's schemes…with the belt of truth…the breastplate of righteousness… the gospel of peace…the shield of faith…the helmet of salvation and the sword of the Spirit, which is the word of God. And pray in the Spirit on all occasions with all kinds of prayers and requests."

"There is nothing more calming in difficult moments than knowing there's someone fighting with you."
Mother Teresa, nun/founder of Missionaries of Charity

2 Samuel 22:2-4, Psalm 4:8, Proverbs 29:25, John 16:33

PAID THE PRICE

If we had not previously realized the dangers of the job, we soon do when we serve in the law enforcement community. We know that we may have to give up our own lives in the line of duty. When an officer stopped a car, the driver exited his vehicle and fired back at the patrol car, but the officer was not hit. After the suspect was taken into custody, the officer examined the bullet holes in the patrol car and became unnerved as he realized how close he had come to the end of his life. The following day, he went to the sergeant and resigned. He was not ready to pay the ultimate price. A line in the Pennsylvania State Police Call of Honor says, "if need be, to lay down my life as others have done before me." In 2017, officers across the country paid the ultimate price, including: Detective Steven McDonald- NYPD, Cause of Death- gunfire; Det. Jerry Walker- Elm, TX, Cause of Death- gunfire; Sheriff Colt Allery- Rolette ND, Cause of Death- gunfire; PO Keith Boyer- Whittier, CA, Cause of Death- gunfire; Sgt. Shawn Anderson- Baton Rouge, LA, Cause of Death- gunfire; Cpl. Stephen Ballard- Delaware SP, Cause of Death- gunfire; Isaac Morales- US Border Protection, Cause of Death- Stabbed; S.A. Michael Walker- VA SP, Cause of Death- gunfire; Trooper Landon Weaver- PSP, Cause of Death- gunfire...and the list goes on and on and on. Although none would have chosen this way for the end of their watch, we always recognize it as a possibility, one we never forget.

Jesus Christ, the only Son of God, came to Earth in human form and actually volunteered to give up His life. Although He was sinless, He willingly laid down His life, thus paying the ultimate price for the penalty we deserve. Why would our Creator sacrifice Himself for each of us? It was because of His unconditional love for His creation. He did not hesitate to offer Himself so that we could spend eternity with Him. Romans 6:23: "For the wages of sin is death, but the gift of God is eternal life in Christ Jesus our Lord."

"It was Christ who willingly went to the cross, and it was our sins that took him there."
Franklin Graham, evangelist/CEO Samaritan's Purse

Isaiah 53:3-5, Romans 5:8, 1 Peter 3:18

DAILY WARFARE

Every day on the job, we start our shift not knowing all that we will encounter. In the last few years, there appears to be a war on cops like never before. The number of on-duty deaths is disheartening, but some off-duty officers died because they chose to go to work to help others. Pennsylvania Trooper Robert Lapp was off-duty and doing yard work. Two fellow officers were on their way to serve an arrest warrant and stopped their car when they saw him. After they told Lapp the details, he volunteered to assist. When they entered the home, the suspect rushed out of a room, aimed a weapon, and fired. Trooper Lapp was struck and killed. That night and for many years to follow, there was an empty chair at the dinner table, one that could never be filled.

Officers today are equipped with firearms, Tasers, handcuffs, Chemical Mace, and sometimes, shields. They also have extensive training on methods to ensure their safety. However, because Christians will daily engage in spiritual warfare, they will need additional "equipment." In 2 Corinthians 10:3-4, Paul says, "For though we live in the world, we do not wage war as the world does. The weapons we fight with are not the weapons of the world. On the contrary, they have divine power to demolish strongholds." In Matthew 26:41, Christ said, "**Watch** and **pray** so that you will not fall into temptation." In 1 Peter 2:11, Peter urges us to "**Abstain** from sinful desires which war against your soul." Paul tells us in I Corinthians 16:13-14, "**Be on** your **guard; stand firm in the faith**; be men of **courage**; be **strong. Do everything in love.**" James 4:7-8 advises us to "**Submit** yourselves, then, **to God. Resist the devil**, and he will flee from you. **Come near to God**, and He will come near to you." Many, many other weapons are defined for us in Scripture, and we should study to learn about them, but practicing just these few will provide good under-armor.

"The Lord made provisions for our nakedness in battle. He hasn't sent us to war unprotected."
Dr. Charles Stanley, pastor/author

Deuteronomy 31:6, Isaiah 41:10, John 10:28-30

BLOODY SIN

Past notorious criminals such as Jack the Ripper, Charles Manson, and Ted Bundy shared one common trait, a desire to take human life. In the book, *Infamous Murders* (Verdict Press), the unnamed author says, "Ever since Cain slew Abel, the murder of a fellow human being has been regarded in all societies as a crime of exceptional horror. Often, it was punished with the death penalty, even when capital punishment had been abolished for other offenses." Whenever I was involved in a homicide investigation, it took top priority, and we worked diligently to gather evidence. On rare occasions, the accused was found "not guilty" and was freed, even though we felt that we had an air-tight case. At such times, my discouraged colleagues and I were stunned and frustrated, for we were convinced that the suspect had spilled another's blood.

Jesus was found guilty of a crime for which there was no evidence, and He was sentenced to the ultimate penalty. Tortured and beaten, He suffered excruciating pain on the cross without resisting, for He knew that His innocent blood was required to rescue humanity from their sins. In Mark 14:24, at the Last Supper, Jesus had said to the disciples, "This is my blood of the covenant which is poured out for many." That includes even those responsible for His crucifixion. They would have been pardoned by Him if they later recognized the wrong that they had committed, believed that He was the Son of God, and asked Him for forgiveness. In Luke 23:34, sinless Christ cried out, "Father, forgive them for they know not what they are doing." Was He speaking about the Roman soldiers who had just nailed Him to the cross, or about the religious leaders who were so determined to have Jesus die in this vicious manner... or perhaps about you and me?

"With Jesus's last breath on the cross, He declared the debt of sin cancelled, completely satisfied. Nothing else required. He paid our debt in full by giving His life so that we might live forever." Charles Swindoll, pastor/author

Isaiah 53:3-5, Ephesians 2:13, 1 Peter 3:18

GOD'S LOVE

As I so often dealt with the dark side of society, I sometimes wondered if there were more bad people in this world than good. From Sandy Hook, Connecticut, to Parkland, Florida, innocent children in schools have lost their lives at the hands of mass murderers. On June 17, 2015, a White Supremacist interrupted a Bible study at an historic Black church in Charleston, SC. He fatally shot nine church members and wounded numerous others. At his hearing, families of the victims spoke one after another to express their forgiveness and prayers for his soul. One said, "We are the family that love built. We have no room for hating, so we have to forgive." However, Reverend Sharon Risher, who lost her mother, two cousins, and a beloved friend, could not speak. On Martin Luther King Day in 2018, she told a college audience that it took her two years to process her loss and emotions. "My journey of moving toward total forgiveness has been hard, lonely, and complicated." However, as she has healed and since publicly professed her forgiveness, her mission now is "to help other people know that hate won't win."

Many of us have heard the expression, "Hate the sin, but love the sinner." Although that is not always easy to do, God has already set an example for us to follow. "For God so loved the world, (not just a few of us, but the entire world) that He gave His one and only Son, that whoever believes in Him shall not perish but will have eternal life." John 3:16. In reality, not one of us deserves God's love, but He offers it to us nonetheless. Although we may not feel any love or compassion toward some, in Matthew 22:39, Jesus commands us to, "Love your neighbor as yourself." In Ephesians 4:32, we are reminded to model Christ's behavior: "Be kind and compassionate to one another, forgiving each other, just as in Christ God forgave you."

"Forgiveness is one of the most beautiful words in the human vocabulary."
Billy Graham, pastor/evangelist/author

Romans 5:8, Romans 8:37-39, Colossians 3:12-14

CARING ENOUGH

Lord, some days it's really hard for me
to care about those I often see.
Many are the dregs in this world;
without them, how better life would be

So many around me are reeling in pain
caused by others who don't even care.
Why should I show them compassion
when their actions are so hard to bear?

Some are self-destructive, bitter, and angry--
violent beyond what words can say.
Do You really want me to love them
when Your laws they refuse to obey?

And then somehow You remind me
that the treatment to Christ was unfair.
It was cruel, vicious, and heartless,
all of which You were aware.

He was unjustly condemned and beaten,
punished on that old, wooden cross.
Yet, You loved those responsible
in spite of Your terrible loss.

If all You are asking of me, Lord,
is to show Your love each day,
I pray You will continue to help me
and teach me the perfect way.

rfg

IN THE LIGHT

Most in law enforcement find that working night shift is often more difficult than working in daylight hours. Criminals often use the cover of darkness to elude officers and conceal their activities. In September 2014, a lone gunman secreted himself at night in a heavily wooded area across the road from the Blooming Grove State Police barracks. At shift change, he fired a .308 caliber rifle toward the barracks, killing Corporal Bryon Dickson II and severely injuring Trooper Alex Douglass. In the ensuing 40 days, federal, state, and local law enforcement officers searched the dense woods to capture the killer. At times, helicopters from several jurisdictions searched overhead. However, the incredibly dense foliage had not yet fallen, so even the infrared thermal imaging, could not detect the perpetrator.

In the daytime, we will also face those who are intent on doing evil. Scripture tells of many who fell prey to the evil desires of others, but also of those who escaped and stayed the course. So that we do not fall into the hands of the evil one and begin to justify things that we know are wrong, we must rely on God's word, our constant source of light. We can be confident knowing that we do not go through dark periods alone, for the Lord is standing with us. As we remain in God's word, we will see more clearly as it sheds light on every area of our lives. "Your word is a lamp to my feet and a light for my path." Psalm 119:105.

"For the God on the mountain, is still God in the valley. When things go wrong, He'll make them right. And the God of the good times is still God in the bad times. The God of the day is still God in the night."
Tim Spencer, Tracy Dartt, songwriters *

John 8:12, Hebrews 4:12, 1 John 1:7

*You may want to go to YouTube and see Lynda Randle on video as she sings "God on the Mountain." When my wife's beloved friend was lying in a hospital bed, we shared this video with her and her husband. As they both broke into tears, her friend said, "I always knew **about** Jesus, but I never **knew** Him before this." Although she passed away shortly afterwards, we **know** that we will all be reunited one day in heaven.

DIFFERENT EYES

Dispatched to a robbery in progress, several officers and I converged at a bank. The perpetrator had already left, but as we entered the bank, we found four female tellers still visibly shaken and huddling behind the counter. To get an accurate description of the event, we separated the victims, and I escorted one woman, who appeared to be most in control, into a back office. I asked how many came into the bank, and she said only one, but a woman sat at the wheel of a tan vehicle parked in front. When I asked her to describe the robber, she said that he was a white, heavy-set male, about 6"2, with brown hair and glasses, and a bandanna covered his face. He held a small black gun which he pointed at them. I then joined another officer and asked for the description provided by the victim that he had interviewed. She said that the perpetrator was Asian, thin, about 5"6, and balding, and the mask covered only his mouth. He held a silver semi-automatic and pointed it at the floor; the car was black; a male drove it. It is not uncommon for witnesses of a crime, who are totally rattled, to have very different recollections.

Often when we Believers try to live a better life by seeking wisdom and direction from the Lord, Satan will cause us to see our sinful ways through his eyes so that we justify what we know is wrong. The evil one strives to tempt and corrupt us. He is real. In John 14:30, Christ referred to him as "the prince of this world" and in John 4:44 as "a murderer...and a liar and the father of lies." 2 Corinthians 11:14 says, He "masquerades as an angel of light." Yet, the Bible encourages us: "For we do not have a high priest who is unable to sympathize with our weaknesses, but we have one who has been tempted in every way just as we are--yet was without sin. Let us then approach the throne of mercy with confidence so that we may receive mercy and find grace to help us in our time of need." Hebrews 4:15-16.

"Hell is the highest reward that the devil can offer you for being a servant of his."
Billy Sunday, Christian evangelist

James 4:7-8, 1 Peter 5:8-9, Revelation 20:10

SHACKLED

When the officer obtained an arrest warrant for someone that he had previously arrested several times, he told a younger officer that he needed assistance in serving the warrant. They went to a location where the suspect frequently hung out. The seasoned officer, who was driving the police vehicle, saw their target and pulled to the curb. Both officers got out of the vehicle and approached the wanted person. When they got alongside the man, the younger officer was told to take him to the patrol car and "hook him up." As he got closer to the car, he went to put his cuffs on the prisoner. Seeing what was about to happen, the suspect began running down the street. After the younger officer chased him for several blocks, he handcuffed the criminal and brought him back to the vehicle where the older officer was waiting. Breathing heavily, the younger one said to his partner, "Can you believe that?" The older officer replied, "Yeah. He did that the last time I tried to arrest him." Outraged, the younger one blurted, "Why didn't you tell me that?" The answer, "I thought he just didn't like **me.**"

Being restrained or shackled and losing one's ability to move freely is an oppressive experience. It is similar to the feelings some have because of the past sins in their lives. It is not uncommon to hear someone say, "There is no way God would ever forgive me for what I have done in my past." However, that is not the God that we serve. "Who is a God like you? You do not stay angry forever but delight in showing mercy." Micah 7:18. "I, even I, am He who blots out your transgression, for My own sake, and remembers your sins no more." Isaiah 43:25. God's word is specific and complete. He forgives all who acknowledge that Christ is the Son of God who died for our sins; confess that they sinned, and ask for forgiveness. Sins are no longer kept on file; our record is blotted out, destroyed, and we are unshackled.

"God will use your mess for good. We see a perfect mess; God sees a perfect chance to train, test, and teach." Max Lucado, author

Psalm 103:12, Luke 7:48, 1 John 2:1-2

SEARCHING

The five-year-old child visiting relatives with his mom and dad was having a happy time. Since he was autistic, his parents had to be attentive so that he would not wander off. As guests continued to arrive, everyone was in a celebratory mood, and the home became crowded with family and friends. After a while, the parents of the young boy lost track of their son. When several minutes passed with no sign of the child, it was evident that he was no longer in the home. Everyone quickly scattered throughout the neighborhood, hoping that he soon would be located, for the temperature was below freezing, and his winter coat remained in the home. When anxious minutes turned into an hour, the police were notified and joined the ongoing search. The area of the search expanded, but still the boy was not found. After several agonizing hours, an officer found the toddler a good distance away from the home. He was face down at the edge of a pond, and his life had ended.

On the job, we conduct many types of searches, such as for missing persons, escapees, contraband, stolen property, as well as crime scenes. Some have to be done quickly because of exigent circumstances while others allow us more time. As people seek answers for many things, what is most important is knowing where we will go when our life here is over. Some are uncomfortable thinking about that, and others believe that they have no control over their final destination. The truth can easily be found if we take time and search God's word. It does not require us to be scholarly theologians. If we accept His offer of eternal life, confess our sinfulness, past, present, and future, and then seek to live a God-honoring life, we can have true peace, knowing that we will spend eternity with Christ in heaven. In John 11:25-26, Jesus said to Martha, "I am the resurrection and the life. He who believes in Me will live even though he dies; and whoever lives and believes in Me will never die." 1 John 2:25 tells us, "And this is what He promised us—even eternal life."

"There is a reason why life can feel empty. Man was created with a yearning that God alone is able to satisfy." Dr. Charles Stanley, pastor/author

John 1:12, Romans 5:8, Ephesians 2:8-10

TESTING

When we confront a suspect that we believe to be responsible for a crime, we are often told that someone else did it. After being dispatched to a home that had just been burglarized, I entered to find open drawers that had been emptied and personal items strewn throughout the home. Immediately, I recognized that it would be difficult to process the crime scene. As I rummaged through the chaos looking for evidence, a black leather wallet that was partially covered by clothing caught my eye. Inside was a photo driver's license which did not belong to any occupants of the home. Later that day, I located and confronted the suspect who, as expected, denied any involvement. However, when I asked for his driver's license, his look of resignation revealed that he knew he could not pass the test to prove his innocence.

In 1 Thessalonians 2:4, Paul tells Believers that God does "test our hearts." However, we are never tested beyond what we can handle. Paul explains, "No temptation has seized you except which is common to man. And God is faithful; He will not let you be tempted beyond what you can bear. But when you are tempted, He will also provide a way out so that you can stand under it." 1 Corinthians 10:13. God does allow things into our lives that we, ourselves, would not choose. Although it may be difficult for us to grasp, these trials [tests] are for our own good. He will guide us and help us through them and ultimately reward us. James 1:12 encourages us with a promise: "Blessed is the man who perseveres under trial because when he has stood the test, he will receive the crown of life that God has promised to those who love Him."

"God has a special purpose for my trial. It is designed to meet a certain need, to be an example to others as they watch how we deal, and we can say to them, 'I have been there.' The trial will be if I trust in faith and demonstrate perseverance under pressure."
Dr. Charles Stanley, pastor/author

2 Corinthians 13:5-8, I Peter 4:12, 2 Peter 2:9

SAFELY HOME

Matt is a New York City Fire Fighter. His shifts are long and often dangerous, and he has seen many tragic incidents, often including loss of life. In 2017, a fire considered to be the worst since 1990, broke out at an apartment complex. The fire began in the apartment of a three-year-old boy who was playing with the gas stove. The stairwell in the building acted like a chimney, allowing flames to spread quickly through the complex. Matt was one of the first responders and together with his team quickly attempted to extinguish the inferno as outside temperatures fell into the teens. In addition to the searing flames, the firefighters also had to deal with ice and equipment freezing up. As Matt and the other responders realized that there was very little they could do, a feeling of helplessness overcame them. Ultimately, twelve were killed in this tragedy, including several children.

As we enter our homes after being away for the day, we often feel a sense of peace and security. In most cases, home is a place where we can feel safe, but that does not always hold true. The families in the blazing apartments had probably felt that they were out of harm's way just minutes prior to the eruption. As Believers, we know that the only place where we will be totally safe and secure is when we are in the presence of our Lord in Heaven for Eternity. 2 Timothy 4:18 says, "The Lord will rescue me from evil attack and will bring me safely to His heavenly kingdom." "Surely this is our God; we trusted in Him, and He saved us." Isaiah 25:9.

"He who lays up treasures on Earth spends his life backing away from his treasures. To him, death is loss. He who lays up treasures in Heaven looks forward to eternity; he's moving daily toward his treasure. To him, death is gain."
Randy Alcorn, pastor/author

Isaiah 25:8, John 14:2-3, Revelation 21:4

DON'T WANT TO FAIL

Whenever I was called upon to assist in the protection of a United States President, a governor, or a foreign dignitary, I recognized that their safety and even their lives might be in my hands, and I sensed a great flood of responsibility. Because the demands on those in law enforcement are enormous, it is humanly impossible to meet all of the needs of our society with "success." When the thirty-fifth President of the United States, John F. Kennedy, was assassinated, Secret Service Agents felt the great burden of failure. Special Agent Jerry Parr, who protected four vice-presidents and was the Special Agent in Charge for Presidents Carter and Reagan, was then a rookie with one year on the job. Eighteen years later in 1981, he was responsible for saving President Reagan's life after an assassination attempt. Afterwards, he openly expressed his belief that God had led him to save Reagan. Four years later, he left the Secret Service and studied to become a pastor. Parr's book, *In the Secret Service,* details some of the burdens on this elite security agency: "Their professional life has one mission: to protect the principle."

At times, we, too, are expected to go beyond what most people consider to be almost impossible. As Believers, we have an advantage, for we can always rely upon the wisdom and direction from the Lord in whatever we are called to do. We should be turning to the Holy Spirit throughout each day to give us discernment in all that comes our way. He will do so. Even if things do not go according to the way that we believe they should, we cannot lose sight that God is still in control. Ultimately, things will unfold according to His perfect plan.

"Our greatest fear should not be of failure, but of succeeding at things in life that don't really matter." Francis Chan, pastor/author

Joshua 1:9, Isaiah 41:10, 1 Peter 3:14

FOES

Even though our ultimate goal is to help others to resolve an incident to which we have been called, it has become more commonplace to experience opposition from many we encounter. At times, before all the facts have been determined, the news media joins in on second-guessing the split-second decisions that we had to make in difficult and sometimes dangerous situations. When an officer returned to the station, he was immediately called to the office of his sergeant who related that he had just been contacted by someone claiming to have been physically mistreated during an incident. The caller gave a description of the officer and the number of his patrol car. The sergeant said to the officer, "I sure hope for your sake that there is nothing to this." He did not ask the officer to explain anything about the incident and told him to report to his office the following morning. After an agonizing night, the officer returned to work and entered the sergeant's office. Somewhat sheepishly, the sergeant said that after he reviewed the in-car camera in the officer's cruiser, he deemed that no actions by the officer were inappropriate. He concluded, "I hope you charge the complainant not only with disorderly conduct but also for assaulting you."

When we start our day in prayer, asking God to direct our path and to give us wisdom, we can do so knowing that He is with us always. His word tells us that He actually delights in our calling out to Him. He will direct our steps, helping us to face our foes appropriately. Psalm 3:1-4 reminds us, "O Lord, how many are my foes! How many rise up against me! Many are saying of me, 'God will not deliver him.' But you, Lord, are a shield around me, O Lord; You bestow glory on me and lift up my head. To the Lord I cry aloud, and He answers me from His holy hill."

"And our wise Father in Heaven knows when we're going to need things, too. Don't run out ahead of Him."
Corrie ten Boon, author/protector of the Jews in WW II/ Auschwitz survivor

Psalm 109:2-5, Psalm 138:7, Romans 12:14

COURAGEOUS

Perseverance, sensitivity, determination, and courage are but a few of the many attributes that those in law enforcement are expected to have. In the PSP Academy, we were required to take boxing and self-defense, and our instructors attempted to match each cadet with another of similar stature and build. As Joe and I entered the boxing arena, he exclaimed, "This is going to be fun!" Assuming that this bout was probably going to hurt one if not both of us, I asked why he was so enthusiastic. He responded that he was a boxer and had been training for several years. My courage dwindled once he started to punch, for I realized that he was not joking. The more his fist landed on my head and face, the more the instructor encouraged him, yelling, "Hit him harder." Between blows, I tried to tell Joe discreetly to take it easy, but he was having too much fun. However, I did learn a valuable lesson that day and determined that it would be far better for me to avoid physical confrontations on the street whenever possible.

On the job, we can become overwhelmed by the expectations of the many people who are in desperate need of our help. In our humanness, we will become discouraged and sometimes fail. When our well-being is threatened, we can become fearful, and we may lose courage. As Believers, we must remember that we are never alone, and God's word can provide us with the encouragement we need. In Psalm 56:3-4 we read, "When I am afraid, I will trust in You. In God, whose word I praise, In God I trust; I will not be afraid. What can mortal man do to me?"

"Courage is resistance to fear, mastery of fear, not absence of fear... Do the thing you fear most, and the death of fear is certain... It is curious--curious that physical courage should be so common in the world, and moral courage so rare."
Mark Twain, humorist/author

Psalm 27:1, Ephesians 6:10, 2 Timothy 1:7

THE COMFORTER

In 2006, on a rural country road in Lancaster County, Pennsylvania, several children in the Nickel Mines Amish community met in their one-room schoolhouse on a typical morning. Suddenly and without warning, this day turned into a parent's worst nightmare. A lone gunman, a non-Amish resident of the quiet community, burst into the school and fired weapons, killing five and injuring five other young girls. Pennsylvania Troopers were called to the scene and smashed through secured windows and a door to subdue the gunman. This tragedy had a tremendous impact on both the survivors and those who had lost loved ones. It also had a profound impact on the responding troopers, many of whom had young daughters close to the ages of the murdered and brutally injured girls. Shortly afterward, one trooper, a father of young children, resigned from the department, knowing that he could no longer deal with the atrocities that he often faced on the job. Many of the troopers involved in this horrific incident continued to interact with this close-knit community that is usually not open to outsiders. Some of the Amish later said that ongoing interactions with the troopers and first responders brought them great comfort and healing, helping them to lessen their grief.

Believers know that just prior to Jesus's leaving this world, He told His disciples that He was going to leave a Comforter for them. And Jesus said, "And I will ask the Father, and He will give you another Counselor to be with you forever--the Spirit of truth." John 14:16. At the moment that we accepted Christ, we, too, received the gift of the Comforter, the Holy Spirit, who dwells within each one of us. He continues to watch over us and will never leave us. He intercedes for us in our prayers when we cannot find the words that we need. He will provide wisdom, peace, and comfort every day of our lives when we reach out to Him.

"God speaks through a variety of means. In the present, God primarily speaks by the Holy Spirit, through the Bible, prayer, circumstances, and the church."
Henry Blackaby, pastor/author

John 14:26, Acts 2:38, Romans 8:26

NO LONGER SPEAKING

Eugene Francois Vidocq was a 19th century detective and former criminal who helped police solve "cold case" homicides. In 1990, the Vidocq Society formed as a non-profit organization in Philadelphia. Members meet monthly to examine evidence and investigate seemingly unsolvable homicides and disappearances in the USA that are at least two years old. The 100+ members have diverse backgrounds including: anthropological reconstruction experts, firearms examiners, forensic pathologists, financial investigators, bloodstain pattern analysts, arson investigators, psychological profilers, handwriting analysts, and document authenticators. Many crimes have ultimately been solved through the efforts of the Society. In one such case, which had gone unsolved for fourteen years, a young woman was murdered inside a fast-food restaurant, and the case was considered a "robbery gone wrong." Ultimately, the efforts of the Vidocq Society led to the arrest of an ex-boyfriend who received a life sentence without parole. In their pursuit of justice, the Society is determined to speak for those who can no longer speak for themselves.

A time will come when we will leave this world and face our Maker. If we have not already accepted Jesus as our Lord and Savior while we are alive on Earth, we will have no further opportunity. At that point, nothing more can be said that will cause a holy, righteous God to grant us permission to enter heaven. Jesus is still calling to the unsaved to accept His gift of salvation, but He leaves the choice with us. Jesus said, "Here I am! I stand at the door and knock. If anyone hears my voice and opens the door, I will come in and eat with him, and he with Me. To him who overcomes, I will give the right to sit with Me on my throne...He who has an ear, let him hear..." Revelation 3:20-22. Calling out to Jesus with a very simple prayer will take us from death to life eternal. The time to speak to Him is now--before it is too late.

"With God, life is an endless hope. Without God, life is a hopeless end."
Bill Bright, evangelist

John 5:24, Romans 6:23, Ephesians 2:8-9

EVERYTHING RECORDED

Today, digital forensic science plays an intricate part in solving many crimes. This includes the examination of computers, cellular phones, and GPS devices. Computer-related crime has increased over the years to include hacking, child pornography, cyberstalking, and espionage. Cell phones have provided international and domestic terrorists a means to detonate bombs. Photographs, calendars, phone numbers, and notes seized from a cell phone can provide valuable information that can lead to arrests. A serial killer was convicted for murders committed over a sixteen-year period after a search of his computer led to his arrest. Michael Jackson's doctor was convicted on digital evidence seized from his computer which showed that lethal amounts of a drug were provided to Jackson. Sometimes suspects have argued that they were not in the vicinity of a crime, but an examination and the "pinging" of their cell phone proved otherwise.

Some people may believe that if they have to face their Creator when they leave this world, perhaps He will not remember all the sinfulness of their life. To think that our omnipotent, omniscient God would not remember every incident in our lives and every word spoken is more than foolish. Consider Psalm 147:4, "He determines the number of stars and calls them each by name." Matthew 10:30 tells us, "And even the very hairs on your head are numbered." Matthew 12:36 addresses the words we speak, "But I tell you that men will have to give account on the Day of Judgment for every careless word they have spoken." However, the good news is that when we accept Jesus as our Lord and Savior and determine to live a life more pleasing to Him, He becomes our advocate before our all-knowing Father God. Because our profession of faith in Christ's redeeming blood will also have been **recorded,** we will be welcomed into His kingdom.

"Remember the tongue speaks only what is in the heart."
Theodore Epp, evangelist/author

Hebrews 6:10, Revelation 20:12, Revelation 20:15

CALM IN THE STORM

Extreme weather conditions were causing an increase in accidents, power outages, wires and trees obstructing the highways, and stranded motorists. Late one afternoon, dispatch advised me to proceed to a crash on an interstate highway. Severe winds and icy roads had brought traffic to a standstill, and it was difficult to navigate around vehicles which were almost impassable. Finally, I came upon a passenger car on its roof and two tractor-trailers which had both jackknifed. Once I determined that the couple in the car was not injured, I was able to pull the distraught husband and wife out of the overturned vehicle and lead them to my car. Since their car had to be towed, I took them to the nearest hotel. As they entered the lobby, their anxiety was replaced by obvious relief, for they were safe and felt calm in the midst of the storm.

Many with whom we interact experience storms of a different nature in their lives. During these times, they sense that there must be something better, since everything seems to be going well for those around them. Often, those who struggle do not seem to know where to find the relief that they long for. If our contact with these people is supportive and helpful, they may be receptive to hearing something from us that will point them in the right direction. During these vulnerable times, they may even be willing to learn about the peace that we have through our relationship with the Lord. In Matthew 11:28-30, Jesus said, "Come to me, all you who are weary and burdened, and I will give your rest. Take my yoke upon you and learn from me, for I am gentle and humble in heart, and you will find rest for your souls. For my yoke is easy, and my burden is light." Although we cannot calm a storm caused by nature, we can lead others to a calming of their spirit, which is far more important.

"Sometimes God calms the storm. Sometimes He lets the storm rage and calms His children." Leslie Gould, author

Psalm 23:1-4, Mark 4:35-41, 2 Timothy 1:7

REAL LOVE

During my years on the job, I encountered many who felt unloved and were looking for attention. Homeless, abused, wounded, or abandoned, they found it difficult to believe that anyone genuinely cared about them. One night, a friend of one of my best informants, told me that my informant, a prostitute, had been beaten with a coat hanger and was in the hospital with significant injuries. I immediately went to see her and found her in bad shape. When I asked her who was responsible for her injuries, she would not tell me. Even after I offered her protection, she still would not name the attacker. When I asked if her pimp had done this to her, she reluctantly admitted through her tears that he had. After I told her that she needed to press charges, she cried out, "No! I am not going to do that. I deserved what I got. He takes care of me, and I didn't work hard enough tonight." As perplexing as that sounded, I realized that for some, any attention, even hurtful attention, is better than having none at all.

People will sometimes disappoint us, turn against us, disrespect us, or indicate that they do not care about us. Our best and most consistent source of comfort can be found in the One who went to the cross because of His love for us. Evangelical author and speaker, Jerry Bridges, assures us that, "God's unfailing love for us is an objective fact affirmed over and over in the Scriptures. It is true whether we believe it or not. Our doubts do not destroy God's love, nor does our faith create it. It originates in the very nature of God, who is love, and it flows to us through our union with His beloved Son." Romans 8:38-39 reminds us, "For I am convinced that neither death nor life, neither angels nor demons neither the present nor the future, nor any powers, neither height nor depth, nor anything else in all creation, will be able to separate us from the love of God that is in Christ Jesus our Lord."

"God proved His love on the cross. When Christ hung, and bled, and died, it was God saying to the world, 'I love you.'" Billy Graham, pastor/evangelist

John 3:16, Romans 5:8, Ephesians 2:4-7

ON THE FRONT LINE

In law enforcement, we are regularly called upon to be on the front line. When disruption, tragedy, or danger is present, someone has to move ahead and quell the disturbance. It takes courage to assume that position, and not everyone in our society can or wants to do that. Even situations that seem somewhat mundane can turn tragic. All too often, we hear of an officer who comes upon a fallen tree, a dead animal, construction material, or another large object lying in the middle of the highway. As the officer attempts to drag it off the highway to prevent an accident, a vehicle suddenly comes out of nowhere and strikes and kills the officer. Frequently, we hear of other officers killed in the line of duty. Recently, a U.S. Marshall was shot and killed while assisting in serving a fugitive warrant, and police officers in two states were shot and killed. Knowing how dangerous and difficult the job can be, we still go out each day with the intention of coming to the aid of someone in danger or distress.

As Believers in Christ, we are also required to take a front-line position and stand strong, especially when facing a confrontation or act of disobedience. If we do so in a peaceful, fair way, without being judgmental, we may be able to make a difference, not only in resolving the issue, but also in showing that we are different and why. So many around us do not know the Savior or His saving power and the peace that is available to everyone, but the Lord can use us to help them see Him. In 2 Timothy 4:2-5, Paul instructs Timothy: "Preach the Word; be prepared in season and out of season; correct, rebuke, and encourage—with great patience and careful instruction…keep your head in all situations, endure hardship, do the work of an evangelist, discharge all the duties of your ministry." All Believers who accept the responsibility to be ambassadors for Christ can then say as Paul did, "I have fought the good fight." 2 Timothy 4:7.

"Every believer is a witness whether they want to be or not."
Donald Barnhouse, pastor/author

1 Corinthians 16:13, 2 Timothy 1:7, Hebrews 4:16

CHANGING IN APPEARANCE

Over the years, several criminals have attempted to change their physical appearance in an effort to go unnoticed. In his book, *Cleveland Curiosities,* Ted Schwartz tells of two well-known criminals of the day: Alvin Karpis, a professional criminal who specialized in bank robberies and kidnappings, and Fred Barker, who was the son of the notorious "Ma" Barker. In 1934, these two criminals decided to change their appearance to reduce their risk of being caught. They paid a doctor to surgically alter their facial appearance and to destroy their fingerprints with acid. The doctor removed the top layer of skin on their fingers and cut their faces in a painful procedure. When the criminals saw the results, they were displeased, for their appearance was not significantly altered. Then, they murdered the doctor for his unacceptable treatment.

When we become Believers in Christ, signs of significant change should emerge, not in our physical appearance, but in our outward expression toward others, even to those we do not care for. A change in our language should be obvious. A sense of peace now in our life, even during stressful and painful times, should be evident. In our own strength, we can never achieve all of that, for in our humanness, we will fail. Although we will continue to sin, regular, positive growth should become evident. It should be apparent in what we say or do not say, and also in the way we act. The Lord is patient and knows that change in our lives may not come quickly, and we are prone to backslide. However, Romans 12:2 says, "Do not conform any longer to the pattern of this world, but be transformed by the renewing of your mind. Then you will be able to test and approve what God's will is--His good, pleasing, and perfect will."

"I'm not perfect. I'm never going to be. And that's the great thing about living the Christian life and trying to live by faith, is you're trying to get better every day. You're trying to improve." Tim Tebow, former NFL quarterback and MLB player.

Isaiah 55:8-9, 1 Corinthians 11:1, Ephesians 2:10

October 12

ONE MORE MISTAKE

Our experiences in the PA State Police Academy were probably similarly demanding, both physically and mentally. Eventually, I understood why I was being pushed to the max. If I could not endure the stringent discipline in a secure environment, I would never survive the streets. Often unannounced, the instructors conducted a random room search. Any discrepancies resulted in extra chores that added pressure to our schedule. One day while taking a break outside of the classroom, I stood against the wall with hands in my pockets. The instructor called me to attention and standing inches from my face asked why my hands were in my pockets. Having no real reason, and knowing that he did not want to hear any, I admitted having none. He then ordered me to run around the large parking lot for thirty minutes. Upon my return to the classroom, he said, "You're not finished. Go to your room and sew up all the pockets in your pants." Not sure where to find a needle and thread, I sheepishly asked him. "Sounds like your problem," he replied. From that day forward, I did all in my power not to make one more mistake in the PSP Academy.

When we get to a place where we realize the presence of God and the need to follow Him, we try to keep from sin. Eventually, we realize that to live a sinless life is impossible. Try as we may, we will continue to make mistakes, which often are sins. Yet, we can have peace in knowing that these "mistakes," past, present, and future, are forgiven because of the sacrifice made by Jesus on the cross. Often, we keep dredging them back up, for it is difficult to understand the full redemption that comes through trusting in Christ. We do not have to keep going back to ask for forgiveness of sins that we have already confessed. He forgives, once and for all. "If we confess our sins, He is faithful and just and will forgive us our sins and purify us from all unrighteousness." 1 John 1:9.

"Our old history ends with the cross; our new history begins with the resurrection."
Watchman Nee, Christian teacher

2 Corinthians 5:17, Ephesians 1:7-8, Hebrews 10:17

NEVER ALONE

We are often exposed to dangerous situations, and even a typical traffic stop can quickly escalate into a serious, threatening incident. The trooper was standing at the side of the highway and speaking to the operator of the tractor trailer that he had just pulled over. Suddenly, he sensed that something was wrong, and he turned to see an oncoming rig heading toward him. Apparently, the driver had just noticed the trooper, and as he attempted to slow down quickly, his breaks locked. His truck fishtailed, but at the last second, the driver was able to pull it back into the lane, narrowly avoiding the trooper. When the trooper returned to his patrol car, he viewed his in-car camera which he had activated at the beginning of his stop. Only then did he realize how quickly his life could have ended that day, especially since the approaching vehicle was a tanker truck, most likely transporting a combustible liquid. Even backup would not have saved the trooper.

As Christians, we are not promised a life without trouble, sorrow, or difficulty while we are on Earth. Paul's description of his circumstances in 2 Corinthians 4:8-9 reveals the troubles that he and the early Christians endured: "We are hard-pressed on every side, but not crushed; perplexed, but not in despair; persecuted, but not abandoned; struck down, but not destroyed." Today, Christians around the world are being persecuted in both subtle and overt ways in ever-increasing numbers as Paul predicted in 2 Timothy 3:12: "In fact, everyone who wants to live a godly life in Christ Jesus will be **persecuted."** Nevertheless, we can hope and trust in the Lord to meet all of our needs in the way that He sees fit for us. "I will say of the Lord, 'He is my refuge and my fortress, my God, in whom I trust.'" Psalm 91:2. Remember that the shortest part of our lifespan is the time we spend on Earth, and we will be forever in His care when we meet Him face to face. **Praise God; we are never alone!**

"The Lord watches over us every moment of every day. He is there—and He cares—about every step and every breath." Dillon Burroughs, author

2 Samuel 22:2-4, Psalm 46:1, 2 Thessalonians 3:3

PEACE BROTHERS

Years ago, during a time when our country was at war, some in our society promoted what was called a "peace movement." In their minds, the answer to achieving peace was simple: no more war. Anti-war demonstrations erupted throughout the country. Many participants were "flower children" who also believed that people should release their inhibitions and do whatever made them feel good. Promoting "free sex" and illegal drugs, they rallied against those who did not agree with them. Because the gatherings often became violent, it was a challenging time for those in law enforcement. At this time, I had recently graduated from the PSP Academy, and a few weeks later, I received a draft notice to serve in the U.S. military. However, because of the widespread violence and angry protesting around the country, the federal government recognized the need to maintain law and order here at home, and my draft was rescinded.

Today, so many people try to achieve peace through self-help gurus and rituals, abusing mind-altering substances, acquiring material possessions, and chasing after wealth. Believers, on the other hand, have found the true answer to achieving peace in this world. Isaiah 26:3 reminds us, "You will keep in perfect peace him whose mind is steadfast, because he trusts in You." Philippians 4:7 tells us, "And the peace of God, which transcends all understanding, will guard your hearts and your minds in Christ Jesus." As Jesus prepared His followers for the coming days of confusion and the crucifixion, He spoke these words: "Peace I leave with you; My peace I give you. I do not give to you as the world gives. Do not let your hearts be troubled and do not be afraid." John 14:27.

"Anxiety does not empty tomorrow of its sorrows, but only empties today of its strength."
Charles Spurgeon, pastor/author

Isaiah 53:5, 1 Corinthians 1:2-3, Colossians 3:15-17

LEFT BEHIND

Responding to a crash with apparent injuries outside a small town, I found an elderly man slumped over the wheel of his car that had smashed into a tree. Damage to the car's rear indicated that another vehicle was involved but had fled the scene. Although the driver's external injuries seemed minor, closer examination revealed that he was not breathing. When the victim was removed, I examined the scene closely and found a chip of paint of an unusual bluish-green color imbedded in the crashed vehicle. After removing it, I went into town and drove up and down several streets. When I noticed fresh tire tracks running through a well-manicured lawn, I followed the tracks to the rear of a residence where a car covered with a tarp was parked closely against the home. Further examination revealed that the color of the car was the same as the chip in my possession. An arrest was subsequently made based on the paint chip left behind.

Psalm 90:10 tells us, "The length of our days [on Earth] is seventy years--or eighty, if we have the strength..." And then what? Jesus said, "For God so loved the world that He gave His one and only Son, that **whoever believes in Him shall not perish** but have everlasting life." John 3:16. True peace comes when we understand His promise of Heaven. To think that there is nothing good for us after this life or that there is nothing at all afterwards is beyond foolish. In Revelation 1:18, Jesus also said, "...I hold the keys of death and Hades," and in John 3:18, Jesus said..."**Whoever does not believe** stands **condemned** already because he has not believed in the name of God's one and only Son." Those who reject Christ will be left behind to spend eternity in the only other place—Hell, the place of "everlasting burnings," Isaiah 33:14. Believers can rest in the promise Jesus made to the thief on the cross, "I tell you the truth, today you will be with me in paradise." Luke 23:43.

"The moment we take our last breath on Earth, we take our first in Heaven."
 Billy Graham, pastor/evangelist

Job 14:5, Revelation 20:1-15

LIFE IS FRAGILE

Two officers were assigned to the midnight shift on a miserable night. Hurricane-like winds blew fiercely as torrential rains made it difficult to stay on the highway. Even though traffic was less than typical, some travelers were still on the road, and officers knew that they were probably in for a busy shift. When they came upon a vehicle that was down a small ravine with the front end resting up against a tree, they were relieved to see that the car was empty. As they returned to their car, dispatch reported downed wires on a roadway. Upon arrival, they realized that poor visibility made it difficult to see the wires. The first officer to get to the area where the electrical wire appeared to be down took several steps and landed on a live wire. His body jolted, and he dropped to the ground. After his partner called for help, he rushed to drag him to safety and began CPR. When emergency personnel arrived, the officer was transported to the nearest hospital, but he was dead upon arrival.

We often go through our days without thinking about the fragility of life. Since our lives may unexpectedly end in an instant, it is wise to consider, then, how we should be living. Ephesians 5:15-20 says, "Be very careful, then, how you live—not as unwise but as wise, making the most of every opportunity, because the days are evil. Therefore, do not be foolish, but understand what the Lord's will is. Do not get drunk on wine, which leads to debauchery. Instead, be filled with the Spirit. Speak to one another with psalms, hymns, and spiritual songs. Sing and make music in your heart to the Lord, always giving thanks to God the Father for everything, in the name of our Lord Jesus Christ." Paul's letter shows a life that is lived thoughtfully, carefully, happily, cordially, and thankfully with brothers and sisters in Christ.

"It is nothing to die. It is frightful not to live."
Victor Hugo, French poet/ novelist/dramatist.

Proverbs 27:1, Psalm 90:12, Matthew 6:34

FREE WILL

We were on an organized crime wiretap of members of the Philadelphia mafia where Nicodemo "Little Nicky" Scarfo reigned over the crime family. In George Anastasia's book, *Blood Honor,* the author described Scarfo as, "a greedy, ruthless despot, who reveled in wanton, ruthless, and senseless violence." Scarfo, one of the bloodiest mob bosses in history, took over when Philip "Chickenman" Testa was killed by a nail bomb that exploded at his front door. Scarfo, a long-time soldier in the family, became prominent in the mob after the assassination of Angelo "Docile Don" Bruno led to an on-going mob war in which over two dozen mobsters were killed in a five-year period. Often, these murders occurred when a mob member, expecting to be taken out next, gunned down potential threats. As feuding members discussed and carried out retaliation, I not only read about it in the news, but also heard it on the tapped phone. While the violent rampage continued, I often wondered who was going to be next. Although no one was forced to be in this violent group, I could not understand why they joined, knowing that their life could be cut short either by death or extended incarceration.

We all enter this world having received free will. Often, we do make the right choices, but many times throughout our lives, we do not. The Bible tells us in 1 Corinthians 10:13 that any temptations that we face are not new, and we also have the ability to choose not to give in to them. "No temptation has seized you except what is common to man. And God is faithful; He will not let you be tempted beyond what you can bear. But when you are tempted, He will also provide a way out so you can stand up under it." When Jesus was about to be crucified, He told His disciples that He would leave a Counselor to be with them to help them while He was gone, and He offers the same Holy Spirit to each of those who believe in Him. John 14:26.

"Free will carried many a soul to hell, but never a soul to heaven."
Charles Spurgeon, pastor/author

Proverbs 16:9, Galatians 5:13, Ephesians 5:17

BREVITY OF LIFE

In our profession, it is not uncommon to meet with death. Calls that we respond to, where one has died of natural causes, are commonplace and easier to process. Far more difficult are those where some died at the hands of another or when some felt that they could not go on any longer and, in desperation, ended their own lives. Although I had to go into a morgue many times, either to witness an autopsy or to gain information to identify the victim, it never became commonplace. A house fire investigation in which I was called to assist the Fire Marshall was especially troublesome. The wife and three children had succumbed from the raging inferno. Seeing the children lying on a cold slab in the morgue was very difficult, as I thought of my own children, similar in age. Knowing that these family members were gone from this life, I wondered where they would spend eternity. Shortly afterwards, the husband was charged and convicted on four counts of homicide.

The Bible tells us in James 4:14, "Why, you do not even know what will happen tomorrow. What is your life? You are a mist that appears for a little while and then vanishes." Although Hebrews 9:27 affirms our future, "Just as man is destined to die once, and after that to face judgment, ..." many people still are unwilling to address life after death and choose not to reflect on such issues but rather hope for the best. This is foolish, especially when we consider the length of eternity--endless. How much better it is to have God's peace in knowing exactly where our final destiny will be. There is a far better place than this world, and we can easily make a reservation while here on Earth. "For God so loved the world that He gave His only Son, that all who believe in Him shall not perish but have eternal life." John 3:16.

"Those who go to Heaven ride on a pass and enter into blessings that they never earned, but all who go to hell pay their own way." John R. Rice, pastor/author

Psalm 90:12, Ephesians 2:8-10, 1Timothy 1:15-16

RECURRING OFFENCES

After receiving a call of a burglary in progress, I headed toward the neighborhood and saw a teenage boy walking down the sidewalk in the opposite direction. As my patrol car got closer, he averted his eyes toward the sidewalk and began to walk more quickly. A sack resembling a full pillowcase was slung over his shoulder. As I turned around and headed toward him, he began to run. Exiting my car, I ran after him and tackled him to the ground. When questioned, he refused to tell me his name or age. In the pillowcase were items that I sensed came from the home that had just been burglarized. Ben, the sixteen-year-old, was turned over to his parents and later sent to juvenile court. At the hearing, this boy had a defiant, antagonistic attitude that caused me concern. Afterwards, as I walked toward the door in the courtroom, I turned to Ben and said, "I will see you again." Several years later, two brothers and their cousin committed a horrendous, extremely violent homicide. The two brothers mercilessly slaughtered their parents and younger brother. Their accomplice in the killing was Ben.

When we get to a place in our lives where we genuinely desire to get serious about our relationship with God, we determine to change the areas in our lives that we know are not pleasing to Him. Although our intentions are good, we often fail and fall again into sin. The Lord already knows that because of our sinful nature, we will continue to struggle with temptation and sin. However, He is always ready to forgive us of our sins: past, present, and future. I John 1:9 and 2:1-2 encourages us: "If we confess our sins, He is faithful and just and will forgive us our sins and purify us from all unrighteousness...My dear children, I write this to you so that you will not sin. But if anybody does sin, we have One who speaks to the Father in our defense--Jesus Christ, the Righteous One. He is the Atoning Sacrifice for our sins, and not only for ours, but also for the sins of the whole world."

"God forgets your confessed sins; so should you." Woodrow Kroll, pastor/author

Isaiah 1:18, Acts 3:19-20, Romans 3:23-24

WHO IS THE ENEMY?

The loss of the life of any law enforcement officer in the line of duty is so difficult to accept, not only for family members, but also for others on the job. Often, when plain-clothed or undercover officers conduct an investigation or a raid, or during the arrest of a wanted criminal, shots are fired. When the lighting is poor, suspects are running, and guns are drawn, it becomes very difficult to determine who the enemy really is. Consequently, "friendly fire" may sometimes be responsible for the tragic death of an officer. Try as we may, at times, it is unavoidable. Such deaths are especially wrenching for those involved in the incident.

We do all that we can to protect society from the criminal element. We attempt to stay aware of trends, illegal groups, and locations where someone may become vulnerable and subject to attack. As much as we try to identify evil people who are intent on inflicting harm on others, we especially need to be aware of someone else who can be very subtle in his strategies. Satan loves to attack people, especially Believers, because we oppose all that he stands for. In Ephesians 4:27, Paul warns Christians to examine their behavior, "and do not give the devil a foothold." If we are not careful to walk the line, Satan can cause us to stumble and fall, and he considers that a huge victory. We need to be ever vigilant against our spiritual enemy who cannot be visibly seen. Ephesians 6:10-11 reminds us, "Finally, be strong in the Lord and in His mighty power. Put on the full armor of God so that you can take your stand against the devil's schemes." By remaining regularly in God's word, by spending quiet devotional time with Him each day, and by seeking His will and asking for continued wisdom while in prayer, we put up the best possible defense to thwart the single biggest enemy of this world.

"But as long as we live on the Earth, we are still on Satan's turf. He will try to rule our lives by deceiving us into believing that we still belong to him."
Neil T. Anderson, author

2 Thessalonians 3:3, James 4:7, 1 Peter 5:8-9

CHILDLIKE FAITH

Nearing the end of an extremely busy shift, I was called to be the lead investigator in a possible murder. A hunter had found the badly beaten body of a young woman in a field, and she had obviously been dead for days. As we began our search of the crime scene, I knew how crucial the collection of evidence is in determining the identity of both the victim and the perpetrator. After hours of seeking leads along with other detectives who had joined me, I could no longer think clearly. At 2 AM, as I prepared to drive home, I informed the lieutenant that the investigation would resume in the morning. He told me to sleep until I was fully rested, and soon I fell into a deep sleep. At 6:00 AM, my two-year-old son came into the bedroom and opened the drapes on the sliding door windows just as the sky lit up with a spectacular sunrise. With his hair tousled in curls and his big blue eyes beaming, he shook me awake while exclaiming in his loudest voice, "Look what God did today!"

Often on the job, we are called into the activities of the day, which may include major investigations needing our total attention. The success or failure in solving a crime or in helping someone with a significant need is dependent on us. During such times, we may easily lose sight of other things that are also important. Our families suffer during those long periods of time when we are out of the picture. We need to trust God to remind us of what is important in our lives and seek direction to prioritize those things that bombard us each day. Ephesians 5:15-17: "Be very careful then how you live--not as unwise but as wise, making the most of every opportunity...understand what the Lord's will is." Psalm 39:4: "Show me, O Lord, my life's end and the number of my days; let me know how fleeting is my life."

"Make sure of your commitment to Jesus Christ and seek to follow Him every day. Don't be swayed by the false values of the world and goals of the world, but put Christ and His will first in everything you do." Billy Graham, pastor/evangelist/author

Psalm 31:14-15, Ecclesiastes 3:1, Ephesians 5:8-10

KEYS

Taking a person to jail always made me feel very uncomfortable. It was especially daunting when it was a state prison where the worst, most hardened, and violent criminals were incarcerated. Upon entering the facility, protocol required me to place my firearm in a lock box before going through the first set of security doors. Although a guard accompanied the shackled prisoner and me, that walk to the cell was unsettling as I was in uniform and without a gun. I consciously tried not to look apprehensive as prisoners tried to intimidate me by staring me down. As gate after gate closed behind me with loud clangs that resounded through the sterile corridors, all that I could think about was how secure and available the keys were that would ultimately ensure my release.

Even Believers will likely have times when we feel shackled. Although we now have freedom over sin and darkness, the evil one will continue his attempts to discourage us and pull us down as he tries to cause us to doubt our security in Christ. He wants nothing more than to stifle our walk with Christ by dredging up our past sinfulness and enticing us in new ventures. He comes to us not in a red suit with a pitchfork, but in the likes of "bold and arrogant" men who "…blaspheme in matters they do not understand…For they mouth empty, boastful words and, by appealing to the lustful desires of sinful human nature, they entice people…They promise them freedom while they themselves are slaves of depravity." 2 Peter 2:10-19. In time, Satan will lose all his power over us, for Revelation 1:18 says that the living Lord holds "…the keys of death and Hades." Revelation 20:10 says, "And the devil, who deceived them, was thrown into the lake of burning sulfur, where the beast and the false prophet had been thrown. They will be tormented day and night forever and ever." Until then, the key to overcoming Satan's schemes is to remember the promise of John 8:36: "So if the Son sets you free, you **will** be free indeed."

"Don't let your yesterday take up too much of today." John Wooden, NBA coach

Acts 13:38-39, Galatians 5:1, Ephesians 3:12

IN TIMES OF TRAGEDY

Some incidents that I experienced on the job are still difficult to fully process or forget. Brothers and sisters on the job have seen great tragedy, devastation, and loss of life in their communities, as well as in events of great magnitude such as the World Trade Center devastation, the bombings at the Boston Marathon, active shooters in Connecticut, Virginia Tech, a prayer meeting in South Carolina, and a shooting at a Las Vegas concert with 58 dead and 851 injured. Etched in our memories, such incidents cause us to become even more vigilant as we continue to serve. When the public gets a closer look at what we do in the line of duty and realizes the magnitude of our job, they often develop a better understanding of our profession. Yet, violence against law enforcement remains out of control, and many officers lost their lives just because they wore a uniform. Over the past years, leaders in law enforcement have come to understand that de-briefing, counseling, and time-off are often the most important steps for an officer to be able to move on. In some departments, chaplains provide spiritual counseling which is often valuable in officer recovery.

Believers have someone who is always there to listen, to advise, and to provide needed peace. God is aware of the times when we are in a spiritually dry or difficult place. He is waiting for us to call out to Him. "But if from there you seek the Lord your God, you will find Him if you seek Him with all your heart and with all your soul." Deuteronomy 4:29. Since He knows us and our inner struggles better than anyone else does, who is better able to help us through times of tragedy? Psalm 31:14-15: "But I trust in You, O Lord; I say, 'You are my God.' My times are in Your hands."

"We tend to be preoccupied by our problems when we have a heightened sense of vulnerability and a diminished sense of power. Today, see each problem as an invitation to prayer."
John Ortberg, pastor/author

Deuteronomy 33:27, Joshua 1:9, 2 Corinthians 12:9-10

NEVER MISSING

In 1971, John List, a mild-mannered accountant living in New Jersey, was experiencing significant financial issues. In desperation, he decided to kill his mother, wife, and three children, and then himself, thus putting an end to his struggles. He followed through with part of his plan and killed them all. Then he came to the realization that now he would no longer have such a financial burden, so he decided to re-locate, change his identity, and start a new life. Eighteen years later, "America's Most Wanted," television show asked Frank Bender, a forensic sculptor to create a clay bust of what an aging John List would look like. Several days after it was publicized, a woman in Virginia recognized List as her neighbor. Fingerprints confirmed his identity, and he was arrested, convicted, and sentenced to five life-terms in prison.

Since God created all humans in His own image, not one is ever truly missing. He knows us all by name. At the end of our journey in this world, we will have the opportunity to meet with the Lord, and He will accept some to live with Him in heaven for eternity. "He calls His own sheep by name and leads them out." John 10:3. The Book of Life will list all who will be eligible to enter into Heaven. "If anyone's name was not found written in the book of life, he was thrown into the lake of fire." Revelation 20:15. If during our life here on Earth, we have acknowledged Christ as our Lord and Savior and accepted His forgiveness for all our sins, our names **will not be missing** from the book. "He who overcomes will, like them, be dressed in white. I **will never blot out** his name from the book of life but will acknowledge his name before my Father and His angels." Revelation 3:5.

"Grace teaches that God loves because of who God is, not because of who we are."
Philip Yancey, author.

John 14:2-3, Philippians 3:20, Revelation 21:4

UNJUSTLY ACCUSED

A few times, I was accused of doing or not doing something expected of me while on the job. Realizing that it is impossible to be right all the time, I accepted the criticism. However, an unjustified accusation is difficult to accept. Working a night shift, I was surprised to see the lieutenant in charge of the detective bureau still at his desk at 10:00 PM. He called me in and chastised me for not developing any leads or arrests for the considerable number of home burglaries in our area. He indicated that he was getting complaints not only from the victims of the burglaries, but also from others living in the area. I went to my office and quickly returned with documentation that I had gathered over several months, which identified similar methods of operation, times the burglaries were committed, as well as some possible suspects. Furthermore, I had documentation about arrangements with several undercover officers to assist me for the next three nights in surveillances in the neighborhoods being attacked. After my explanation, the only thing he said was, "I want to see results quickly and this crime wave stopped."

Even if we are unjustly accused, Believers are called upon to respond appropriately because of our relationship with Christ. Pastor David Jeremiah said, "The secret of the Christian passion is simple: Everything we do in life, we do it as to the Lord and not to man." No one knows better the feeling of being unjustly accused than Christ. In Luke 18:31-33, Jesus said to his twelve disciples, "We are going up to Jerusalem, and everything that is written by the prophets about the Son of Man will be fulfilled. He will be handed over to the Gentiles. They will mock Him, insult Him, spit on Him, flog Him, and kill Him." Our pain pales in comparison with what our Lord was willing to suffer for us. Our goal in the work we do in this life is to do our best, attempt to please the Lord, and remember that we really are working for Him.

"If you want to see what judgment looks like, go to the cross. If you want to see what love looks like, go to the cross." D.A. Carson, theologian/professor

John 10:11, John 15:13, Romans 5:9-11

PRIDE BEFORE THE FALL

After many grueling months of PSP Academy life, I accomplished the goal that I had originally set. Upon graduation, I entered a profession that many seek, but fewer are able to achieve. As I prepared for my first tour of duty, my uniform crisply pressed, my leather gear highly polished, I have to admit that I was impressed by the person looking back in the mirror. Driving around my first day, I quickly became aware that I did not go unnoticed. At lunchtime, I pulled into a diner, and as I was getting out of my car, I inadvertently activated the siren from a button on the floor. Drawing further unwanted attention, I put on my emergency lights and quickly pulled away.

Although it is good to take pride **in** what we do, we have to realize that the evil one will take every opportunity to prod us to **be** proud and puffed up. Because we are able to help so many on a fairly regular basis, it is easy to become prideful, forgetting who has endowed us with all of our gifts and talents. Since the Bible refers to pride as "sinful" and "wicked" because it distracts us from a healthy relationship with God, we need to check regularly for signs of it seeping into our behavior. One way to determine if we are being prideful is to examine our motives for doing what we do. Those who continue to wallow in pride without trying to overcome it are eventually going to fall. Proverbs 16:18-19 warns us, "Pride goes before destruction, a haughty spirit before a fall. Better to be lowly in spirit and among the oppressed than to share plunder with the proud." 1 John 2:16-17 describes a better choice: "For everything in the world--the cravings of sinful man, the lust of his eyes, and the boasting of what he has and does--comes not from the Father but from the world. The world and its desires pass away, but the man who does the will of God lives forever."

"We cannot free ourselves from pride and selfish ambition; a divine rescue is absolutely necessary." C.J. Mahaney, pastor/author

Proverbs 8:13, Psalm 10:4, 2 Corinthians 10:13

RESPECT

Laird is a Believer who has a demanding profession as an officer in a local, county prison. During each shift, he is responsible for the male inmates on Tier 3, many of whom believe that the charges against them were trumped up and are bogus. Each day, he is locked up with those who have been incarcerated for various crimes, up to and including significant felonies, and some have been repeatedly incarcerated. However, Tier 3 also houses many who seem genuine about wanting to change their lives. A number of them have a faith in the Lord, attend Bible studies, and are trying to become better people. Laird has developed a reputation among them of being fair, but demanding when necessary. A newly incarcerated inmate was having a difficult time adjusting to his surroundings. Approaching Laird, he said, "Give me some f###### soap." Laird responded, "First, those on this Tier don't swear in front of me. And, there is a way to ask for something you may need." Laird then walked away. About fifteen minutes later, the same inmate approached Laird and said, "Hey man, I am sorry for the way I acted. It won't happen again." Surprised but pleased at this quick turnaround in behavior, Laird accepted the apology. Then as he looked over the inmate's shoulder, Laird saw a seasoned inmate staring at him with a big grin and giving him a "thumbs up." This second inmate had come to realize that Laird was always fair and treated the inmates with respect. When he passed that on to the new arrival, he quickly changed his behavior. The inmates on Tier 3 recognized that Laird was different from most other officers. Laird's attitude and demeanor were Christ-like, and as a result, he turned what could be a hostile environment into one of peace. Laird had credibility when he explained to the inmates on Tier 3 that they could be forgiven, for Christ loved them, regardless of what they had done.

"Every human being, of whatever origin, of whatever station, deserves respect. We must respect others even as we respect ourselves."
U Thant, Burmese diplomat/ third Secretary General of the United Nations

Matthew 7:12, Titus 2:6-8, 1 John 3:11-14

TEMPTATIONS

Several of us in the vice unit had been called to assist officers in another county after the district attorney directed them to raid about twenty-five establishments known to have illegal gambling machines. Believing that it was more important to seize drugs rather than to be involved in gambling-related activities, I reluctantly participated in the assignment. Shortly after the raid, I was sitting at my desk in the vice office when the phone rang. The caller asked if I had been involved in a recent, large-scale raid on video poker machines. Immediately assuming that I was going to be blasted with, "Don't you guys have anything better to do with your time? Get out and arrest some real criminals," I hesitantly said that I had been. When she said, "I just want to thank you," I was speechless. She then told me that over a year ago, her husband began playing video poker machines at a local tavern and became addicted. In the past week, she came home to find that, again, some of her furniture was gone. After she questioned her husband, he told her that he had sold it to get money to pay off some of his gambling debts. This woman certainly changed my outlook on such illegal activity.

Regardless of where we are in our walk with the Lord, we will face continuing temptations. Even Jesus was tempted while on Earth, and "Because He Himself suffered when He was tempted, He is able to help those who are being tempted." Hebrews 2:18. When we are tempted to sin, we should recognize that the evil one wants nothing better than to see a Believer fall. We can also find comfort in knowing that we do not have to try to resist temptation on our own. 1 Corinthians 10:13 says, "No temptation has seized you except what is common to man. And God is faithful; He will not let you be tempted beyond what you can bear. But when you are tempted, He will also provide a way out so that you can stand up under it." James 4:7 provides our attack plan: "Submit yourselves, then, to God. Resist the devil, and he will flee from you."

"It is not a sin to be tempted." Rick Warren, pastor/author

Proverbs 1:10-15, Matthew 26:41, James 1:2-3

ALWAYS WATCHING

The call came in to dispatch that a passerby saw a car parked on a city street, and a man was slumped over the steering wheel with a significant amount of blood on his shirt. Responding officers found a dead man with two bullet holes in his head. He was identified, but there were no apparent witnesses. Since a number of cameras were in the area, the investigators began to search them for possible evidence. One camera revealed a potential suspect leaving the location of the parked car and traveling down a side street. Additional cameras showed his direction of travel as he came to a trashcan, pulled something from his coat pocket, and threw it in. Officers quickly retrieved the object, which was determined to be a gun. When bullet cases left in the vehicle were compared with those still in the firearm, they matched. In time, the owner of the gun was identified, but he was not willing to take the rap for his friend. However, he did tell the officers the name of the friend that he had loaned the weapon to, and shortly afterward, an arrest was made.

Police work has advanced significantly over the years, and technology is often responsible for helping to solve crimes. Cameras in police cruisers as well as body cameras worn by the police provide compelling information about those who have committed crimes. As Believers, we may sometimes forget that all of our actions are being observed as well, but by our Creator. "For a man's ways are in full view of the Lord, and He examines all his paths." Proverbs 5:21. Sometimes those actions please the Lord; at other times, we would rather that God did not see our every action. It is far better to consider our actions beforehand than to have to account for them later. Hebrews 4:13 says, "Nothing in all creation is hidden from God's sight. Everything is uncovered and laid bare before the eyes of Him to whom we must give account."

"We need never shout across the spaces to an absent God. He is nearer than our own soul, closer than our most secret thoughts." A.W. Tozer, pastor/author.

Job 31:4, Job 34:21, Psalm 69:5

SET FREE

In 1962, Nelson Mandela was arrested for trying to overthrow the state and was sentenced to life in prison for breaking the laws of South Africa. Leader of the antiapartheid revolution, this activist, politician, and philanthropist continued his work in prison and even earned his law degree while incarcerated. He was not broken, but energized and more determined than ever as he said, "The greatest glory in living is not in never failing, but in rising every time you fall." After his release, he eventually served as the first Black President of South Africa and received more than 260 significant awards recognizing his tireless work, including The Nobel Peace Prize. It is difficult to fathom the irony that this crusader for freedom and global advocate for basic human rights and social justice was forced to spend nearly three decades of his life in prison before being set free.

We Believers were also set free when we understood and acknowledged the true reason for Jesus's crucifixion and accepted Jesus as our Lord and Savior. Romans 6:6-7 says, "For we know that our old self was crucified with Him so that the body of sin might be done away with, that we should no longer be slaves to sin--because anyone who has died has been freed from sin." Consequently, we should seek to deepen our understanding of Jesus so that we grow and learn as we follow Him. In John 8:31-32, Jesus said, "If you hold to My teaching, you are really My disciples. Then you will know the truth, and the truth will set you free." This truth is found in the infallible Word of God, the Bible. When we, with a child-like faith, believe that God sent His only Son, Jesus, to take the penalty for our sins so that we can have everlasting life in heaven, we are then truly set free. "It is for freedom that Christ set us free. Stand firm, and do not let yourselves be burdened again by a yoke of slavery." Galatians 5:1.

"In almost everything that touches our everyday life on Earth, God is pleased when we're pleased. He wills that we be as free as birds to soar and sing our Maker's praise without anxiety." A.W. Tozer, pastor/author

John 8:36, Romans 8:1-2, 2 Corinthians 3:17

EVERYONE GOES HOME

In 2016, 56 volunteer, 23 career, and 10 wildlife agency firefighters died while on duty. The 89 deaths were a result of stress, over-exertion, heart attack, blunt force from a fall, asphyxiation, and building collapse. These heroes never turned away from calls that could potentially be a fatal event. Matt has been a New York City Fire Fighter for seventeen years. His shifts are a total of twenty-four hours and require him and his brothers and sisters to remain at the "House" for the entire time, ready to be activated at any minute. Their ultimate goal is to save lives and to do it in such a way that they go home safely after each shift. Several years ago, members of the "House" were fighting a raging fire while on top of a large roof. Suddenly, the area where they were standing collapsed, and they were soon engulfed in flames. All perished, never to return home. The loss to the others in the "House" will never be forgotten. Hopefully, the heroes had accepted Jesus as their Lord and Savior and are in their eternal home in Heaven.

Such unexpected tragedies are reminders that our life in this world is temporary. As evangelist Billy Graham said, "My home is in Heaven. I'm just traveling through this world." When our lives on Earth are over, there will be one of two places where we will spend eternity. As real as Heaven is, so, too, is Hell. In Matthew 13:41-43, Jesus said, "The Son of Man will send out His angels, and they will weed out of His kingdom everything that causes sin and all who do evil. They will throw them into the fiery furnace, where there will be weeping and gnashing of teeth. Then the righteous will shine like sun in the kingdom of their Father." Jesus is painting an awful picture of hell to illustrate how awesome and bright heaven is in comparison. God wants us to be with Him for eternity, and He has provided a simple plan to get us there. The decision either to follow Christ or to reject His offer is left to each of us to make.

"I have all that I need here, and heaven hereafter! How much richer could anybody want to be?" Lester Roloff, pastor

Matthew 25:46, John 14:1-6, Revelation 21:1-4

UNDERCOVER

Upon graduation from the PA State Police Academy, I was quickly thrust into the limelight. A sharp uniform, a shiny badge, a marked patrol car--all signified that I was a part of a unique profession, and I was proud to tell others that I was in law enforcement. In time, however, when I accepted a new assignment, it was important that my police identity was not known. What was most stressful in this role was my concern that someone with whom I had previously been involved or someone in an ongoing investigation would learn who I really was. It is easy to become paranoid. One day as I sat over lunch with a coworker on this new assignment, he unraveled right before my eyes. As he described a recent dangerous encounter, be became disoriented and broke down into tears. After taking time away from the job, he recovered and was assigned to another division. Thereafter, I was careful to remember that living a double life can take a serious toll.

Believers sometimes choose to live in an undercover capacity and are often hesitant or unwilling to tell others that the peace that we enjoy comes from our knowledge of Christ's saving promise in Romans 10:9-10. However, sharing the good news is not optional, for Jesus told Christ-followers to, "Go into all the world and preach the good news to all creation." Mark 16:15. At times, doing so will require us to be bold in our faith, but that does not allow us to be pushy or overbearing. In sharing, it should be apparent that we are different and have a calm confidence about something that others would want: the assurance of eternity in Heaven. "But in your hearts set apart Christ as Lord. Always be prepared to give an answer to everyone who asks you to give the reason for the hope that you have. But do this with gentleness and respect..." 1 Peter 3:15.

"We may live in a culture that believes everyone will be saved, that we are 'justified' by death, and all you need to do to go to heaven is die. But God's word certainly doesn't give us the luxury of believing that." R.C. Sproul, pastor/author

Acts 4:31, Acts 13:47-48, Ephesians 6:19-20

November 2

UNINTELLIGIBLE

Many law enforcement agencies have an intelligence division that relies on confidential sources for information about on-going criminal activity. Depending on the significance of the criminal enterprise, the agency may apply for a court-authorized telephone wiretap. However, it is extremely difficult to obtain permission for a wire-tap through a superior court judge because infringing on personal privacy is taken very seriously. Once permission is obtained, strict guidelines establish the length and manner by which only authorized officers can conduct the wiretap. Any failure to follow the directions from the court could result in significant discipline, including termination of the officer involved in the violation. Listening to phone conversations can become tedious, but officers must remain alert. Sometimes they will experience difficulty in distinguishing exactly what is being said. During such a time of listening, the monitor must then document that the conversation was "unintelligible" since it cannot be discerned.

For Believers, the infallible words of God found in the Bible are the most important words that we could ever hear. Although some may say that the Bible is just too hard for them to grasp, God provided the Bible for us to study, and His words are never unintelligible. However, sometimes we may need to read them repeatedly, and if we persevere, they should provide us a new insight. "Your word is a lamp to my feet and a light for my path." Psalm 119:105. When we set aside time to explore the word, we will see that the truth is always there. "And we also thank God continually because, when you received the word of God, which you heard from us, you accepted it not as the word of men, but as it actually is, the word of God, which is at work in you who believe." 1 Thessalonians 2:13.

"The Bible is God's word to keep you from the bottom of the sea, and to show you where the harbor is, and how to reach it without running on rocks and bars."
Henry Ward Beecher, clergyman/social reformer/abolitionist

Psalm 119:9-11, Matthew 24:35, 2 Timothy 3:16

JUST LISTEN

Within a short period of time on the job, we in law enforcement can begin to think that we have all the answers. This comes, in part, because so many around us need assistance and often ask us tough questions, hoping we can resolve the issue or problem. My Friday 3-11:00 PM shift had extended into the early morning hours. Knowing that I had the weekend off, I was looking forward to sleeping in on Saturday morning. About 6:30 AM, the ringing phone awakened me, and I picked it up to hear the voice of an acquaintance calling to tell me of a problem. I thought that it must be something serious for him to awaken me at this hour. Then he related that he was just out driving when another driver cut him off and almost caused a collision. He said he was confident that I would want to track down this obvious violator, and he could even provide the vehicle registration to get me started on an investigation.

Sometimes we foolishly do not feel the need to pray for wisdom, even though God is always there to listen. While responding to this caller, I had to pray immediately for wisdom and patience--and again the next time I saw him. When we pray for wisdom, God listens and does provide. Conversely, though, we often become very poor listeners. Sometimes people just need to be heard, and they want us to listen and give our undivided attention. That is becoming more difficult to do as ever-encroaching technology interrupts with incoming cell phone calls and text messages. We allow them to disrupt conversations with family and friends because we feel that we must answer that call. Such behavior suggests that the call we are taking is more important than they are. We should pray regularly that the Holy Spirit would convict us about the time that we need to speak as well as the time to listen. Ecclesiastes 3:1,7: "There is a time for everything...a time to be silent, and a time to speak."

"Good listeners believe they can learn something from everyone."
Charles Swindoll, pastor/author

Proverbs 13:3, Proverbs 17:28, James 1:19

SAVE A LIFE

The nature of our job requires us to enter into situations that most had never been in nor would ever want to be in. In time, we are able to respond to a need without a second thought. One Sunday morning as I was traveling on a highway with my wife, a car several vehicles ahead of me spun out of control, traveled down a steep embankment, and rolled on its roof. After pulling over, I ran toward the vehicle. Smoke was billowing from the car, and the operator inside was obviously dazed. After prying open the door, I grabbed him by the arm and shoulder and, with sustained effort, extracted him from the car. I quickly led him away, and within seconds, the visibly shaken driver and I saw the vehicle become engulfed in a raging blaze. After the ambulance arrived, I walked back to my car to find my distraught wife looking at me through tears as she said, "You could have just been killed trying to save that man." In law enforcement or as first responders, we rarely take the time to consider that possibility. We just do what we know we need to do.

In some situations, we have great success and can even prevent a tragedy and save a life. At other times, our efforts are in vain, and those vivid memories stay with us forever. In our Christian walk, we must remember that, as Believers, we will face times when we can help to save a soul. Many have not heard about the Lord and the power that He has to remove our sins and open up Heaven to us for eternity. Since eternity is forever, leading one to the saving knowledge of Jesus Christ and eternal life in heaven is far more important than saving a mortal life here on Earth. "For everyone who calls on the name of the Lord will be saved. How then can they call on the One they have not believed in? And how can they believe in the One whom they have not heard? And how can they hear without someone preaching to them? ... As it is written, 'How beautiful are the feet of those who bring good news.'" Romans 10:13-15.

"A life of significance is about serving those who need your gifts, your leadership, your purpose." Kevin Hall, author

Luke 12:8, John 3:16-17, Romans 6:23

OUR HELPER

Early in our law enforcement career, most of us begin to understand that life on the job often is not going to be easy. Countless times, I had to call home toward the end of a shift to relate that I was going to be late, possibly for many hours. Sometimes I had to miss special family events or holidays, causing me to feel that I had let my family down. Feeling guilty at times, I tried to erase my family's disappointed voices by rationalizing that what I was doing was very important to society. For the most part, our families learn to adapt to or at least cope with the interruptions of a normal life as time goes on. Sometimes, though, working this job may cause us to feel as helpless as if we are in a winless tug of war. However, since we have agreed to protect and serve, we must discipline ourselves to stay focused on what is important while on duty. On the other hand, thinking about things that are important to us and our families must sometimes be suppressed until we are off duty.

Believers must not lose sight of the fact that our source for direction, stability, awareness, and a clear mind comes from our Creator who wants only the very best for us. Regardless of one's intelligence, it can never supersede the power of the Holy Spirit that we receive when we accept Jesus as our Lord and Savior. Christ sent this Counselor to provide us with greater wisdom, discernment, peace, and direction. He is the third part of the Trinity that many Christians have not learned much about, so they are missing out on an invaluable Helper. He indwells each Christian, and each of us needs to become acquainted with Him. Jesus said, "I am going to send you what my Father has promised; but stay in the city until you have been clothed with power from on high." Luke 24:49.

"We have been given divine power! We have weapons that are not of this world--the most powerful on Earth." Phil Robertson, Duck Dynasty

Proverbs 3:13, John 14:16-18, Acts 1:8

MESSED UP

Early in my career, I recognized the need to do things well, to the best of my ability, and without mistakes; yet, I still messed up some situations. One summer day, I was assigned to a Civil War reenactment in Gettysburg, Pennsylvania where a large but orderly group of history buffs were having a good time. My sergeant assigned me a new marked vehicle to drive through the fields where tents were set up. Friendly "soldiers" and their families, dressed in the clothing of the era, waved as I passed. Suddenly, I struck a big rock that had been covered by high grass in the field. After continuing for several feet, my car abruptly halted, and I could no longer drive. Sheepishly, I called the command post, and a tow truck was dispatched. Sitting in the passenger seat of the truck with the patrol car in tow, I felt humiliated as many looked at the sight with amusement. I still cringe as I recall this humbling incident.

Believers should always attempt to do their best, seeking to be an example of our faith. However, even in a Christian walk, it is easy to fall into temptation and sin. Some sins are more outward than others, but the Holy Spirit knows that we messed up and prods us to get back on track. We can choose to dwell on our transgressions, or we can ask for God's forgiveness, which He will always provide. "Jesus doesn't avoid but enters our mess in order to clean it up. Jesus transforms us from messy sinners to messy sons and daughters who have hope. As He does, Jesus transforms us and wants us to be willing to enter into the mess of others and help them when we can." Joseph Henseler, pastor.
"Live by the Spirit, and you will not gratify the desires of the sinful nature." Galatians 5:16.

"Jesus doesn't avoid those who mess up. Jesus runs to those who mess up."
Matt Chandler, pastor/author

Isaiah 43:25-26, Daniel 9:9, Colossians 2:13-14, 1 John 1:9

SET APART

Anyone on the job who has worked undercover realizes the importance of looking totally different from our days in uniform. Tom had been working undercover in a large city for a few months after previously achieving significant success in interacting with those involved in criminal activity. He knew that his appearance was critical if he were going to fit in with the criminal element. One day, a Field Training Officer, on patrol with his new recruit, told him that they were going to check out an area where a great deal of illegal activity occurred, including prostitution, drug sales, and the sale of stolen property. As they drove down the main street of the town, the recruit looked over to see a disheveled, unkempt, and dirty-looking man sitting on a bench. He appeared to be either drunk or on drugs. The recruit said to the FTO, "Look at that bum. I will bet he's up to no good." The senior officer kindly said, "Kid, he's on the job." Tom had obviously done well to be set apart.

All too often, we Believers seek to walk in the Lord's will but are not willing to give up the things of the world that we have become accustomed to, but which are not in God's will. Psalm 4:3 tell us, "The Lord has set apart the godly for Himself." 1 Peter 2:9 calls us "a chosen people," chosen by the living God and saved through Christ! We can see then, that since the Lord has already claimed us, if we continue to walk outside the parameters that He has clearly defined, we can expect internal conflict as long as we cling to what is unacceptable to a holy God. 2 Corinthians 5:17 reminds us, "Therefore, if anyone is in Christ, he is a new creation; the old has gone, the new has come."

"You and I were created by God to be so much more than normal. Following the crowd is not a winning approach to life. In the end it's a loser's game, because we never become who God created us to be by trying to be like everyone else."
Tim Tebow, former NFL player, professional baseball player

John 15:19, Romans 12:2, Colossians 3:10

BLOOD COVENANT

Michael Franzese, the son of an underboss in the New York Columbo crime family, initially planned on going to medical school. However, he knew what his dad did for a living and, instead, decided that he would join the "family." He became one of the biggest moneymakers for the mob, accruing an estimated 30 billion dollars for them--equivalent to 86.3 billion in 2017. As part of the ritual to become a "made member," of the family, the initiation required him to prick his finger with a needle, allowing drops of blood to fall on a card bearing the likeness of a saint. The card was then set on fire. This blood covenant is an oath, promising to be faithful to the "family." Years later, after meeting his current wife, Michael left the mob, turned his life around, and began serving the Lord. Walking away from the mob is unheard of. Traditionally, the only way to leave the mob is in a body bag. In his book, *Blood Covenant,* retired FBI expert and mob hunter, Bernie Welsh, said of Michael, "He will get whacked." However, to this day, Franzese is living a mob-free life, and he knows it is because of his walk with the Lord.

Hebrews 9:1 refers to "the first covenant" in Old Testament times. This law required the sacrifice of animals, for their blood made an atonement for the sins of the Jewish people. However, when Jesus went to the cross, He made a new blood covenant with anyone who accepts Him as their Lord and Savior. In Luke 22:20, during the Last Supper, Christ explained, "This cup is the **new covenant** in My blood, which is poured out for you." Hebrews 9: 14-15 affirms this: "How much more, then, will the blood of Christ, who...offered Himself unblemished to God, cleanse our consciences from acts that lead to death so that we may serve the living God...Christ is the mediator of a **new covenant**, that those who are called may receive the promised eternal inheritance—now that He has died as a ransom to set them free from the sins committed under the first covenant."

"Be assured that there is no sin you have ever committed that the blood of Jesus cannot cleanse." Billy Graham, evangelist/author

Matthew 26:27-28, 1 Corinthians 11:25-26, Ephesians 1:7-8

November 9

WORDS RECORDED

When we made a significant seizure of cocaine, we arrested Rick, a major drug dealer with several prior arrests. Knowing that he was facing jail time, he quickly asked for a deal in exchange for information on a recent homicide. Since we had run out of leads in that case, we agreed to speak on his behalf in court if he cooperated. Rick told us that several weeks prior, he and a friend, John, went to a farmhouse late one night. John had learned that Ben Jones had received two kilos of cocaine and intended to rip Ben off. After entering the home, John asked about the coke, and Ben eagerly showed them how he had "scored." Once the dope was in plain sight, John pulled a gun from his waistband and fired at close range, hitting Ben numerous times. Then John quickly searched for any available cash, grabbed the kilos, and they left the home. Without hesitation, Rick agreed to wear a wire, meet with John, and talk about the murder. The eavesdropping equipment had limitations since background noise could be easily picked up and obscure conversations. When the recording was later played, parts of the conversation could not be discerned, but enough words were clearly recorded to allow us to bring charges of murder against John.

Believers in Christ know that when we go before God with a clean heart, He clearly hears our every word. Nothing is obscured or misunderstood when we call out to Him for help. Psalm 18:6 says, "In my distress I called to the Lord; I cried to my God for help. From His temple He heard my voice." He hears all we ask of Him and will answer in accordance with His will. 1 John 5:14 says, "This is the confidence that we have in approaching God: that if we ask anything according to His will, He hears us." Let us also remember that the Lord is pleased when He hears us simply praising Him. "Let everything that hath breath praise the Lord." Psalm 150:6.

"The greatest tragedy in life is that some prayers go unanswered as they go unasked."
Mark Batterson, pastor/author

Psalm 18:1-3, Psalm 66:17-20, Ephesians 6:18

THE MESSENGER

In my civilian life and prior to going into law enforcement, I cannot recall having to pass on to anyone what would be life-changing information. Once I was on the job, I soon realized that sometimes we have to deliver very difficult messages. After a fatal motorcycle accident investigation, I knew that for the first time, I would have to go to the home of a young man to carry this news. Mentally reviewing what I had learned prior to giving a death notice, I knew that it was important to try to interact with a neighbor or relative to determine the health of the person receiving the tragic information so as not to exacerbate health issues. Learning whether the family had a member of the clergy who could console them would also be helpful. However, as much as I tried to prepare for the encounter, there was no easy way to do that. When I rang the doorbell, and a middle-aged woman answered, I saw her expression turn to fear as soon as she saw my uniform. After being invited inside, I did my best to convey the horrible news to the weeping mother. It was terribly difficult to maintain my own composure, and ensuing encounters never got any easier.

On the other hand, Believers can also find it difficult to give to others the good news about the saving message of Jesus Christ, even if they are a member of our family. Our concerns may be that it will not be well received; that they may not believe in what we have to say; that they may reject our friendship; or that a family relationship may be severed. However, if we really care about where they will spend eternity, sharing Christ is not an option, and God will help us to do this. Romans 1:14-16 says, "I am obligated to both Greeks and non-Greeks, both to the wise and the foolish. That is why I am so eager to preach the gospel also to you who are in Rome. I am not ashamed of the gospel, because it is the power of God for the salvation of everyone who believes: first for the Jew, then to the Gentile."

"We ought to be living as if Jesus died yesterday, rose this morning, and is coming back tomorrow afternoon." Adrien Rogers, pastor

Luke 18:27, 1 Peter 3:15, 1 John 4:15

MORE MONEY

Many people today have bought into the belief that having money and material things will cause them to experience true joy and peace. On the job, we frequently come in contact with those who have no legitimate way to gain power and wealth. To acquire what they believe will give them happiness, they commit illegal acts such as drug trafficking, robbery, burglary, petty thefts, or even falsifying tax returns. When I formed an executive protection detail for a very wealthy individual and his extended family, the agents and I were initially impressed by the expensive cars, large mansions, and several vacation homes, both in this country and abroad. A haunting memory that remains for my daughter was a $25,000 birthday party for the three-year old grandson, whom she occasionally babysat. Guests enjoyed pony rides, clowns, musicians, food fit for royalty, and multiple cakes shaped like construction vehicles while expensive gifts covered the tables. At the end of the night, the solitary child played with the empty boxes.

James 1:17 encourages us to be thankful and view what we have as God-given instead of desiring more: "Every good and perfect gift is from above, coming down from the Father of the heavenly lights, Who does not change like shifting shadows." Romans 13:14 is far more than an anti-fashion statement as it cautions us about fulfilling worldly desires: "Rather, clothe yourself with the Lord Jesus Christ, and do not think about how to gratify the desires of the sinful nature." 1 Timothy 6:6,10 reminds us, "But godliness with contentment is great gain...For the love of money is a root of all kinds of evil. Some people, eager for money, have wandered from the faith and pierced themselves with many griefs." This security detail experience affirmed once again for me: "Do not store up for yourselves treasures on Earth, where moth and rust destroy, and where thieves break in and steal." Matthew 6:19.

"I never saw a hearse towing a U-Haul." Chuck Swindoll, pastor/author

Matthew 6:24, Philippians 4:19, 1 John 2:15-17

CALL OFF THE SEARCH

During an extremely cold winter, temperatures were often in the teens and frequently fell below zero. At 10:00 PM, the temperature was near zero when I was dispatched to a senior living facility where an elderly woman with dementia was missing. Upon arrival, I was told that after a two-hour search of the entire facility, the woman had not been located. The woman, who was in her early 60's, was wearing nothing more than a robe and slippers. Realizing that only a short time frame remained to find the woman viable, I called for assistance to begin a search immediately and for other first responders to assist. Although dressed in a uniform fit for the winter temperatures, I became very cold after two hours, and a feeling of despair set in. About an hour later, after the woman had been missing for over four hours, a radio call went out, advising that she had been located. Her robe was still covering her, but her slippers were missing. Her condition was immediately obvious, and a coroner was contacted. Unsuccessful searches are always difficult to accept, no matter how many times we conduct one.

One search, however, will never turn up void. A sincere search for our Lord will always provide positive results with eternal consequences and blessings. Deuteronomy 4:29, 31 tells us, "But if from there you seek the Lord your God, you will find Him if you look for Him with all your heart and with all your soul…For the Lord your God is a merciful God; He will not abandon or destroy you or forget the covenant with your forefathers, which He confirmed to them by oath." Many in today's world do not believe that there is a need to seek God. Sadly, someday, and into eternity, they will realize the terrible mistake that they made. Then, it will be too late.

"Knowing we will be with Christ forever far outweighs our burdens today. Keep your eyes on eternity." Billy Graham, pastor/evangelist/author

1 Chronicles 16:11, Acts 17:27-28, Hebrews 11:1,6

EXPUNGEMENT

Patrolling a highway one summer evening, I observed a car driving erratically. After pulling it over, I smelled alcohol as I questioned the middle-aged driver, Allen. He regretfully admitted that he had too much to drink at a friend's retirement party. Embarrassed and ashamed, this mild-mannered family man took full responsibility for his behavior. Pennsylvania offers a pre-trial intervention program for non-violent offenders as a rehabilitation and intervention tool to prevent additional, similar incidents. After no more than two years, a defendant can petition the court to have any record of an arrest or charge expunged. In addition, names on related documents may be redacted for legal or security purposes. At Allen's hearing, I stated that I agreed with a decision to expunge and redact his record, for he had no previous citations and had fully cooperated.

When we accept Jesus as our Lord and Savior, our sins are forgiven and expunged from our records. Our names are immediately placed in the "Lamb's Book of Life," a registry that God keeps which allows us entry into Heaven. Once a Believer's name is put in the book, it will **never** be redacted. Revelation 3:5 assures that, as Jesus said, "He who overcomes will, like them, be dressed in white. I will **never** blot out his name from the book of life, but will acknowledge his name before My Father and His angels." The "Throne of Judgment." described in Revelation 20:11-15, is not a judgment for Believers, but for non-believers who will be judged for what they have done, for, "Without faith, it is impossible to please God." Hebrews 11:6. However, God is pleased with those who, by faith, accepted the free gift of Jesus by believing in His cleansing blood. It could not get any better for Believers for now and into eternity!

"For a small reward, many will hurry away on a long journey; while for eternal life, many will hardly take a single step."
Thomas a` Kempis, 15th century theologian/author

John 10:28-29, Romans 8:37-39, Revelation 20:15

PLANS INTERRUPTED

Finishing an exceptionally busy 3-11:00 PM shift after a stretch of ten consecutive shifts, I was looking forward to having the next several days off. All I wanted was to get home to my family. As I returned to the station, heavy snow had accumulated on the roads. When I rounded a curve, flashing lights ahead revealed a downed tree obstructing the highway. I now had to take an alternate route. Complaining to myself over this interruption and certain delay, I turned onto an unfamiliar rural road. Suddenly, I saw a vehicle on the side of the road in a snow bank. Walking to the driver's side of the car, I found an elderly woman slumped over the wheel. The ignition was in the on position, but the motor was not running. Apparently, she had run out of gas while attempting to stay warm. She appeared to have been there for a while, and her breathing was very shallow. Returning to my patrol car, I grabbed emergency blankets and rushed back, hoping to save her. After wrapping the blankets around her, I took off my heavy uniform coat and threw it over her. As I continually talked to the woman, her breathing started to improve. Picking her up, I placed her in my car where the heater was blasting. Many minutes passed before the old woman looked over at me with a small smile on her wrinkled face. She made it! Although I was late getting home that night, I was very glad that my plans had been interrupted.

Often, those in law enforcement who do not have a faith or dependence on the Lord are put in a place where they perform acts of kindness. It is our job. But when we realize that our Creator allows things to happen in our life, even situations that we had not planned for, it is a comfort to know that He is in full control. When we do not shut Him out and watch for His leading, we become grateful and know how blessed we are. "Commit to the Lord whatever you do, and your plans will succeed." Proverbs 16:3.

"Trust whatever He (God) has for you. It will be better than anything you can plan yourself." Francis Chan, pastor/author

Psalm 56:3-4, Psalm 91:1-2, Psalm 143:8

GRACE ABOUNDS

In *Moments for Fathers,* Rev. Thomas Strand tells of a large church in London that started three mission churches in the city's slums. At a combined communion celebration for the three churches, a judge knelt next to a burglar that he had once sentenced to seven years in prison. Afterwards, as the judge and the pastor were walking home, the judge asked the pastor if he had seen who was kneeling next to him for communion, and then he exclaimed, "What a miracle of grace!" When the pastor agreed, the judge asked, "But to whom do you refer?" Somewhat confused, the pastor said, "Why, the conversion of the convict, of course." When the judge replied, "But I was referring to myself," the pastor was more bewildered. The judge then said, "It did not cost the burglar to get converted when he came out of jail. When he saw Jesus as his Savior, he knew, then, salvation and a hope for him. But look at me. I was taught from infancy to live like a gentleman; that my word was my bond; that I was to say my prayers, go to church, take communion, and so on. I went through Oxford, earned my degrees, was called to the bar, and eventually became a judge. Pastor, nothing but the grace of God could have caused me to admit that I was a sinner on a level with that burglar. It took more than grace."

When we commit to following Christ, Believers first must cast off pride and admit that we are sinners. Usually, the more we have accomplished in life before making this life-changing decision, the prouder we grew through the years. Ephesians 2:8-9 reminds us, "It is by grace you have been saved, through faith--and this not from yourselves, it is the gift of God—not by works, so that no one can boast." James 4:6, 10 says, "He gives us more grace…God opposes the proud, but gives grace to the humble…Humble yourselves before the Lord and He will lift you up." The more we grow in humility, the greater will be the evidence of God's grace in our lives.

"Your worst days are never so bad that you are beyond the reach of God's grace
Jerry Bridges, pastor/author

Ephesians 2:8-9, Ephesians 4:7, Hebrews 4:16

WEAKNESS

I always thought that I was in relatively good physical condition until I entered the PA State Police Academy. I soon realized that I had to work to keep up with the physical rigors we experienced each day. The two entrances to the PSP Academy each have a long, steep roadway leading up to the building. As I arrived for my first day and drove up the hill, I realized how steep it was. That these roads would be used to get the cadets in shape never entered my mind. That evening we were told to report to the parking area behind the PSP Academy at 05:30 the next morning. When the instructor met us in the morning darkness, he began to bark out orders. Before he led us on a very long run, he made it clear that anyone who could not complete the run would receive negative consequences. As we returned, another staff member met us at the door with a smirk on his face and said, "You have no idea what we have for you in the next six months while you are our guests." From the first day at the PSP Academy, we were groomed to be strong, bold, and courageous; however, in our humanness, that is impossible to achieve all of the time.

Sometimes, when the task that we face seems to be more than we can humanly handle, we may feel that we cannot go on. It pleases God if we then call out to Him in our weakness and tell Him that the situation is impossible. We find specific instructions in 1 Peter 5:6-7: "**Humble** yourselves, therefore, under God's mighty hand, that He may lift you up in due time. **Cast** all your anxiety on Him because He cares for you." Isaiah 40:30-31encourages us: "Even youths grow tired and weary, and young men stumble and fall; but those who **hope** in the Lord will renew their strength. They will soar on wings like eagles; they will run and not grow weary, they will walk and not be faint."

"Look at our armor! We've been equipped with truth, righteousness, readiness, faith, salvation, and the Spirit-- what more do we need? Once we are suited up, all God asks us to do is stand." Phil Robertson, Duck Dynasty

1 Corinthians 16:13, Ephesians 6:10, 2 Thessalonians 2:16

THE OPEN DOOR

Carlos was an incredible confidential informant who provided information on many high-level heroin dealers. One day, he called to say that several times during the past week, he had been in the residence of Jake, a large-scale dealer who had been on my radar for many months. Carlos had learned that a kilo of heroin was to be delivered to Jake the following day. After he gave me the address and description of the duplex, he said that the front door was solid and would take great effort to break down. When the raiding team arrived at the home, I picked the biggest member, knowing that with a battering ram, he could take down any door. Moving quickly to the front door, we announced our presence, and within a few seconds, the ram hit the door and slammed it open. Rushing into the living area, we found only a terrified, elderly woman. When I demanded to know where Jake was, she meekly said, "He lives next door."

The Lord sometimes closes the door to situations and desires that we may want to pursue. In Acts 16:6-7, Paul and his companions set out to preach the word, but the Holy Spirit twice closed the door and prevented them from going to places that they had planned to visit. Yet, at another time, in the city of Troas, Paul relates that "The Lord opened a door for me," to preach about Christ. 2 Corinthians 2:12. Although it can be difficult to understand why He does not allow us to walk through a closed door, He never closes a door that He wants us to walk through. In Matthew 6:33, 7:7, Jesus says that the Heavenly Father knows our needs, and He directs us to, "Seek first His Kingdom and His righteousness...Ask and it will be given; seek and you will find; knock and the door will be opened to you." Walking in the Spirit leads us to the best of all doors. "I have opened a door for you that no one can close." Revelation 3:8.

"God in His love always wills what is best for us. In His wisdom, He always knows what is best, and in His sovereignty, He has the power to bring it about."
Jerry Bridges, author

John 10:2-3, John 16:13, Acts 14:27

PEACEMAKERS

When tempers flare and volatile situations are evident, we are often called upon to be peacemakers, but this role can be very difficult. For the third time in a month, several neighbors called the barracks about a horrific argument between a married couple on their street. Dispatch directed Mike to go to the home that he had visited in the previous months. When he arrived, the couple was still engaged in a loud and profane disagreement. After futile efforts to calm them, Mike announced, "That's it! He is going to have to leave this house immediately!" At these words, the wife broke into heaving sobs, and the husband tenderly tried to comfort her. Somewhat stunned, Mike asked if they seriously intended to change their behavior because this was their last chance. When both agreed to mend their ways, Mike asked if they wanted to renew their wedding vows. Eagerly, they stated that they did. Mike went to his patrol car and returned with *The Pennsylvania Crimes Code* manual. After asking them to place their hands on the small book, he led them in a somewhat unorthodox recitation of the traditional wedding vows. That was the last visit made to that home by any officers.

God's word tells us that, as Believers, we should always seek to bring about peace. This effort may be for those we encounter during our tour of duty, for acquaintances, coworkers, family, or friends who are in turmoil. When we face a difficult situation that needs a peaceful resolution, our first step should always be to seek wisdom through prayer. James 3:17-18 says, "The wisdom that comes from heaven is first of all pure; then peace-loving, considerate, submissive, full of mercy and good fruit, impartial and sincere. Peacemakers who sow in peace raise a harvest of righteousness." Jesus said, "Blessed are the peacemakers because they will be called the sons of God." Matthew 5:9.

"Happy is he that attains the character of a peacemaker in the church of God."
John Wesley, English cleric/co-founder of the United Methodist Church

Psalm 34:12-14, Proverbs 12:20, Romans 14:19, Hebrews 12:14

OVER MY HEAD

It is impossible for anyone who is not on the job to fully understand the requirements, challenges, demands, dangers, and disappointments that those in law enforcement experience. What we see on television or in the movies is entertaining, but often very unrealistic. Before becoming a trooper, I naively looked from afar at what appeared to be not only a prestigious, but also an exciting profession. When new assignments became available, I was eager to put in for them. If additional work on a specific case or incident needed to be done, I was quick to jump in, even before the days of overtime. Even when challenges or requests outside of the job were presented to me, my attitude was, "Sure. I can do that!" More often than not, after accepting additional responsibilities, I would later think, "How am I going to do that?"

Because we are often trying to make things better, we may think that we can do almost anything. We need to realize that we will not always have the answers. When we turned our lives over to Christ, God sent the Holy Spirit to enter into us. In John 14:26 and 16:13, Jesus said, "But the Counselor, the Holy Spirit, whom the Father will send in my name, He will **teach** you all things...He will **guide** you into all truth." In 1 Corinthians 6:19, "Do you not know that your body is the temple of the Holy Spirit who is in you, whom you have received from God?" Romans 8:26, "The Spirit **helps** us in our weakness. We do not know what we ought to pray for, but the Spirit Himself intercedes for us..." The Believer's Counselor and Helper wants us to talk to Him so that we do not get in over our head.

"The Spirit-filled life is not a special, deluxe edition of Christianity. It is part and parcel of the total plan of God for His people." A.W. Tozer, pastor/author

Psalm 54:4, Philippians 4:13, Hebrews 13:6

NOISE ALL AROUND

In today's society, it is often difficult to find quiet time during each day. Restaurants frequently blare music. Elevators are known for their unique tunes. Medical offices have speakers and TVs to overcome the silence. Many drivers turn on car radios as soon as they get in the car. Technical advances have provided us with so many electronic devices that bombard us with data, messages, and alerts which also require our time to respond. In law enforcement, we are constantly interacting with people in person, over radio communications, and on job-related cell calls. When we are off duty, we converse with family and participate in the activities of their lives, which often requires loudly cheering them on from the sidelines. People have become so used to background noise that many are uncomfortable in a quiet atmosphere. However, those who desire peace and quiet find that it has become more difficult to acquire.

Although Believers cannot control much of the external noise, we should remember the primary source of internal peace. In John 14:27, Jesus said, "Peace I leave with you; My peace I give you. I do not give to you as the world gives. Do not let your hearts be troubled and do not be afraid." Psalm 23:1-3 reminds us of our caring Lord: "The Lord is my Shepherd, I shall not want. He makes me lie down in green pastures, He leads me beside quiet waters, He restores my soul." Philippians 4:7 says, "And the peace of God that transcends all understanding will guard your hearts and your minds in Christ Jesus." Peace is a common theme in the Bible, perhaps because the Lord knows that finding internal peace will lead us to a more productive and fulfilling life. Jesus said, "I have told you these things so that in Me you may have peace. In this world you will have trouble. But take heart! I have overcome the world." John 16:33. "Let the peace of Christ rule in your hearts." Colossians 3:15

"The most frequent promise in the Bible is, "I will be with you."
John Ortberg, pastor/author

Psalm 29:11, Romans 15:13, Philippians 4:8-9, 2 Thessalonians 3:16

DO WE HAVE TIME?

After a couple years in the patrol unit, I needed a change of pace. Typically, at the end of each day, I submitted citations made during the shift, finished a report that I had started while on the road, and ended my shift, only to begin a similar routine the following day. Accepting a transfer to the Criminal Investigations unit, I found a significant change of routine with new responsibilities. My first investigation was challenging and somewhat overwhelming as I conducted interviews and reviewed evidence from the scene. Although I was immersed in the investigation, two days later, I received two additional investigations for follow-up. Doing criminal investigations did not leave any downtime and often left me frustrated that I was not able to devote the time that I needed for some cases. With endless paperwork, reports, scheduled hearings, court, on-going investigations, in-service training and updates, I felt that there was never enough time. Such circumstances can wear on us if we are constantly reflecting on what must be done next.

Ecclesiastes 3:1 tells us, "There is a time for everything, and a season for every activity under heaven." We can be at peace when we understand that God put into place the number of our days and years, and we use this gift of life wisely. "Teach us to number our days aright, that we may gain a heart of wisdom." Psalm 90:12. When we fully acknowledge that He is sovereign and in total control, and we turn over each day to Him, He will show us our next steps. "The heart of a man plans his ways, but the Lord establishes his steps." Proverbs 16:9. A good practice is to start each day with a prayer of thanksgiving and a request for guidance. "Seek first His kingdom and His righteousness, and all these things will be given to you as well. Therefore do not worry about tomorrow, for tomorrow will worry about itself." Matthew 6:33-34.

"The remarkable thing is, we have a choice everyday regarding the activity we will embrace for that day." Chuck Swindoll, pastor/author

Psalm 31:14-16, Ecclesiastes 3:11, Ephesians 2:10

CONDEMNATION

Jerry and Marge lived a quiet life in a typical suburban development. They had successfully raised two children who were now gainfully employed college graduates. Through the years, neighbors had many pleasant interactions with them, but in the last year, Jerry had no time for anyone. When neighbors reported that newspapers were piling up at their home, officers forced entry and found Mary dead on the sofa with no apparent cause, and Jerry could not be located. A check of the home computer revealed a search for chemicals to poison a human, and an autopsy ruled poisoning as the cause of death. Eventually, Jerry was located, charged with first-degree murder, and found guilty. He was stoic through it all. At his sentencing, he sat emotionless next to his attorney until the death penalty was announced. Then he broke into uncontrollable, heaving sobs and had to be escorted from the courtroom.

Believers know that regardless of how much we may strive to be sinless, we will never be able to live without committing sin. We also know that only Jesus, our Lord and Savior, can atone for our sins. Suffering a horrible death on the cross, Jesus, alone, took the penalty that we so rightly deserve. 1 John 2:2 attests, "He is the atoning sacrifice for our sins." Pastor Charles Stanley explains the concept that many have not grasped: "As a believer, you will never be judged by your sins. That is a settled issue. It is so settled in the mind of God, that at the moment of your salvation, knowing full and well all the sins you were yet to commit, God adopted you into His family." Romans 8:1-2 says, "Therefore, there is no condemnation for those who are in Christ Jesus, because through Christ Jesus the law of the spirit of life set me free from the law of sin and death."

"If you want to see what judgment looks like, go to the cross. If you want to see what love looks like, go to the cross." D. A. Carson, theologian/author

Psalm 34:22, Romans 8:1, 1 Peter 2:24-25

LISTENING

After a lengthy investigation involving an organized crime family, we developed enough probable cause to obtain permission from a superior court judge to install a non-consensual wiretap. Although such investigations often reveal information which leads to subsequent arrests, they are labor-intensive and require hours of listening to and reviewing tapes of conversations. One intercepted call was especially suspicious, but determining what criminal activity might be occurring was difficult. Because the words were often spoken quickly, they were difficult to decipher. Over an extended time, we noted that one suspect repeated the name of a company where he had gotten more "stuff." Further investigation revealed this to be a pharmaceutical company that sold laboratory equipment, which could be used to manufacture illegal drugs. This information, along with additional facts that I learned, allowed another wire on other suspects and led to future arrests.

In our everyday lives, we have to be sensitive to the presence of God and be ready to listen. When we decide to follow Christ and walk in His will, we should be aware that at times, He will speak wisdom to us. Sometimes, it will come while we are doing devotions and reading His word. Sometimes, we will sense His response while we are praying. I have never experienced an audible voice, but I certainly know that because of the way something happened and the decisions that I ultimately made, God had nudged me in that direction, and I did make the right decision. We will also experience times when those around us are facing difficulties, and they do not know where to turn. If they sense that something is different about us and believe that we genuinely care, they may turn to us and listen to our advice. "My dear brothers, take note of this: Everyone should be quick to listen, slow to speak, and slow to become angry." James 1:19.

"Of all human activities, man's listening to God is the supreme act of his reasoning and will." Pope Paul VI

Psalm 116:1-2, Jeremiah 33:3, 1 John 5:14

NOT EXPECTED

When Evan accepted a position in the vice unit, he was already aware of ongoing drug activity. Because he did not yet have an undercover car, he hitched a ride to the location and went into a "head shop." Asking the attendant, Carl, where he could "score," he was told to return that evening to pick up his drug request. After making several other purchases from Carl, Evan expressed interest in buying a large quantity of "weed." Carl set up the deal with the main supplier and told Evan to bring $15,000. When they met that night, Carl asked for the cash, but Evan would not let the money walk out of his sight. Carl then agreed to allow Evan to lie down in the back seat of his car while he drove to meet the dealer. After exiting his car, Carl dashed into the dealer's car, and they drove off. Since Evan had previously received a signal that his backup was not yet in place, and determined that he was not going to lose all that money, he jumped out of the back seat and began running after the car. Shortly, he tripped and fell to the ground, dislocating his elbow as his gun went off. Scrambling to his feet, he was relieved to see that his backup had stopped the get-away car and taken the two dealers into custody.

Our well-intentioned plans are often interrupted by something or someone. When we begin to fully believe and trust God in every aspect of our lives, we soon realize that we will still experience trials and difficult circumstances. Unexpected situations will continue to happen, but we can find peace in knowing that He is in control of all things. 1 Peter 5:6 advises us, "Humble yourselves, therefore, under God's mighty hand that He may lift you up in due time." At times, I have wondered why God has allowed certain things to happen while at other times, His purpose soon became evident. "Trust in the Lord with all your heart and lean not on your own understanding; in all your ways acknowledge Him, and He will make your paths straight." Proverbs 3:5-6.

"Those who walk with God always reach their destination."
Henry Ford, industrialist/businessman/founder of Ford Motor Company

Psalm 9: 9-10, Psalm 55:22, 1 Peter 3:13-14

AN ESCAPE FROM EVIL

The Chief of a bustling, medium-sized town contacted me and asked for assistance with a growing drug problem in his community. Two people had recently overdosed and died from injecting heroin, and a number of others had come very close to death. Several of us began an undercover investigation and were aided by a confidential source that the Chief provided. The investigation lasted for several months and went well beyond what the Chief had expected. We had developed enough information to arrest thirty people, not only for drug trafficking but also for numerous burglaries and a recent vicious armed robbery. On the day of the raid, I entered a small apartment and arrested a pregnant woman who held a small child in her arms. The stories of others who were arrested were varied, but just as pathetic. I wondered where these people went wrong. Why did they pursue such a life? Didn't they have anyone to come alongside them and be a source of encouragement and strength? Did they ever learn about God?

From previous interactions with the Chief, I knew that he had a strong faith. Moreover, he was concerned not only for the physical welfare of those in his community, but also for the welfare of their souls. Hopefully, the arrests that day allowed him to interact with some on a personal level. Perhaps being arrested caused some to consider changing the way they were living and gave them pause to think about their eternity. Our Lord God eagerly offers forgiveness to all who call upon Him and accept His Son, Jesus, as their Lord and Savior. At that moment, He sends the Holy Spirit into our lives to nudge us along while providing peace and direction. He does not want us to give up. Jesus said, "And I will ask the Father, and He will give you another Counselor to be with you forever—the Spirit of truth...The world cannot accept Him because it neither sees Him nor knows Him. But you know Him, for He lives with you and will be in you. I will not leave you as orphans." John 14:16-18.

"You were made by God and for God, and until you understand that, your life will never make sense." Rick Warren, pastor/author.

2 Corinthians 5:17, Galatians 5:16-26, Colossians 3:12

WHY?

Austin, Texas was recently the site of six terrifying explosions of package bombs. The law enforcement community agonized as they attempted to gain clues from each bombing. Three packages were left at the doorsteps of residents; one was tripped on a city street, and two were found at a Fed-Ex facility. As each explosion increased fear in the community, investigators desperately sought DNA, fingerprints, video camera images, bomb fragments, and any other forensic evidence. A well-respected federal profiler was also brought into the investigation. Ultimately, the twenty-four-year-old suspect killed two and injured five. As officers approached his stopped vehicle, he detonated another bomb, killing himself. In a pre-recorded message, this self-described psychopath said, "I wish I were sorry, but I am not." He came from a stable family whose daily lives reflected their strong faith. The family released a statement saying, "We are devastated and broken at the news...We had no idea of the darkness that Mark must have been in." Neighbors, friends, and investigators joined his family in asking, "WHY?"

The Bible teaches that when God created man and woman, He chose to give them free will. Adam and Eve were the first to exercise free will, and they made a rebellious choice. Because they introduced sin to all generations to follow, humans will forever commit sins, sometimes against each other. Yet, it is still difficult to fathom some of the heinous decisions that people make. Why was this young man totally devoid of a sense of right and wrong and natural emotions? Why were these hateful bombs allowed to take two lives and harm others? Although some things are beyond our comprehension, our God has always been in control, and He continues to be. "Those who know Your name put their trust in You, for You, Lord, have not forsaken those who seek You." Psalm 9:10. He promises that one day, "He will wipe every tear from their eyes. There will be no more death or mourning or crying or pain." Revelation 21:4.

"With Jesus, even in our darkest moments, the best remains, and the very best is yet to come." Corrie ten Boom, survivor of the Holocaust/author

Psalm 46:1, John 14:27, 1 Peter 5:10

DEATH NOTICE

Ed was a detective assigned to a Major Case investigative team in a large city police department. Over the years, there was little that he had not seen or dealt with. Too many times, it was his responsibility to deliver a death notification to the family of the deceased. Ed's son, Chris, joined the armed forces early in his life because he, like his dad, wanted to help people and protect the United States from terrorist attacks. While serving oversees, Chris was regularly involved in face-to-face combat on the enemy lines. Ed knew that his son was always in danger, probably much more so than others were. Often, when a car pulled up close to his home in the middle of the night, he wondered if the dreaded time had come when someone was coming to the door to notify him that his son had been killed in combat.

A day will come when each living person will receive notice that life on Earth is over. In his book, *Revealing the Mysteries of Heaven,* Dr. David Jeremiah says that 250,000 people go either to heaven or to hell every day. Many may hope that because they have lived a fairly decent life, perhaps the Lord will allow them to join Him in heaven. However, that is not what the Bible tells us. Rather, there is but one way to heaven, and that is by the grace of God through the salvation offered by the death of Jesus Christ. Romans 10:9 says, "Because, if you confess with your mouth that Jesus is Lord and believe in your heart that God raised Him from the dead, you will be saved." Because it sounds too easy, many feel a need to make the path more difficult and insist that something else must be done. 2 Peter 3: 9 says, "He (the Lord) is patient with you, not wanting anyone to perish, but everyone to come to repentance." Ultimately, those who enter heaven will be those who have recognized the only route to eternal life: "For by grace you have been saved through faith. And this is **not** your own doing; it is the gift of God, **not** a result of works, so no one may boast." Ephesians 2:8-9.

"Christ took our Hell so we could take His Heaven."
Dr. Donald Barnhouse, pastor

John 3:36, Philippians 3:20, Revelation 21:6

THE HELPER

At some point, most on the job will encounter uncontrollable and irrational people. It quickly becomes obvious that outside intervention is necessary when mental imbalance appears to be causing a problem. A large state mental hospital was located in our patrol zone. One night, I received a call from dispatch that the hospital needed assistance with a patient. When I arrived, a nurse met me at the front door. Her concerned expression caused me to realize that the issue was significant. As she led me to a room down the hall, I could hear screaming and thumping sounds. Walking into the room that was in complete disarray with furniture thrown all around, I saw two nurses, a male and a female, trying to subdue a ranting patient who was totally out of control. He was banging his bloodied head against the wall and any other objects that he could reach. I was greatly comforted when my backup walked into the room. I really needed help.

We are likely to face many situations where we cannot go it on our own. These may not be as serious as dealing with a raving patient, but we may encounter someone looking for direction or discernment. Those who are in the family of God have been given the privilege of having a full-time Helper who is always available to us. When the Lord was preparing to leave His disciples to return to Heaven, He told them that He was leaving a Helper for them and all others who accepted Him as their Lord and Savior. The Holy Spirit, then, dwells within each one of us and is always available to us at the mere calling of His name. We no longer have to try to do it on our own. Dr. Charles Stanley said, "Sometimes the Father (God) permits His children to walk through dark valleys, but always the protective Shepherd remains by their side."

"No matter what storm you face, you need to know God loves you. He has not abandoned you." Franklin Graham, evangelist

Ezekiel 36:27, John 16:13, 1 Corinthians 3:16

WAY TOO SINFUL

Ted Bundy, a serial killer, rapist, kidnapper and burglar, had a university degree in psychology and had been accepted into law school. Intelligent, articulate, charming, and good-looking, he was well-liked by his peers and professors. However, he had a dark side that led to unspeakable things. He often lured and then kidnapped young women from college campuses. Once he tried to abduct a woman by pretending to be a police officer. Ultimately, he was arrested and admitted to twenty-eight murders, although some believe that he had committed over one hundred murders. Sentenced to death, he was to be executed in the electric chair. Just prior to his execution, he told psychologist and author, Dr. James Dobson, a Christian, that although he did not want to die, "I deserve the most extreme punishment society has." In his final interview, Bundy told Dobson that he had accepted Jesus as his Lord and Savior and was now a Believer in Him.

Many believe that this man who committed so many horrific crimes, who tortured and snuffed out so many innocent lives, who caused countless family members to suffer as well, certainly did not deserve to be redeemed. Because of all that he had done, his sins were far too grievous. However, God's word is inerrant and clearly says that when Jesus went to the cross, He did not rank some sins as being unforgivable because they are more severe than others are. 1 John 1:9 states the only path to forgiveness from all sins: "If we confess our sins, He is faithful and just and will forgive us our sins and purify us from **all** unrighteousness." We are all sinners; our focus should not be on judging others but on being thankful for a forgiving Lord. Remember the thief on the cross, the woman at the well, the woman caught in adultery, and countless others--all forgiven! "For all have sinned and fall short of the glory of God and are justified freely by His grace through the redemption that came by Christ Jesus." Romans 3:23-24.

"The wonderful news is that our Lord is a God of mercy, and He responds to repentance." Billy Graham, evangelist/pastor/author

Psalm 14:2, Romans 3:10, Romans 5:8, 1 Peter 2:24

A LIFE OF SERVICE

Lynn G. Adams joined the US Army in 1898, served 30 months during the Spanish-American War, and was honorably discharged as a First Sergeant in 1903. In 1905, he was appointed Sergeant of the Pennsylvania State Police and was promoted through the ranks, becoming Captain in 1911. As World War I raged, he reentered the US Military in 1917 as Captain in the USA Signal Corps. Promoted to Major, he joined the Provost Marshal's Department in France. Returning to the PSP in 1919, he was appointed Deputy Superintendent in 1920. Two months later, he was appointed Superintendent. Eventually promoted to Colonel, he served as Commissioner until 1943. As World War II escalated, he rejoined the military as a Colonel in the PA National Guard. In 1945, the War Department returned Adams to federal service, and he was assigned to the Allied Councils and Commissions in the European Theater of Operations. When Adams had completed nearly a half century of service and retired in late 1945, his life exemplified his love for and his desire to serve both his country and the Commonwealth of Pennsylvania.

Jesus Christ came to Earth with the sole purpose of serving. Although His life of thirty-three years was brief, His goal was to teach His creation how to love and serve one another. John 13:12 gives a powerful example of this as Jesus washed the feet of each of His disciples at the Last Supper. As Believers, we, too, are also asked to serve one another. In Matthew 25:35-36, Jesus said, "For I was hungry and you gave Me something to eat, I was thirsty and you gave Me something to drink, I was a stranger and you invited Me in, I needed clothes and you clothed Me, I was in prison and you came to visit." Questioned by His disciples about when they had done such things, Jesus said, "The King will reply, 'I tell you the truth, whatever you did for one of the least of these brothers of Mine, you did for Me.'" Matthew 25:40.

"The measure of a man is not the number of servants he has, but the number of people he serves." John Hagee, pastor/teacher

Galatians 5:13, Philippians 2:3-5, Hebrews 6:10

SEPARATED

As Ed worked an undercover investigation in a large city, each drug purchase took him closer to high-level dealers. When he indicated his desire to purchase a significant amount of methamphetamine, a supplier offered to take him to his source in Canada. Ed agreed on the condition that "Big John," (an undercover officer) could go with them. After purchasing the meth in Canada, they now had to get it over the border and into the United States. At the border, they were stopped, and their vehicle was searched. Upon finding the meth, two border agents, carrying assault rifles, ordered them out of their vehicle. During a pat down, their weapons were discovered, and they were thrown to the ground and cuffed. They were taken into a large complex and immediately separated. Later, after agents contacted the Governor's office and the U.S. Attorney General to confirm Ed and John's story, they were subsequently released. Both officers indicated that the most frightening aspect was being separated from one another, not knowing what was going to happen to them. For both, this ordeal was the most harrowing one of their entire careers.

While we are on Earth, we can choose our final destination for eternity, heaven or hell. Isaiah 59:2 tells us that "Your iniquities [sins] have separated you from your God…" 2 Thessalonians 1:8-9 says that those who reject God and His Son, Jesus, "…will be punished with everlasting destruction and shut out from the presence of the Lord…" Nevertheless, God still loves sinners, and He wants us to be with Him in eternity! He sent Christ to Earth because of His love for us. Romans 6:23 tells us, "…the Gift of God is eternal life in Christ Jesus our Lord." As we celebrate the birth of Christ, let us offer thanks for the full and complete gift of eternal life for all who accept Jesus as our Savior.

"Earth leads directly into Heaven or directly into Hell, affording a choice between the two. The best of life on Earth is a glimpse of Heaven; the worst of life is a glimpse of Hell."
Randy Alcorn, author

Luke 10:20, Philippians 3:20-21, 1 John 1:9

WHAT DO YOU DO?

When we enter into the law enforcement profession and, especially, when we don a uniform, others have no doubt about what we do. I remember the first of what would become many times when I was in a social setting and meeting people for the first time. The conversation among the group soon turned to the typical question, "So, what do you do?" After others briefly defined their professions, my turn came. Once I indicated that I was a police officer, ongoing side conversations stopped, and the group focused on me. Because people are often fascinated by the frequently distorted TV and movie versions of our lives, where crimes are often solved within the allotted hour, they are interested in knowing more. Many have little idea of what those on the job really do; in fact, some of the things we routinely do are totally foreign to others.

When we become Believers, our lives should be visibly different. One of our responsibilities is to make others aware of how Christ changed us. In Mark 16:15, Jesus directed us, "Go into all the world and preach the good news to all creation." Yet, we are sometimes uncomfortable telling others about our relationship with the God of creation because we focus on ourselves and do not want to be rejected, criticized, or mocked. The apostle Paul leads by example as he emphasizes God's power instead of personal inadequacies in Romans 1:16: "I am not ashamed of the gospel, because it is the power of God for the salvation of everyone who believes..." If we focus on the lost instead of ourselves and consider what eternity will be like for them without the saving grace of Christ, we should find courage to risk leaving our comfort zone. Jesus came to Earth, knowing that He would eventually suffer and die so that we would not have to. "Always be prepared to give an answer to everyone who asks you to give the reason for the hope that you have." 1 Peter 3:15.

"Testify boldly and without fear, regardless of the response, and you will know God's favor upon your witness for Christ." James McDonald, pastor

Isaiah 40:8, 2 Timothy 3:16-17, Hebrews 4:1

GO-BETWEEN

Sources told me about a major heroin dealer now in the area who was not a user, but was in the business strictly to make a lot of money. This repulsed me, and I determined to take him down. When I went into the area known for considerable drug trafficking, an obviously strung out young male approached me and asked if I wanted to score. Knowing that he was not a high-level dealer but was selling to support his own habit, I indicated that I did. After telling him that I needed a new supplier and was looking for "Proud Mary" because I heard that she had good dope, he claimed to have direct contact with her and could get whatever I needed. As much as I asserted that I needed to meet her, he insisted on being the go-between. He indicated that if I gave him the money for a buy, he could score quickly from Mary and would bring the dope back to me. From experience, I knew that if I fronted the money to this addict, I would never see it again.

For all who accept Jesus as their Lord and Savior, He acts as an intermediary between the Father and us. He advocates for us before the Father and allows our prayers to reach Him. In Romans 8:34, Paul reminds us, "Who is He who condemns? Christ Jesus, who died--more than that, who was raised to life--**is** at the right hand of God and **is** also **interceding for us**." While Believers understand the value of a relationship with Jesus and the peace and joy we find in knowing Him as our Lord and Savior, this good news may be foreign to some. The Lord wants us to tell them about the saving knowledge of Christ, just as someone once shared it with us. Although people do not need a human go-between to approach God, we need to remember that we are a part of people's lives for a reason, and not by chance. Perhaps we will be used to draw them closer to Him.

"Jesus Christ carries on intercession for us in heaven; the Holy Ghost carries on intercession in us on Earth; and we the saints have to carry on intercession for all men."
Oswald Chambers, evangelist/author

John 14:6, 1 Timothy 2:5, Hebrews 7:25, 1 John 2:1

DROPPING OUR GUARD

When we first enter the law enforcement profession, we quickly learn the importance of being vigilant, steadfast, inquisitive, and always on top of our game to ensure our safety as well as that of others. Failing to do so could also result in the loss of evidence. Armed with a search warrant for a residence occupied by a large number of people, we approached the door and announced our identity and the purpose of our presence. As we forced the door open, I heard yelling and saw a suspect racing down the hallway. Immediately, I took off after him, knowing that he could have a weapon. When he ran into a bathroom and began pouring white powder from a cellophane bag into the toilet, I grabbed him by his long hair, threw him on the floor, and subdued him before he was able to flush. In my hand, was a large clump of hair that I had pulled out of his head as he attempted to destroy evidence. We retrieved the powder along with the bag that had remnants of the powder still inside. Although a complete search revealed no other drug evidence, the suspect was later charged with possession with intent to deliver cocaine.

When Believers attempt to live a life that is pleasing to our Creator, the evil one is not happy. Therefore, he will do all that he can to disrupt our relationship with God so that he can invade our lives. Sometimes, his attacks are so subtle that we do not even realize that we are unwittingly imitating improper behaviors that have become acceptable in society. When we start to become lax in our time spent in God's word or in prayer, attend church irregularly, or allow our language to be no different from that of others in society--coarse and inappropriate--we are dropping our God. Satan wants nothing more than for us to drop our guard. It is then that he takes advantage and subtly leads us down an inappropriate path. Ephesians 6:11 advises, "Put on the full armor of God so that you can take your stand against the devil's schemes."

"Surely what a man does when he is taken off his guard is the best evidence for what sort of man he is." C.S. Lewis, Christian apologist/author

Psalm 119:36-37, 1 Corinthians 15:33, 1 John 5:2-5

OBVIOUSLY

Years ago, those seeking a first-time driver's license and those renewing licenses in Pennsylvania had to take a driving test at an exam unit. Called to assist with exam duty one afternoon, I anticipated a much-needed break from the day's stress. The first driver, an elderly woman, was very nervous when I got in her car. After I instructed her to proceed into the course and to follow the road, she drove at an agonizingly slow pace. Next, she had to pull into a stall to demonstrate her parking skills. As she neared the end, the car suddenly lurched forward, mounted the curb, and continued onto the top of the guard rail. Instead of hitting the brake, she had stepped on the accelerator. Sheepishly glancing at me, she began to sob and said, "I guess this means I am not going to pass."

Often, the truth becomes obvious through physical evidence. The twitching lip of our son as he explained why he unfairly received a speeding ticket or the darting eyes of our daughter as she justified her missed curfew were indicators of unfounded excuses. Believers seeking to follow the Lord's will acknowledge the need to be different in our behavior, language, and appearance. 1 Peter 1:13-15 instructs us: "Prepare your minds for action; be self-controlled…do not conform to the evil desires you had when you lived in ignorance. But just as He who called you is holy, so be holy in all you do." Yet, we often find this difficult to put into practice. Sometimes, we hesitate to express our faith, especially among non-believers, and they do not see any difference in us. While we may claim that we have a peace that can come only from our faith in God, unless we exhibit a positive difference, others will see no reason to learn about our faith. "But you are a chosen people…a people belonging to God that you may declare the praises of Him who called you out of darkness into His wonderful light."

"People look at me and see a calm, cool guy on the sidelines and I want them to know that my Christian faith affects my coaching and everything I do."
Tony Dungy, former NFL player and coach

Romans 12:2, 2 Corinthians 5:17, Ephesians 4:31-32

LINE OF FIRE

The police radio broke the silence of the night as dispatch advised of a domestic situation in progress. An estranged husband was holding his wife and five-year-old son at gunpoint. Arriving at the remote, wooded area, the officers cautiously approached the residence. As they briefly discussed their plan, the junior officer offered to enter the home first while another would follow, and the third would cover the rear entry. In seconds, it was over. The husband was subdued, and mother and son were set free. Back at the station, one of the officers asked the junior officer why he was adamant about being first to enter the home. He said, "You have young children at home. They need their dad tonight and for years to come. If something happened to me, I know with certainty that I would then be in heaven with my Savior forever. I don't know if either of you has a relationship with the Lord or if you know where you will be going when you leave Earth."

Being a Christian does not keep us out of the line of fire. Instead, statistics indicate that just being a Christian can set us up for harm and/or persecution. The U.S. Department of State notes that Christians in 60+ countries are persecuted just because they believe in Christ. In 2018, Open Doors Ministry stated that **every month**, 255 Christians are killed; 104 abducted; 160 detained and imprisoned without trial; 180 Christian women raped, sexually harassed, or forced into marriage; 66 churches attacked. However, Paul realized that his trials strengthened his faith. 2 Corinthians 12:10: "For Christ's sake, I delight in weaknesses, in insults, in hardship, in persecutions, in difficulties. For when I am weak, then I am strong." Christ knew that His followers would suffer: "Blessed are you when people insult you, persecute you, and falsely say all kinds of evil against you because of Me. Rejoice and be glad, because great is your reward in heaven." Matthew 5:11-12.

"My home is in Heaven; I'm just traveling through this world."
Billy Graham, evangelist/author

John 11:25-26, 1 Corinthians 12:26, I John 5:13-14.

PREPARED

Prior to entering law enforcement, we do not know what we do not know about the job. Soon, however, we realize the need to always be prepared. When planning a raid on a residence where known or wanted criminals were hiding out, I knew our team had to be ready, so I considered the many possibilities. Could we adequately cover exits of possible escape? Were the doors fortified in a way that entry could be difficult and slowed, thereby making our ingress more dangerous? Did we know if the bad guys were believed to possess firearms? Did we have an adequate number on the raiding team, especially if we encountered resistance? Were there trained attack dogs that might confront us? Did any arrest warrants exist for possible occupants? Did any of the "enemy" believe that they had a great deal to lose should they be captured, found guilty, and incarcerated for many years? Consideration of all of these possibilities is critical to being well-prepared, for lives could be dependent upon it.

From a spiritual perspective, our life on Earth is relatively insignificant compared to our life to come. Our preparations to face experiences in this life should pale in comparison to our need to be prepared for eternity. "What is your life? You are a mist that appears for a little while and then vanishes." James 4:14. Regardless of our age, someday, perhaps soon, each of us will be heading to our "forever" home. Some, "without hope and without God" (Ephesians 2:12) foolishly think that after this life on Earth, there is nothing, but we will all be going someplace. Only while we are on Earth will we have the opportunity to determine our life after death. "And this is the testimony (of God): God has given us eternal life, and this life is in His Son. He who has the Son **has life**; he who does not have the Son of God **does not have life**." 1 John 5:1-13. Our choice should be simple: "Believe in the Lord Jesus, and you will be saved…" Acts 16:31.

"People do not have to do something to go to hell. They just have to do nothing to go to hell." John MacArthur, pastor/author

Matthew 24:42-43, Mark 13:33-37, Romans 13:11-12

SACRIFICE

Each of us is required to make sacrifices from time to time. In fact, every day on the job, we probably have to make some type of sacrifice, although most will not be significant. On November 22, 1963, Secret Service Agent Cliff Hill was running directly behind the open limousine carrying the thirty-fifth President of the United States, John F. Kennedy, and his wife, Jacqueline. As shots rang out, Hill dove into the back seat of the President's limo, throwing himself over the wounded President and his wife. Hill consciously and courageously was ready to make the ultimate sacrifice in an attempt to avoid any further gunshots to the Kennedys. In the attack on the Twin Towers in New York City, many heroes ran toward what they knew was beyond anything that they had ever trained for, and brave men and women paid the ultimate sacrifice and lost their lives. When they began that day, none knew that they would not see their loved ones again. Their families, as well, had to make the sacrifice of living without them.

The most significant sacrifice in history was made by Jesus Christ on a rugged cross. However, it was a unique and unequaled sacrifice of such magnitude that it is humbling to comprehend. Christ, who was in the glory of Heaven with the Father, consciously left that realm to assume the life of a simple human, born to a lowly family. He came to Earth knowing that in thirty-three years, He would be brutally sacrificed to pay the sin debt for humankind. Standing before Pilate, Christ said, "You are right in saying I am a king. In fact, for this reason I was born, and for this I came into the world, to testify to the truth." John 18:37. To save us from the eternal punishment that we deserve for our sins, Jesus, out of His undying love for us, chose to make the ultimate sacrifice.

"No sacrifice should be too great for Him who gave Himself for us."
Harry Ironside, pastor/theologian/author

John 15:13, Hebrews 9:28, 1 Peter 1:18-19

December 9

HOOKED

Tom and I had been assigned a brutal homicide investigation. For three weeks, we worked long hours with no time off. We helped to process the crime scene, recorded and processed evidence, and interviewed those who might have information that would bring the investigation to a successful conclusion. Soon, our diligence paid off, and an arrest was made. We were exhausted, so I suggested that we take the following day off and go fishing. Needing no convincing, Tom and I headed to the lake the next day. About twenty minutes after we got in the boat, the bass started to hit, and we pulled in one after another. Eager to get his lure back into the water, Tom made a cast which resulted in a loud "whap" sound. Puzzled that he could not see where his lure went, he turned to find it imbedded in my ear lobe. Although he was very upset, he soon began to laugh. His favorite lure dangling from my ear was too funny a sight. Then he feverishly began to try to remove this hook, often interrupting his efforts with peals of laughter. Although I was uncomfortable, I soon joined Tom in uncontrollable laughter. Tom later told me that this prized lure was so good that it was banned in several states. I think I know why.

When Jesus was here on Earth, He called Simon Peter and Andrew, two fishermen, and said, "Come, follow Me, and I will make you fishers of men." Matthew 4:19. Over time, He instructed them and challenged all Believers--including us today: "Go into all the world and preach the good news to all creation. Whoever believes and is baptized will be saved..." Mark 16:15-16. Because He later died on the cross for our sins, believing in Him as Savior will allow us to live with Him for eternity. If we truly believe that Jesus is Lord and that His sacrifice was made so that we could have eternal life, how selfish it would be not to share the best news we could ever receive this side of heaven.

"We are not just thrown on the earth like dice across a table. We are lovingly placed here for a purpose." Chuck Swindoll, pastor/author

Psalm 96:3, Matthew 28:19-20, Romans 10:13-15

POSITIVE CHANGES

Established in 1905, the Pennsylvania State Police has changed dramatically since its inception. In the early years, troopers received an Honorable Discharge from the Department every two years and had to reapply for their current position. In 1927, a new regulation prohibited troopers from marrying without first getting permission from the Superintendent. Then, the intended wife and her family underwent background checks. Finally, troopers had to sign an agreement stating that they would not allow their marriage to interfere with performance of duty. Telephone calls to the stations were accepted by a trooper whose shift assignment was to answer and then direct calls by inserting a wire into a switchboard. Troopers worked six days each week followed by twenty-four hours off. They were required to live at the barracks, where they ate and slept for the entire six days on duty. Fortunately, over the years, many positive changes have occurred.

When we join the ranks of those who have accepted Christ as their Savior, we are also expected to make changes in the way we live. One change is to accept others even when it is difficult: "Accept one another, then, just as Christ accepted you, in order to bring praise to God." Romans 15:7. He also calls us to be honest: "The Lord detests lying lips, but He delights in men who are truthful." Proverbs 12:22. As we walk closer to Him, we will experience greater peace. "I have told you these things, so that in Me you may have peace. In this world you will have trouble. But take heart! I have overcome the world." John 16:33. He will strengthen us. "Have I not commanded you? Be strong and courageous. Do not be afraid. Do not be discouraged, for the Lord your God will be with you wherever you go." Joshua 1:9. "Therefore, if anyone is in Christ, he is a new creation; the old has gone, the new has come." 2 Corinthians 5:17.

"Living in this world is unavoidable, but we do have a choice about how we live. And Scripture is clear about the kind of lifestyle God's people are to live."
Phil Robertson, Duck Dynasty

Proverbs 3:5-6, Ephesians 5:4, Colossians 3:9

COMMON BOND

Early in our career, we recognize the common bond that we share not only with those within our separate departments, but also with first responders and others in law enforcement. The statement, "I have your back," is not a glib cliché, but a pledge to do whatever we can to ensure that we all go home safely at the end of our shift. In 2009, when Pennsylvania Trooper Joshua Miller entered his patrol car to begin his shift, he accessed his in-car computer and sent out this message to troopers on the shift: "I will not let anything happen to my brothers on my watch." Soon after, a radio message broadcast the route of travel of an estranged father who had kidnapped his son. Trooper Miller was in close proximity and began pursuit as another trooper joined him. Eventually, the two troopers stopped the vehicle. As Miller approached the driver's door, shots rang out, hitting him in an area not protected by his vest. The other Trooper was able to pull the child through the passenger door to safety. Trooper Miller soon succumbed to his injuries, and his End of Watch was documented at 20:38 hours that day. This tragedy rocked the entire law enforcement community as word spread around the country.

We understand that as humans, we are limited in the ways that we can physically and emotionally help one another. As Believers, however, we are bound together by an incredible power and peace that "covers our back" in all situations. "He who dwells in the shelter of the Most High will rest in the shadow of the Almighty…He is my refuge and my fortress, my God, in Whom I trust." Psalm 91:1-2. Only God knows why trooper Miller was taken that day, but perhaps it was because he had been a faithful servant, and his ultimate reward was waiting for him in Heaven. "…God Himself will be with them…He will wipe away every tear from their eyes. There will be no more death or mourning or crying or pain…" Revelation 21: 3-4.

"God does not remove us from all harm; He uses harm to move us close to Him."
Dillon Burroughs, author

Romans 5:3-5, Romans 8:28, 2 Corinthians 12:9, Philippians 4:19

OYEZ, OYEZ

The culmination of an investigation often ends in a trial. I usually enjoyed presenting my criminal cases because I had the opportunity to match wits with a defense attorney who would try to pull my case apart and discredit my testimony. However, sometimes testifying was not a pleasant experience. In an attempt to prove their client innocent in any way that they could, some defense attorneys became arrogant and aggressively unpleasant. Interestingly, one of the most arrogant and contentious attorneys that I faced was later arrested for fraud and had to appear in court. However, most were professional and treated me with respect. Nevertheless, I was aware that such consideration was almost guaranteed if they were going to plea bargain. Since they were looking for some of the charges on the list to be dropped, they wanted me to agree with the plea.

In 1 John 2:1-2, we read, "My dear children, I write this to you so that you will not sin. But if anybody does sin, we have One who speaks to the Father in our defense--Jesus Christ, the Righteous One. He is the atoning sacrifice for our sins, and not only for ours but also for the sins of the whole world." A time will come when we all are going to appear in a "court" which will render a decision of far greater magnitude. Before the Judge, God the Father, our advocate, Jesus, will tell the Father that He has already paid the price for our sinfulness. Because we accepted Him as Savior, we have been forgiven and are not guilty as charged. "He who overcomes will, like them, be dressed in white. I will never blot out his name from the book of life but will acknowledge his name before My Father and His angels." Revelation 3:5.

"God does not regret saving you. There is no sin which you commit which is beyond the cross of Christ." Matt Chandler, pastor/author

Job 16:19-21, Psalm 103:12-13, Romans 5:8

WAKE UP

In January 2018, another tragic shooting at a high school occurred in a small town in Kentucky. At the end of the carnage, two students had been killed, and eighteen had been injured. The first trooper who arrived at the scene initially thought that one victim was his daughter since she and the actual victim were wearing similar clothes. Parents, not just those of the victims, but most around the country are asking why the educational system and law enforcement cannot, at the least, minimize the number of casualties that occur every year. Kentucky Governor Matt Bevin challenged Americans to "wake up" and recognize that what is happening is a "cultural problem." He further stated, "We can't celebrate death in video games, celebrate death in movies, celebrate death in musical lyrics. Our culture is crumbling from within."

As horrifying as these incidents are, those who read God's word are not surprised at the condition of the world. Jeremiah17:9 tells us, "The heart is deceitful above all things and beyond cure." In the beginning of the Bible, Genesis 6:11-12 says, "Now the earth was corrupt in God's sight and was full of violence. God saw how corrupt the earth had become, for all the people on earth had corrupted their ways." In Genesis 6:13, God dealt with this corruption: "So God said to Noah, 'I am going to put an end to all people, for the earth is filled with violence because of them.'" Although the Lord reestablished the earth and gave people another chance, many are again searching for peace in a crumbling world. In John 16:33, Jesus says, "In this world you will have trouble. But take heart! I have overcome the world." Only by accepting Jesus as our Lord and Savior can we have the assurance of an inner peace. In John 14:27, Jesus offers comfort that abides in all situations: "Peace I leave with you; My peace I give you. I do not give to you as the world gives. Do not let your hearts be troubled and do not be afraid."

"You and I cannot change or control the world around us, but we can change and control the world within us." Warren Weirsbe, pastor/author

Isaiah 26:3, Romans 15:13, 1 Peter 5:7

CONTAMINATED

Protecting a crime scene is the most critical step to ensure that evidence may be gathered which could lead to a successful investigation. Answering a call for a bank robbery in progress, I quickly headed in that direction. As I pulled into the lot, the first officer on the scene was exiting the bank. The look on his face told me that what I was about to see was going to be gruesome. Entering the lobby, I saw blood spattered on the wall behind the tellers' stands. On the floor, three women with numerous gunshot wounds were lying motionless. Once we determined that none of the employees had survived, the area was cordoned off, and we waited for the crime scene analysts to arrive. Soon, a newly promoted lieutenant, who had no criminal investigative experience, entered the building. Walking up to the counter, he placed both of his hands palm down and peered over to see the victims. When asked what he was doing, he said, "I have never seen a dead person before." Suppressing my outrage, I responded, "You have just contaminated the crime scene, and now you, too, are going to have to be processed."

It is comforting to know that once we have a relationship with Jesus, we have assurance that, even though we may slip into sinning, our sinfulness, past, present, and future, will not keep us out of heaven. As incredible as it may seem, the sacrifice of Jesus Christ cleansed us, freeing us from the penalty we so rightly deserve. 2 Corinthians 5:17 tells us, "Therefore, if anyone is in Christ, he is a new creation; the old has gone, the new has come!" That is exactly why God sent His Son into this world. "For God did not send His Son into the world to condemn the world, but to save the world through Him." John 3:17. Now that's good news!

"A man should never be ashamed to own that he has been in the wrong, which is but saying...that he is wiser today than yesterday."
Jonathan Swift, author of *Gulliver's Travels*

Exodus 23:25, Psalm 30:1-2, Isaiah 41:13

December 15

MOMENTS OF CRISIS

Recently, an officer on "routine" patrol was contacted by dispatch regarding a medical emergency at a nearby home. Entering the home, he found a woman with a newborn baby in her arms, and the umbilical cord was still attached. He was unaware that the woman was having twins when the arm of the second child suddenly appeared. Knowing that it was impossible to wait for the paramedics, he crouched down as the baby's head began to appear. Soon, he saw that the umbilical cord was wrapped around the baby's neck, and the baby was turning blue. While comforting the mother and patting the baby on the back, he untangled the cord. Soon after, the paramedics entered and quickly cut the cord. Later that day, the officer received several accolades, including those from his chief. The officer replied, "With all of the publicity about police officers, the kind of thing that happened today is what we as police officers do. We want to do this kind of stuff. We want to deliver babies and save people from heart attacks."

Both on and off the job, we are likely to face life-threatening crises. In John 16:33, Christ affirms that life on Earth will not be easy, but He is personally involved in the lives of all Believers and offers us help to endure any situation: "I have told you these things, so that in Me you may have peace. In this world you will have trouble. But take heart! I have overcome the world." Turning to Him in prayer for ourselves, for others, and for the situation should be the first step in responding to a crisis. Paul encourages us in Hebrews 4:16: "Let us then approach the throne of grace with confidence so that we may receive mercy and find grace to help us in our time of need." Psalm 34:15 assures us that, "The eyes of the Lord are on the righteous, and His ears are attentive to their cry." Psalm 121:1-2 rejoices, "I lift up my eyes to the hills—where does my help come from? My help comes from the Lord, the Maker of heaven and earth."

"No circumstance is so big that He cannot control it." Jerry Bridges, author

Psalm 4:3, Isaiah 26:3, John 14:27

ADVERSARIES

As a New Jersey State Trooper, Dirk worked for many years against Organized Crime. After information had been gathered for over a year, enough probable cause was established for a search warrant to be executed at the enterprise where "Fast Eddie" was "The Boss." When the warrant was served and evidence was gathered, Dirk asked Eddie about becoming an informant. Fearing that he would be killed by those at the top, Eddie refused. Following a trial, "Fast Eddie" went to jail. A few years later, Dirk learned that Eddie was out of jail, and word on the street said that he had "found God." Dirk, a man of strong faith, decided to visit him to find out if this were true. When Eddie answered the door, Dirk asked if he remembered him as a trooper. Eddie's expression clearly said, "Go away." Then Dirk said, "I have only one question. Are we brothers in Christ?" Eddie's demeanor totally changed, and for the next three hours, they talked about how God had worked in their lives. Eddie even revealed that he once had a hit out for Dirk. When Dirk asked if it were still active, they both laughed. No longer adversaries, they were, indeed, brothers in Christ.

When people invite God to come into their lives, we often see amazing changes in what had seemed to be impossible situations. The Apostle Paul was dedicated to persecuting early Christians. Michael Franzese was a notorious mob boss and head of the Colombo crime family. Chuck Colson was imprisoned for his involvement in the Watergate scandal. Like so many others, they turned their lives over to God and committed to following the principles that Jesus established for Believers. In 2 Corinthians 5:17-18, Paul says, "Therefore, if anyone is in Christ, he is a new creation; the old has gone, the new has come. All this is from God, who reconciled us to Himself through Christ…"

"God loves you just the way you are but refuses to leave you that way. He wants you to be just like Jesus." Max Lucado, author.

Psalm 51:10-12, Romans 12:2, 1 Corinthians 10:13

THE CAPTAIN

Tammie Jo Shults, one of the first female fighter pilots in the U.S. military to pilot an F/A-18 Hornet fighter jet in the Navy, later became a commercial pilot. On April 17, 2018, she landed a Southwest Airlines Boeing 747 safely after a midflight engine failure shot debris through a window in the passenger cabin and caused it to drop 20,000 feet in 6 minutes. Social media reported that Captain Shults had "nerves of steel" and was "a true American hero." She and the first officer humbly said they were "simply doing their jobs." The Administrative Assistant at the church which Shults attends said, "She wants people to know that God was there with her and that He helped her in getting control of that plane and landing that plane. It was because of Him, not her. She was just a teammate and co-captain. He was the Captain." Captain Shults has never been shy about sharing her Christian faith and was noted as saying that she generally tells people about her God during her workday.

As Believers in Christ, we have experiences on the job with outcomes which cause us to realize that God truly was in control. Sometimes we may not immediately recognize His role, but years later as we recollect a significantly harrowing incident, we realize that God's presence was evident. When we reach out to our "Captain," we can know, without a doubt, that He not only hears us but will also take control in accordance with what is best for us. Psalm 18:6 describes this: "In my distress, I called to the Lord; I cried to my God for help. From His temple, He heard my voice; my cry came before Him into His ears." In fact, our Captain encourages us to call upon Him for help: "Call to Me, and I will answer you and tell you great and unsearchable things you do not know." Jeremiah 33:3.

"Do not strive in your own strength."
Andrew Murray, Dutch missionary/pastor/author

Psalm 61:1-5,8, Psalm 107:27-28, Proverbs 3:5-6, Matthew 11:28, Romans 10:13

EMPTY CHAIR

After investigating so many deaths, I began to take them in stride. I recognized that my emotions had become somewhat calloused, but savage, horrific attacks, the loss of limbs or decapitation, or the death of a young child were still especially difficult to leave behind. At the arrival of the coroner, I was always observant of how he or she handled the deceased. Sometimes I saw coroners gathering body parts as if they were picking up debris from the highway. Perhaps that is how some of us who are exposed to these deaths on a regular basis learn to cope with loss of life. At times, however, I was jolted back to reality, especially when it became my responsibility to inform the family of the victim that their loved one was not coming home. Knowing that they would always be reminded by an empty chair at the kitchen table caused my emotions to surface as I remembered just how fragile life is.

Many people do not want to talk about or even consider the finality of life. However, ignoring the reality of death eliminates the opportunity to receive the peace that they could have. Those who believe in Jesus Christ as our Savior know that He has a plan for each of us, not only for the remainder of our time on Earth, but also for when we pass into eternity. The empty chairs left behind by those who have accepted Christ's promise of eternal life can, instead, provide great peace to loved ones as a reminder that although the chair is now vacant, they will be reunited for eternity. God sees you already seated in Heaven with Jesus. It is a done deal! In John 14:2, Jesus said, "In my Father's house are many rooms; if it were not so, I would have told you. I am going there to prepare a place for you." Before Jesus was betrayed, He prayed, "Glorify your Son that Your Son may glorify You...Now this is eternal life: that they may know You, the only true God, and Jesus Christ, whom You have sent." John 17:1,3

"Knowing we will be with Christ forever far outweighs our burdens today! Keep your eyes on eternity." Billy Graham, evangelist/author

John 3:16-18, Philippians 3:10, 1 John 2:17

NOT WHAT WE THOUGHT

While on the job, we often respond to significant incidents which require intense observation. Frequently, they are similar to others that we had been involved with in the past. As a result, we may begin to judge the cause and determine our response without fully knowing all the facts. As I drove down the interstate highway in a marked patrol car, I approached a motorcycle whose operator was driving well within the speed limit. In a sidecar attached to the shiny, red, motorcycle, the small passenger had on a helmet and eye goggles that resembled something The Red Baron would have worn. A quick glance at the passenger caused me to realize that something was strange and puzzling, so I motioned to the operator to pull over. When the operator got off the cycle, he walked to the sidecar and took the "Snoopy" helmet and goggles off his passenger. Immediately, a big boxer dog jumped out of the sidecar and ran into the woods as the driver said, "My dog never lets me go on a ride without him." Laughing with him, I then walked back to my vehicle thinking, "Some things are just not what I had thought."

Although this incident was comical, it caused me to wonder how many times I had unfairly made a judgment call before I had all the information. Obviously, our profession often requires us to make spontaneous assessments. However, numerous Bible verses caution us against judging others. John 7:24 says, "Stop judging by mere appearances, and make a right judgment." As Believers, it is critical that we are not judgmental. Matthew 7:1-2 tell us, "Do not judge, or you too will be judged. For in the same way you judge others, you will be judged, and with the measure you use, it will be measured to you." Paul tells the Romans in 2:1, "You, therefore, have no excuse, you who pass judgment on someone else, for at whatever point you judge the other, you are condemning yourself, because you who pass judgment do the same things."

"The most dangerous leap is the leap to conclusions."
Woodrow Kroll, preacher/radio host

Matthew 7:5, Luke 6:37, James 1:19-22, 1 Peter 3:8-12

GOD'S PLANS

When two newly posted, special duty positions became available, I applied for both since each interested me. They were in the same bureau, each headed by a lieutenant. After I completed the application and testing process, one of the lieutenants offered me the position in his unit. I was both happy and disappointed because I knew the other lieutenant, and my first choice would have been to work for him. Nevertheless, with a deadline hanging over my head, I fervently prayed about making this important decision and soon decided that "one in the hand" was the best choice. Unexpectedly, about six months later, my lieutenant retired. The lieutenant that I had wanted to work for took the new vacancy, so I began working for him after all. This experience reinforced my belief that when I take something to the Lord and then feel at peace about a decision, I need to move ahead and not look back. Once again, God proved that He was in total control.

Data from Amazon says that the most highlighted passage in scripture on Kindle eBooks was written by the apostle Paul, probably while he was in prison. "Do not be anxious about anything, but in everything, by prayer and petition, with thanksgiving, present your requests to God." Philippians 4:6. Even though this was penned so long ago, it still speaks to us today since anxiety abounds in our society. Hardly a day goes by that we do not experience challenges, some far more significant than others, and God wants to hear all of our concerns. We never want to interfere with God's plans, however, for ourselves or for others. Pastor Charles Stanley advises that we should be careful, for "Stepping into someone's life can block what God is doing with that person." Fortunately, God does not expect us to figure out all of this on our own. As we continue to pray, He will make evident not only how we should respond to our trials, but also how and if we should get involved with others' issues.

"The greatest privilege God gives you is the freedom to approach Him anytime."
Wesley Duewel, author/ missionary

Psalm 94:19, Proverbs 3:5-6, Luke 12:22-26

December 21

SOMEONE TO HELP

Working late on Christmas Eve, a discouraged officer thought of others celebrating this special night with families. When a call from dispatch directed him to a residence, an elderly woman opened the door and said, "He's in there." Unaware of the reason for the call, the officer entered a bedroom where a frail, elderly man lay in bed. He seemed barely alive, for his breathing was labored, and a blank look covered his ashen face. When the officer asked the woman why she had called, she said it was at the request of the old man, who was now staring intently at him, but with a peaceful look. A nearby photo of a young man in a police uniform caught the officer's attention, a youthful picture of the old man now lying before him. As the officer approached the bed, the old man slid his arm from beneath the blanket and took the officer's hand. Soon the hand went limp, and the man passed away. The officer now knew why he had been called. Sensing his impending death, the old man wanted help for his wife and the protection of a fellow cop on his journey. "A caring God had seen to it that His child would be delivered safely to Him. The honor of being his escort fell to me. I no longer feel sorry for myself for having to work Christmas Eve. I have chosen an honorable profession." (Author unknown)

Believers are never alone! **Jesus** said in Matthew 28:20, "...And surely I am with you always, to the very end of the age." John 16:13 tells us that **The Holy Spirit** dwells in us to "guide you into all truth." Hebrews 1:14 tells us that **Angels** are "...ministering spirits sent to serve those who will inherit salvation." In Luke 16:22 Jesus told of the beggar who was carried by angels to heaven. Believers are blessed with unequaled, supernatural protection in every breathing moment on Earth and when we take our last breath, and our spirit travels with angels to heaven where **God the Father** is waiting.

"Heaven is a wonderful place, and the benefits for the believer are out of this world."
Billy Graham, evangelist/author

Isaiah 25:8-9, Isaiah 41:10, John 14:2-4

December 22

AMAZING GIFT

Such a wonderful birth, but
You could have come as a King.
Yet, your arrival that day
caused the Angels to sing.

Your presence was foretold
so very long ago,
though some still denied
or said they did not know.

In a cold, dark stable--
no room in an inn--
began a life so pure,
to take away sin.

Thank God in Heaven
for sending His Son.
Our deserved penalty for sin
Is over and done!

rfg

Isaiah 7:14, Matthew 1:18-25, Luke 1:30-35

PEACE AND MORE

It is not uncommon for most on the job to work on holidays. Unfortunately, holidays are often a difficult time for many, and the number of calls we receive on a shift is likely to increase. For some, holidays bring back memories of special days with loved ones who are no longer here. Others may never have experienced Christmas as a special time; instead, painful memories flood their minds as they try to endure one more season of sorrow. Often, there is an increase in domestic incidents that turn violent as families fight about over-spending or drinking too much. Even during the holiday season, unrest and wars continue to rage around the world, and many in the military are separated from friends and family. Surely, everyone would welcome peace-- not just peace on the job and in our personal lives, but also in the world.

The birth of our Savior occurred, in part, to provide His followers with a different kind of peace as we sojourn through life, a peace that is not dependent upon our circumstances. Rather, it is a peace promised by the Maker of the universe to those who have a relationship with the Christmas Baby. Even if we face personal hardships and the world swirls in tumultuous winds, Believers can achieve an inner peace by remembering that all of this world is temporary and inconsequential in light of the promise of eternity in heaven with our Lord. In Matthew 24:6, Jesus tells us of the signs of the End Times: "You will hear of wars and rumors of wars, but see to it that you are not alarmed. Such things must happen, but the end is still to come." Isaiah 9:6 reminds us, "For to us a child is born, to us a Son is given, and the government will be on His shoulders. And He will be called Wonderful, Counselor, Mighty God, Everlasting Father, Prince of Peace."

"As the bells ring out the joys of Christmas, may we also be alert for the final trumpet that will announce His return, when we shall always be with Him."
Alan Redpath, author

Isaiah 26:3, Psalm 29:11, John 14:27

RETURNED GIFT

"The hour's late, should go to bed,
Near midnight, I believe.
But memories keep me wide awake
This snowy Christmas Eve.

Yes, memories of my kids moved on;
Each has their separate life.
And how the holidays have changed
Since angels took my wife.

The toys, the food, the Christmas cheer,
My wife would bear the load
Because I worked most holidays
State Trooper on the road.

Just sitting in my easy chair
So many years retired,
I reminisce of times gone by
And all that has transpired.

Of all the many happenings
That seem to come to light,
A multitude of them occurred
Right on this very night.

A drunken woman in a wreck
Died on Christmas Eve
Leaves memories of a tragic case
Most people won't believe.

I had to drive to where she lived
To tell the next of kin
And found the rundown mobile home
She had been living in.

The person who answered the door,
I still recall today,
A little girl 'bout four years old.
She said, "I'm Sue McKay."

I asked her if her dad was home
And felt the longest pause.
She said, "My daddy ran away.
You must be Santa Claus."

My mommy said you'd come tonight
If I just stayed in bed
And bring a pretty doll for me.
That's what my mommy said."

I broke the law that Christmas Eve--
Did not call Child's Care.
They'd merely put her in a room,
And that I could not bear.

I picked her up and took her home,
And My wife tucked her in bed
And wrapped a pretty doll for her
Just like her mommy said.

Adopted by a loving home
And soon they moved away.
I won't forget that Christmas Eve
And little Sue McKay.

Another bitter Christmas Eve
A blizzard to behold
Had left a family in a ditch
Just trapped there in the cold.

By grace of God I spotted them
All cold and gaunt with fright.
I drove them to a motel room
To safely spend the night.

One Christmas Eve a homeless man,
shivering and wet,
Was trying hard to get a ride
I'm sure he'd never get.

I picked him up and drove him
To a diner on the hill.
To warm his bones, I left him with
a five-dollar bill.

Strange how when you're all alone
What memories you recall.
You think of everything you've done
And was it worth it all.

I think about my God, my job,
My children and my wife.
Would I do it all the same,
Could I re-live my life?

Then comes a knock upon my door.
This late, who could it be,
A neighbor, or has Santa Claus
Come to visit me?

The figure standing in the cold
Gives me a sudden fright,
A trooper with that solemn look.
Dear God, who has died tonight?

I'm flashing back to bygone years--
How I'd often stood
On someone's porch to bring them news,
And it was never good.

Is this how life gets back at me
For misery I've induced,
Where pain I've caused some other folks
Has now come home to roost?

But looking in the trooper's eyes,
My mind is in a whirl.
I see a pleasant countenance;
The trooper is a girl.

She reached and smiled to shake my hand,
And the silence wasn't broke
Until a tear rolled down her cheek
And then she softly spoke.

"I'm sure you don't remember me,
But thought I'd stop and say
God bless you on this Christmas Eve.
I'm Trooper Sue McKay."

Retired Ohio State Police Trooper, Bob Welsh

THE BIRTH

The Heavens rejoiced
at the birth of the King,
knowing His purpose
was a message to bring.

This child was born
so innocent and pure,
to each generation
God's gift to be sure.

The shepherds, the lowly,
and three kings as well
searched for the Christ-Child
and a story to tell.

Did they truly understand
what happened that night,
or just look to confirm
if the message was right?

The power of this birth
most did not know,
for He came as a Servant,
humble and low,

So marvelous, so precious
so wonderful to see,
arriving to pay
death's price for me.

I want to live each day
in light of that birth.
Nothing else in my life
has so much meaning and worth.

rfg

Matthew 2:5-12, Luke 2:15-20, 1 John 5:11

ASYLUM

In 1973, Joanne Chesimard, a member of a revolutionary extremist organization known as the Black Liberation Army, was in a vehicle with two cohorts that was stopped by two New Jersey State Troopers for a motor vehicle violation. Chesimard, who had changed her name to Assata Shakur, was wanted for several felonies, including bank robbery. The three opened fire on the two troopers, and one, Werner Foerster, was killed, shot twice in the head with his own revolver. The other trooper was also shot, but survived his injuries. Shakur was subsequently arrested and sentenced to life in prison for first degree murder. In 1979, Shakur, confined to the Clinton Correctional Facility in New Jersey, escaped with the help of three BLA members who were visiting her and had concealed firearms. They seized two guards as hostages, and she escaped. After living as a fugitive, she surfaced in 1984 and fled to Cuba where she was granted asylum. The U.S. Government is still seeking her extradition and is currently offering a two-million-dollar reward for information leading to her arrest.

Eventually, a time will come when we all will face our Judge, God the Father. He will ask many why they should not have to pay for sins they committed in their lifetime, but they will have no valid defense to offer. However, those who have accepted Jesus as their Savior will stand before the Father knowing that they have been granted "Asylum." Christ already paid the penalty we deserve by willingly going to the cross on our behalf. 1 Peter 2:24 reminds us, "He Himself bore our sins in His body on the tree, that we might die to sin and live to righteousness. By His wounds you have been healed."

"Love, not anger, brought Jesus to the cross. Golgotha came as a result of God's great desire to forgive, not His reluctance." Richard J. Foster, pastor/author

Isaiah 53:5, 1 John 2:1, 1 Corinthians 6:20, Romans 5:8-9

GOT A SHOT

A familiar expression that many people use is, "I got (have) a shot." Do you think you have a chance of getting into the police academy? "I think I got a shot." Do you think the jury will find your defendant guilty? "I have a good shot." How do you think you did on the promotion exam? "I have a shot." What do you think your chances are to get that special-duty job? "I got a shot." Do you think the Captain is going to grant your request for a transfer? "I think I have a shot." The officers were called to the scene of a hostage situation. They had received a frantic telephone call from a young child who told them that his dad had just shot and killed his mother, and he and his younger sister were afraid they were next. The SWAT team arrived and set up a position where they could watch the home. Suddenly, one more shot rang out. An officer called over his radio and said that the suspect was in view with a rifle in hand, and the officer "had a shot."

In his book, *Revealing the Mysteries of Heaven,* Dr. David Jeremiah tells of a prominent businessman who was asked if he thought he would go to Heaven when he died. He responded, "So as far as Heaven, who knows? I'm sure not perfect, but if there are any points given out for caring for people with every fiber of your being and giving life all you've got every day, then I suppose that I might have a shot." Sadly, many people hope that they have "a shot" at getting into Heaven based solely on their good works. However, the Bible does not support that belief, for Christ freely gave **to those who believe in Him as Savior** the gift of eternal life. "For it is by **grace** you have been saved, through **faith--and this not from yourselves, it is **the gift of God--not by works**, so that no one can boast." Ephesians 2:8-9. Something cannot be called a "gift" if we have to work for it. The best news is that our penalty for any wrongdoing has already been bought and paid for in full--not deserved, but promised.

"Satan's greatest success is in making people think they have plenty of time before they die to consider their eternal welfare." John Owen, theologian/pastor

Romans 3:22-23, Romans 10:9 Romans 11:6

OTHER PLANS

Louis Zamperini was a troubled boy who became involved in criminal mischief and illegal activity early in life. At eight years old, he was drinking alcohol, stealing from his neighbors and local businesses, fighting with his peers, even throwing tomatoes at a cop. In high school, he began to turn around, and he became a top athlete, achieving national records for track. During a Berlin Olympiad, he was nearly shot for trying to steal a Nazi flag. After he enlisted in the Army Air Corps, he flew many missions in WWII. In a search and rescue mission, mechanical issues caused his plane to crash in the ocean, and he and two others drifted at sea for 46 days in shark-infested waters. Their raft was strafed multiple times, but no one was hit. After 33 days at sea, one of his compatriots died. He landed on a Japanese island and was captured and taken to a prison camp. For two years, he and his fellow POW's suffered from regular beatings, starvation, infection, exposure, and disease until they were liberated after the Japanese surrender. His years of torture and PTSD caused him to start drinking heavily. When evangelist Billy Graham came to town, Zamperini attended one of his sermons and asked God to take control of his life. Consequently, he accepted Jesus as his Lord and Savior and overcame his alcohol addiction. He later returned to Japan and met with his primary persecutor, whom he forgave.

Most of us face times in our lives when we attempt to go our own way. We stumble and fall often and have little if any desire to try to walk in faith. However, even in our rebellion and rejection, Christ does not give up on us. He keeps on loving us with an unconditional love, regardless of our attitude and behavior. Eventually, some get to the place where they are willing to give up their past and seek after our Creator, who wants only the very best for us. Regardless of what we may think, He has other plans for us.

"Everyone climbs fool's mountain several times in life. Some just fall off harder than others."
John M. Drann, my late, wise father-in-law

Deuteronomy 5:33, Jeremiah 29:11, 1 Peter 2:21

December 29

METHOD OF OPERATION

Psychological profilers have developed a matrix for pre-crime and post-crime behaviors which have assisted investigators in solving even the most heinous crimes. However, although I had worked hard for several weeks on a series of burglaries in a suburban neighborhood, I met with no success. The Method of Operation was similar in every case. The criminals approached a home in the middle of the day, and after not finding anyone in the house, they went to the rear door, smashed the glass, and entered. Then they proceeded to the master bedroom, grabbed a pillow case from the bed, and filled it with any items of jewelry that they found. Before leaving, they made a cursory search of the refrigerator and always took some items of food. If they saw any alcohol, they removed it as well. Fingerprints were never found, and rarely were other rooms entered and ransacked. The satisfied, well-fed criminals soon ended their spree and disappeared.

For all people, God has created one way and only one way that will allow sinful humans to be welcomed into the Kingdom of Heaven. Some believe that if they live an exemplary life and are not guilty of certain sins, they might enter the "pearly gates." However, God's word is explicit and consistent about the only way to have eternal life. It is only through believing in Jesus Christ as our Savior and accepting Christ's sacrifice for our sins. Romans 3:23 tells us that every human being, **All**, have committed sins, and the cost for that sin is death. "For all have sinned and fall short of the glory of God." Again, Romans 6:23 stresses, "For the wages of sin is death..." Fortunately, the remainder of that verse provides us peace: "...but the **Gift** of God is eternal life in Christ Jesus our Lord." There is only one way to receive eternal life: "If we confess our sins, He is faithful and just and will forgive us our sins and purify us from all unrighteousness." 1 John 1:9. Jesus Christ does not defend our sin, but He defends the sinner.

"The cross is proof of both the immense love of God and the profound wickedness of sin."
John MacArthur, pastor/author

John 10:28, Romans 5:8, Romans 10:9

WHOM DO WE SERVE?

In the trooper's many years of investigating Organized Crime (OC) on various levels, it was clear that OC does not exist without some form of official corruption. Because of that knowledge and awareness of politics, his career decisions were challenging. The questions he often had were, "Whom am I serving, and what is the ultimate choice?" A good friend, a mentor on the job and a brother in Christ, gave him Psalm 75:7, "But it is God who judges: He brings one down; He exalts another." The trooper then began to wonder, "Am I exhibiting Christ-likeness in my life with my investigating and also testifying before a U.S. Congressional subcommittee on my findings?" Because of his public exposure, there was extensive media coverage, and a newspaper editorial regarding his work outlined many details and included personal profiling. The editor wrote, "He believes in his mission to drive the mob from the State; a fundamentalist, he believes fervently in God--in fact, he likes to say that he works for God." It became public knowledge that the trooper saw that his Lord and Savior is Sovereign and that He had sustained him, a sinner saved by His grace.

On the job, we are often pulled in many directions, and, like so many others, it is easy for us to lose track of what is most important in life. At some point, we probably had to work for someone who was a terrible boss. Although such a situation can discourage and distract us, the Bible can help us to refocus. It is very clear about Whom we, as Believers, are to ultimately serve. In Colossians 3:23-24: "Whatever you do, work at it with all your heart, as working for the Lord, not men, since you know that you will receive an inheritance from the Lord as a reward." Remember that recognition for our performance does not always come when we believe that it should. It is comforting to know that the Lord knows all the good that we do, and we will receive our reward in Heaven. Just follow Him.

"Our example can be our most persuasive influence for Christ. Do others imitate us because we model Him?" *Our Daily Bread*

Joshua 24:15, 1 Samuel 12:24, 1 Thessalonians 1:6

IN HIS GRIP

Early on the job, I learned that sometimes it could be critical if I did not have a firm grip. Controlling an unruly person high on drugs or someone just arrested, transporting a prisoner, pulling someone out of a burning car, handling my firearm during qualification, or helping quell a riot scene--all required extra attention and a firm grip. This devotional was written as a result of much searching throughout my life, often taking me one step forward, then several back. Once I found the true answers to life in God's word, I had a firm grip on the purpose for my existence. My life changed, but it certainly did not mean that I never sinned again. As a child, I believed in the existence of God, but a blind-like faith will not provide true peace. I did not yet know about how to have a personal relationship with Him.

In time, I realized the importance of following my Creator's direction through reading His word, the Bible, not by following a particular denomination. To accept the words of others without closely examining them is foolish, so I began reading the Bible. However, I read it as I did any other book, and it was not always clear. What proof did I have that the Bible is infallible and true? Eventually, I realized that the Bible requires close study and calling out to the Holy Spirit for wisdom and discernment. It takes time and effort to finally "get it." Some reading this devotional already get it, while others may still have doubts. What if the messages are absolutely true, yet you are rejecting them? What then?

Many of us have been in an establishment when the bartender said, "Last Call." Perhaps you are close to a "last call." Although some believe that at the end of this life, there is nothing more, biblical truth says that we will spend eternity in either heaven or hell. Eternity can be difficult to grasp, but "forever" means the elimination of time. Our decision now either to accept or reject Christ's invitation will decide our future home forever. So then, how do we receive the best gift ever--the gift of eternal life? We often make it difficult when it really is not. Jesus Himself provides the answer in Luke 18:17: "I tell you the truth, anyone who will not receive the kingdom of God like a little child will never see it."

Therefore, if we **believe in God**; if we **believe** that out of His love for us, He **sent His only Son, Jesus Christ,** to Earth to willingly suffer a horrific death on the cross; if we **believe** that His death **paid the total price** for our sins; and **if we accept that payment** on our behalf, we **will** be in Heaven for **Eternity!**

Remember that Satan wants us to believe that a righteous God would never forgive us because of the persistence of our sins and the fact that even when we try to do right, we continue to sin. That is a lie from the devil, "for **All** have sinned and fall short of the glory of God, and [**BUT**] are justified [declared not guilty, but righteous] **freely** by His **Grace,** through the redemption [the ransom paid for us] that came by **Christ Jesus.**" Romans 3:23-24.

Know that Satan will actively and repeatedly attempt to get a grip on us as well. He delights in our weakness and our shortcomings, and he will take advantage whenever he can. Cling to God's word; study it; grow in it; live it. Remember the promise of this well-known Bible verse, "**For God so loved the world that He gave His one and only Son, that whoever believes in Him may have eternal life.**" John 3:16. Sometimes we may feel that we are slipping from His grip. However, when we denounce the evil one and call out to Jesus, He **will** hold us tightly *In His Grip.*

"God is not about to put a promise out there and then let the devil steal it."
Bill Myers, pastor

Deuteronomy 31:8, Isaiah 41:10-13, John 10:27-28

A Parting Prayer

May the Lord be your refuge and fortress

as you continue to trust in our God.

May you feel Him gently covering you with His feathers

As you take refuge under His wings.

May you not fear any terrors of the night

nor Satan's attacks during the day.

May you feel the presence of His angels keeping you

in all your ways.

May you always be aware of the love

that He has set upon you.

As you abide under the shadow of the Almighty,

may you find victory in the good fight.

Based on Psalm 91
by jdg
(wife of a warrior)

Some helpful books over the years that provided great clarity include:

The Pursuit of Holiness, Jerry Bridges

The Holy Spirit, Dr. Billy Graham

The Jeremiah Study Bible, Dr. David Jeremiah

Revealing the Mysteries of Heaven, Dr. David Jeremiah

Why I Believe, Dr. D. James Kennedy

Traveling Light, Max Lucado

Eternal Security, Dr. Charles Stanley

The Ultimate Conversation, Dr. Charles Stanley

The Case for Christ, Lee Strobel

The Purpose Driven Life, Rick Warren

The Bible Jesus Read, Philip Yancey

Jesus Calling, Sarah Young

Who Made God? Ravi Zacharias, Norman Geisler, eds.

Author contact: inhisgrip2571@gmail.com

Website and blog: http://www.inhisgrip2571.net

Made in the USA
Middletown, DE
14 November 2022

15010952R00224